Direct
Perception

Claire F. Michaels
LAKE FOREST COLLEGE

Claudia Carello
UNIVERSITY OF CONNECTICUT

PRENTICE-HALL, INC., Englewood Cliffs, New Jersey 07632

Library of Congress Cataloging in Publication Data

Michaels, Claire F.   (date)
    Direct perception.

    (Century psychology series)
    Bibliography: p.
    Includes index.
    1. Perception. 2. Environmental psychology.
I. Carello, Claudia, joint author. II. Title.
BF311.M496   153.7   80-28572
ISBN 0-13-214791-2

Editorial production/supervision
  and interior design by *Edith Riker*
Manufacturing buyer *Edmund W. Leone*

In Memory of
JAMES JEROME GIBSON
(1904–1979)

CENTURY PSYCHOLOGY SERIES
James J. Jenkins
Walter Mischel
Willard W. Hartup
Editors

Printed in the United States of America

10 9 8 7 6 5 4 3 2 1

Prentice-Hall International, Inc., *London*
Prentice-Hall of Australia Pty. Limited, *Sydney*
Prentice-Hall of Canada, Ltd., *Toronto*
Prentice-Hall of India Private Limited, *New Delhi*
Prentice-Hall of Japan, Inc., *Tokyo*
Prentice-Hall of Southeast Asia Pte. Ltd., *Singapore*
Whitehall Books Limited, *Wellington, New Zealand*

Contents

6

APPLICATIONS   115

7

SUMMARY AND CONCLUSIONS   155

APPENDIX: DISCUSSION AND DEBATE   171

REFERENCES   189

NAME INDEX   197

SUBJECT INDEX   199

Credits

Figure 3-1. From Karl von Frisch. *Bees: Their Vision, Chemical Senses, and Language.* Copyright ©1971 by Cornell University. Used by permission of the publishers, Cornell University Press and Jonathan Cape Limited.

Figure 3-2. From C.S. Holling. "The Analysis of Complex Population Processes." *Canad. Ent.* 1964, 96, 335–347, Figures 4 and 5. Reprinted with permission of the publisher and author.

Page 88 and Appendix. We thank Herbert Kaufman for permitting us to quote the perception book he is writing. He also reviewed the first four chapters and provided several questions in the Appendix.

Figure 6-3. From R.E. Shaw, M. McIntyre, and W. Mace. "The Role of Symmetry in Event Perception," in R. MacLeod and H. Pick (Eds.): *Perception: Essays in Honor of James J. Gibson.* Ithaca, New York: Cornell University Press, 1974. Copyright ©1974 by Cornell University.

Figure 6-4. From R.E. Shaw and J.B. Pittenger. "Perceiving the Face of Change in Changing Faces: Implications for a Theory of Object Perception," in R.E. Shaw and J. Bransford (Eds.): *Perceiving, Acting, and Knowing.* Hillsdale, New Jersey: Lawrence Erlbaum Associates, 1977. Figure 1.

Figure 6-5. Courtesy of Leonard Mark and Jim Todd.

Figure 6-6. From J.B. Pittenger and R.E. Shaw. "Aging Faces as Viscal-Elastic Events: Implications for a Theory of Nonrigid Shape Perception." *Journal of Experimental Psychology: Human Perception and Performance,* 1975, 1, 374–382. Copyright (1975) by the American Psychological Association. Reprinted by permission.

Figure 6-7. From J.B. Pittenger, R.E. Shaw, and L. S. Mark. "Perceptual Information for the Age Level of Faces as a Higher-Order Invariant of Growth." *Journal of Experimental Psychology: Human Perception and Performance,* 1979, 5, 478–493. Copyright (1979) by the American Psychological Association. Reprinted by permission.

Figure 6-8. From R.E. Shaw and J. B. Pittenger. "Perceiving the Face of Change in Changing Faces: Implications for a Theory of Object Perception," in R.E. Shaw and J. Bransford (Eds.): *Perceiving, Acting, and Knowing.* Hillsdale, New Jersey: Lawrence Erlbaum Associates, 1977, Figure 4.

Preface

There is a movement afoot in psychology. In its early days it was known as the theory of direct perception; it is now known more generally as the ecological approach. Its main assumption can be (over)simplified as follows: The phenomena of psychology reside in animal-environment systems, not merely in animals. A seed of this thought was planted by J. J. Gibson in 1950 and carefully tended and nurtured by his further works in 1966 and 1979 and by the works of others. It has flourished; its roots are starting to crack some of the philosophical bedrock under psychology and its branches are reaching out to influence the entire field.

We believe that the ecological approach should be the wave of the future for psychology and we have tried to muster a cogent case for its serious consideration. The ecological position may appear at first glance to be unorthodox, but it is the inevitable consequence of philosophical and scientific commitments that are themselves very difficult to undermine. This book explores those commitments and the approach to perception that they entail.

Our central goal was to present these fundamentals in a clear way. We tried to be explicit about where we were going and why, where we arrived and how, often pausing along the way to take stock of our progress. We think that this, taken together with carefully chosen examples and meta-phors, makes the approach readily understandable. The style of presentation makes the ecological approach accessible to students, but at the same time the book's content should stir even the most sophisticated professional.

Even if the reader ultimately rejects the ecological approach, adopting it momentarily provides a unique perspective on the field of psychology. It brings into bold relief many of the tacit assumptions of traditional (non-ecological) psychology. Making these assumptions more visible permits their analysis, criticism, and defense. Whether or not the ecological movement holds sway in the decades to come, a serious consideration of the approach and of the controversies it raises cannot fail, in the long run, to improve our science.

Many individuals and institutions have helped us with the book. A Lake Forest College grant-in-aid and a University of Connecticut Predoctoral Fellowship supported the early phases of our work. The following people provided various degrees of comment, criticism, encouragement, and manuscript preparation: Jean Cranston, Roger Faber, Linda Ferrell, Jean Hardisty, Petie Harlan, Herbert Kaufman, Robert Michaels, Katrina Young, and, of course, our parents.

Special thanks go to Michael Turvey, William Mace, and Robert Shaw, who read many versions of the manuscript, fleshed out and interpreted much of the theory explained here, and made every effort to insure that we have not misrepresented the ecological view. Our gratitude to Turvey and Shaw comes from far more than their inspirational and editorial efforts on this book, but we will forego the effusive praise they deserve—it would only make them uncomfortable—and thank them with a case of Guinness.

Our Century Psychology Series sponsor and editor, James Jenkins, was a joy to work with. He was a thoughtful (though prompt) and thorough (though gentle) critic.

We are also tempted to thank Jimmy Gibson here but, after all, this book is our thanks to him.

C.F.M. and *C.C.*

1

Contrasting Views of Perception

An animal's most commonplace successes in behaving give witness to the vastness and accuracy of its perception of its environment. A human, for example, usually walks without stumbling, normally grasps an object without toppling it, and often recognizes a friend even after decades. Such behaviors all illustrate that perceivers know their environments well. It is this fact that theories of perception, ultimately, should explain. The routes taken to explanation may be different, but the goal, we believe, is to account for the fact that animals perceive their surrounds sufficiently to guide discriminating actions (moving among surfaces without collision, catching prey, following verbal instructions, and so on). A theory of perceiving, then, is a theory of knowing the environment.

While theories of perception can be sorted into categories according to various criteria, one set of distinctions, central to this book, sets the theory of direct perception apart from the more conventional approaches to perception. In this chapter, we examine these distinctions and thereby provide a contrast between the two classes of theories, for the contrast itself reveals much about the theory of direct perception.

James Gibson and those who follow his approach adopt an ecological stance: they believe that perceiving is a process in an animal-environment system, not in an animal. Proponents of the ecological view argue that perception is, quite simply, the detection of information. This approach is labeled *direct* because a perceiver is said to perceive its environment. Knowledge of the world is thought to be unaided by inference, memories, or representations. Conversely, a second family of theories conceives of perception as *mediated*—or, to contrast it with Gibson's theory, *indirect*— and is so called because perception is thought to involve the intervention of memories and representations. The latter view, which has enjoyed nearly unanimous support among contemporary psychologists, implies that perception involves the embellishment or elaboration of inadequate stimulus input. Gibson, on the other hand, holds that stimulation is extraordinarily rich and provides such a precise specification of the environment that a perceiver need only detect that information, not elaborate it.

Because it provides a backdrop against which Gibson's theory unfolds, a brief outline of the basic theory of indirect perception is useful here. (For a fuller account of this theory, the interested reader should consult one of the many excellent books that treat it in detail [Gregory, 1970, 1978; Haber & Hershenson, 1973; Lindsay & Norman, 1977; Neisser, 1967; Solso, 1979].) For the purpose of illustrating this contrast of the underlying philosophies, questions, and research strategies of the two approaches to perception, we limit the discussion primarily to vision.

INDIRECT PERCEPTION: THE THEORY OF IMPOVERISHED INPUT

Perceptual theories that can be labeled indirect begin with the assumption that the senses are provided with an impoverished description of the world. That is, the input does not provide accurate or complete information about objects and events. Perceptions, however, are recognized as being very rich, elaborate, and accurate. We know a great number of things about our everyday world. On the assumption of imprecise or equivocal input and on the fact of meaningful, accurate perceptions, it must be assumed that perception involves a complex set of elaborations upon that input to make it rich. That is, it is assumed that the nervous system provides a variety of additions to its stimulation. Such a view lies at the heart of what is termed indirect perception or, in its current methodology, information processing. The latter term, information processing, reflects the accepted notion that stimulus information must be *processed:* cognitive operations must intervene in a constructive way. Such a theory is a necessary consequence of the view that input is inadequate "as is."

It should be noted that the doctrine of insufficient data is firmly rooted in the tradition of experimental psychology. Structuralism of the late nineteenth century asserted that perception was achieved by summing individual meaningless sensations. The rationale was that a sensation merely recorded the physical characteristics—intensity, frequency, wavelength, and so on—of the impinging energy, but not its meaning. Because a single sensation cannot identify an object, sensations must be added together with the memory images associated with them. Moreover, the anatomical layout of stimulation (for example, the retinal image) fails to preserve some very essential aspects of the world. For example, the world is sculpted from three spatial dimensions while an image of it is limited to two dimensions. It is left to memory, therefore, to aid in the re-creation of reality from the limited clues provided by bundles of sensations.

Gestalt Psychology of the twentieth century was of essentially the same bent. While it is true that this approach was primarily concerned with *Gestalten,* or whole patterns, whatever structure had existed in the environment was lost at the retinal mosaic.

> ... the immediate cause of our vision of any object is just such a mosaic of stimulation as that of the photographic plate. And that raises at once the problem: how the enormous richness and variety of our visual behavioral environment can be aroused by such a mere mosaic of light and shade and color. I think, when formulated in these terms, the problem must appear thrilling by the very paradox which it seems to involve. How can such rich effects arise out of such poor causes, for clearly the "dimensions" of our environmental fields are far more numerous than those of the mosaic of the stimulation. (Koffka, 1935)

As with the structuralists, meaning had to be re-created, this time by virtue of innate laws of organization. Again, internal ordering must be *imposed* on otherwise meaningless stimulation.

Nor is the assumption of equivocal input a long-discarded curiosity of too-early attempts at perceptual theory. Rather, it remains at the very core of the discipline today. The currently accepted definition of perception involves an essentially miraculous process by which sense data must be wheedled and cajoled by higher-order processes into accurate knowledge of the external world.

> We are so familiar with seeing that it takes a leap of imagination to realize that there are problems to be solved. But consider it. We are given tiny distorted up-side-down images in the eyes, and we see separate solid objects in surrounding space. From the pattern of stimulation in the retinas, we perceive the world of objects, and this is nothing short of a miracle. (Gregory, 1978)

The doctrine of insufficient input is aptly characterized by Neisser in his influential *Cognitive Psychology* (1967):

These patterns of light at the retina are . . . one-sided in their perspective, shifting radically several times each second, unique and novel at every moment. [They] bear little resemblance to either the real object that gave rise to them or to the object of experience that the perceiver will construct . . . .

Visual cognition, then, deals with the processes by which a perceived, remembered, and thought-about world is brought into being from as unpromising a beginning as the retinal patterns. (pp. 7–8)

The idea that the stimuli for vision are "distorted" or "unpromising" stems from three assumptions about what constitutes the stimulus for vision. These assumptions are that perceivers *see* their retinal images, that retinal images are *frozen* slices, or snapshots, of the environment, and that the stimuli for perception are *discrete* samples carved out of a temporal flow. Let us consider the origins and consequences of these assumptions.

The "image-qualities" of retinal patterns render visual stimuli ambiguous. As Descartes pointed out after inspecting images on the retinae of recently deceased animals and people, images do not accurately portray shape. Curvature and size are distorted and distance is not represented (Pastore, 1971). Given the equivocal nature of images, then, it is small wonder that the proponents of such an approach feel compelled to explicate the mechanisms by which this image or icon is rendered unequivocal. Such comments are echoed clearly in current approaches to perception. Information processing theory, our exemplar of the indirect view, takes the "distorted" retinal image, or more properly, a copy of it called iconic memory, as the departure point for visual cognition.[1]

In like manner, a description of the visual input in terms of frozen slices renders the input ambiguous in another sense. An extreme example might make this clear. Imagine a photo of a moving car. From the picture one would have no way of discerning whether the car was moving forwards or backwards. But if one were to have two pictures of the car and knew the order in which the pictures were taken, one could determine the direction of the car's motion. Thus, to the extent that one conceives of stimuli as frozen, the perception of motion becomes the problem of integrating the stimuli into a continuous event. On the assumption of snapshots, then, the perception of an event must be considered as a *deduction* from the collection of static samples because any single snapshot is ambiguous with respect to the entire event.

---

[1] We should note that the image assumption is not limited to those theories wherein the retinal image is an intact "picture" which is represented as such throughout the visual system. Rather, more abstract representations (for example, structural descriptions popular in the artificial intelligence literature) are heir to the same distortion because they take the retinal mosaic as their starting point.

While such "retinal-snapshot" theory is hard to defend in light of the discovery of motion-detectors (Lettvin, Maturana, McCulloch, & Pitts, 1958) and in light of the importance of optical *flow* (Gibson, 1950), it has not yet been discarded from information processing theory. That the visual input is seen as a succession of frozen images is implicit in (1) the concept of iconic memory, (2) the use in research of tachistoscopic displays (brief, frozen patterns), (3) theories of pattern recognition, and (4) most obviously, in cognitive theory. "There must be an integrative process that transforms a succession of fleeting and discontinuous retinal snapshots into a stable perceived world" (Neisser, 1967, p. 138).

There are many perceptual theorists who would explicitly disclaim the view that the visual input should be thought of as frozen. Nevertheless, a near cousin of retinal-snapshot theory enjoys almost unanimous support. This latter and more general view may be characterized as the *discrete sampling assumption* (this phrase is borrowed from Turvey [1977a], although he used it in the more restrictive sense of snapshot theory). This assumption claims that the visual input is sampled in discrete (individual or distinct) temporal units. These discrete samples of time have been called perceptual moments, the span of apprehension, and the specious present, to name a few. Moreover, the activity called perceiving is limited to that moment. That is, *perception is in and of the present alone*, and the present is a discrete moment, distinct from the past and distinct from the future. The problem introduced by this assumption is how to relate one sample of time to other samples. Current information processing theory would respond that cognitive intervention serves to relate these samples. In particular, memory holds onto a series of these patterns so that they may be integrated to construct a meaningful event.

Here, then, is the scenario. Traditional theory belittles the input, but at the same time praises the quality of the product. In such an analysis, the quality of the percept must come, in part, from the perceiver. With the exception of Gestalt Psychology which proposed innate laws of organization, the primary internal contributor to perceptions was and is memory.

Notice that the logical network underlying theories of mediated perception is a set of nested assumptions. It is assumed that memory is needed in perception because the momentary input, the retinal snapshot, is ambiguous with respect to the entire event. Moreover, the "image," being two-dimensional, is ambiguous with respect to the shapes and spatial arrangements of objects in the environment. These assumptions require that psychological processes deduce or construct shape and spatial arrangement and reconstitute the discrete moments into events.

These assumptions about how one should describe visual stimulation rest on a further set of assumptions at a deeper philosophical level. In the next section we turn our attention to those assumptions; rock-bottom philosophy, however, is deferred until Chapter 5. For now, we ask simply whether the philosophical premises that permit one to partition visual stimulation into a succession of images, each given in a frozen segment of time, are compelling premises. We shall argue that this approach is not only unjustified, but also subverts the endeavor of studying perception. The philosophical surgery that cut the environment into a space component and a time component and that discretized time into moments inadvertently excised that part of the environment that is most salient to animals—its *events*.

Partitioning Environmental Events

Because stimuli are tied to environments, the way one partitions environments determines the way one partitions stimuli. We can seek, therefore, the origins of the partitioning of time and space described in the last section in the way that psychologists have partitioned the environment. As Gibson (1979) has argued, their description of the dimensions of the environment has followed the lead of classical physics.

It is in the classical physics of Newton, in particular, that we see the most obvious historical basis for the separation of time and space and for their individual conceptualizations. First, Newton proposed a notion of *absolute time*. Time, by this account, is thought to flow quite independently of space. Further, time is essentially empty, including neither space nor change; it continues to flow whether there is change or not. Second, Newton formulated his mechanical principles in Euclidean geometry. When so formulated, time emerges as a geometric line, and like all lines, it comprises a collection (succession) of infinitesimal points (moments). This continuum, in turn, can be parceled into arbitrary units (seconds, days, years) on the basis of cycles or divisions of cycles in which the flow of absolute time is more or less accurately manifested.

Building upon this scientific framework, descriptions of the nature of time are further structured, but in this case not by physicists. Here we refer to the trichotomy of time into past, present, and future. This description of time is derived directly from conscious experience; it is based solely on the experience of nowness.

Later, we will criticize these metaphysics. For now, however, our only aim is to explore the consequences of this view of time on perceptual theory. To that end, it is convenient to distill these notions on time into a few general principles: (1) Time is absolute. Time need not be defined in terms of change; rather, it is change that is defined in terms of time. (2) Time is a succession of discrete moments. (3) One moment or a collection of moments can be singled out and labeled "now." Moments not contained in "now" are labeled future or past depending on their position relative to now on the temporal continuum. (4) Now is the only moment that truly exists.

With respect to the issue of stimulus, it is clear that a stimulus must exist only in that discrete and fleeting moment called "now." If the environment is a succession of nows, so too must stimuli arrive in succession. And what of this moment, now? It is singled out, divorced, as it were, from nearby regions. Because it is singled out, it neither contains nor unambiguously describes either the past or the future. Thus, to know why the present is the way it is, we need to know what happened in the past. Put another way, for the present to be meaningful or unambiguous, it must be viewed within the context of the past.

The implications of all this for psychology are fairly obvious. If one speaks of the present as if it were some objectively real entity, it is fair to suppose that perception deals with such a moment. And just as the notion of present required a frame of reference provided by the past, so contemporary notions of perception require the context provided by the past. However, because the past no longer exists, the context must be provided by the psychological record of it, memory. Whenever a moment is taken alone and isolated, it is either equivocal or meaningless.

Thus, in this formulation a stimulus cannot identify an event. The onus of accounting for the perception of events, therefore, falls by default to the perceiver (e.g., to the "integrative processes" proposed by Neisser).

Not only does the discretizing of time pose unnecessarily difficult problems for a theory of event perception, but the separation of time from space complicates the problems of explaining the perception of the shapes and arrangements of objects in the world. It legitimizes the idea that space and depth can be perceived, as if they were real things. The phrase "space perception," which titles a chapter in most perception texts, implies that one perceives some disembodied, X-, Y-, Z-coordinate system in which various objects are located; the space is primary and the objects merely occupy it. Thus, rather than asking how one perceives the positions of objects relative to each other and relative to the perceiver, traditional psychology encourages our asking how the *dimensions* required for this geometric *description* of position are perceived. And, as noted earlier, the perception of those three dimensions is problematic because the stimulus is taken to be two-dimensional.

To summarize, indirect perception takes as its departure point the idea that the input to the senses is inadequate. Where that input is based on retinal images (or iconic memories thereof), it is recognized as imprecise (there are distortions of size and shape, for example), impoverished (the third dimension is absent), and, like all discrete samples of time, are meaningless (without a context provided by the nonexistent past). The problem for a theorist who assumes the equivocality of the input becomes singularly straightforward. How is the inadequate input embellished, organized, structured, and repaired so as to yield an adequate perception of the events of the environment?

Directions for Research and Theory

The overarching question for a theory of indirect perception is: How are equivocal inputs elaborated into meaningful experiences? The current version of such a theory, the information processing approach (e. g., see Solso, 1979), has sought to describe that elaboration as a set of processes, storages, and transformations, ordered in time. In the main, these stages of processing describe how sense data are stored in various kinds of memories (iconic, short-term, long-term), how stored items are selected and elaborated, and how memory influences the perceptual experience.

This particular view of perception dictates that research should proceed in a particular way. This has generally involved such things as tachistoscopic presentations and a consequent attempt to describe what happens inside the perceiver in the few milliseconds or seconds that follow. Typically, research addresses questions on the specification of memory (buffer) sizes, speed and complexity of coding in the various memories, and the speed of information transfer between memories. We see, then, that research in the area of indirect perception generally asks how one brief display is processed. An analysis of perception done in this way has revealed a variety of stages of information storage and transformation. Over the years these stages have been elaborated so that the model today is a complex chain of events that intervene between the presentation of a display and its later report by the observer.

This is, of course, a simplistic account of information processing. It would take us too far afield from our intentions, however, to provide a precise description of the current state of the art. Rather, we simply acknowledge what we see as its two primary contentions: (1) the input does not provide a sufficient basis for an organism's knowing its environment, and (2) the embellishment that is needed for perception is supplied by the organism, usually in the form of memories. As long as these assumptions are accepted, regardless of changes in particular aspects (e.g., the specific nature of various memories), the overarching theory remains the same.

But these assumptions and a good deal of the philosophy behind them are rejected in a direct perception view. This fundamental rejection alters the entire foundation on which notions of perception rest. We are left with a vastly different approach to theory, one that starts with an entirely different set of questions and one, therefore, that will result in an entirely different set of answers.

DIRECT PERCEPTION: THE ECOLOGICAL VIEW

As noted above, the assumptions underlying a theory of direct perception are very different from the assumptions that underlie information processing. Let us make clear at the outset that those who espouse a theory of direct perception in no way belittle the richness of the perceptual experience. Representatives of the direct perception view clearly recognize such richness, but they have sought the basis of that perceptual richness *not* in the elaboration done by cognitive processes but *in the richness of the stimulation.* They propose that a precise specification of the nature of objects, places and events *is* available to the organism in the stimulation.

The source of this richness becomes apparent when we examine the way Gibson has reformulated the notion of stimulus (Gibson, 1960). Traditional descriptions of stimuli are in terms of very low-level physical variables, the metrics of sound or light a physicist would use. We need only look at the structuralists' notion of sensation, or the variables examined by psychophysicists to see that light has been dealt with in terms of intensity and wavelength, sound with respect to amplitudes and frequencies. Gibson, on the other hand, proposed that a more psychologically relevant treatment of stimulus would involve not energy, but *information.* The term "information" has a variety of meanings (for example, computer science) but, as Gibson uses the term, information is structure that specifies an environment to an animal. It is carried by higher-order patterns of stimulation—neither points of light nor collections of such points (images)—but, rather, complex structures often given over time. These patterns are information about the world.

The recognition of these distinctions drives a wedge between the notions of direct and indirect perception. For the indirect view, perceptual richness is a result of processing carried out by the perceiver; impinging stimulation is ambiguous at the outset and knowledge of the environment is a derivative of processing. For the direct approach, the stimulation specifies the environment and no elaboration is needed.

A further redefinition of stimulus drives the wedge even deeper. It will be remembered that theories of indirect perception consider the stimulus to be a discrete time-slice. Naturally, such a moment is thought to be meaningless until it can be related to other moments already identified and held in memory. But ecological psychologists would like to dispose of a notion such as the perception of discrete time-slices. It is their claim that perception is not limited to a present instant captured by a retinal snapshot. Rather, the "stimulus" or, better, information for vision, is in a transforming optic array. Time is not chopped into an arbitrary succession of nows, but organized into naturally occurring events of varying duration. That is, the transforming array is an optical flow or transpiring event which, in a sense, lasts as long as it has to. For example, a falling apple represents one kind of event while a horse race is another, longer event. Moreover, such events are not sequential, but nested. The falling apple is part of any number of longer events: the existence of the apple, the repro- duction of the species, the "discovery" of gravity, and so on. In sum, then, perception is of *events*—not of objects isolated in time or space.

If events are the significant units of the world, the world must be de- scribed in a way that preserves their integrity. The world must be described in terms of both time and space. And if, as we argued earlier, the di- mensions of stimuli must reflect the dimensions of that which they specify, stimuli (information), too, must be described in terms of both space and time. Thus, information, like the events it specifies, lasts over time. This is in bold contrast to the position described earlier, that the "stimuli" for vision are in a narrow interval called "now." If information can last over time, so, too, can perception, which is simply the detection of information. Perception does not produce isolated results which are dealt with at a later time (as is the case in memory-based theories). It is, rather, an ongoing activity of knowing the environment.

One perceives the beginning of an event at a later time because new information that still refers to it becomes available over time. More pre- cisely, a whole event is perceived not by adding parts, but by detecting the continuity of those "parts."

Clearly, the manner in which the direct perception approach deals with time and space is very different from that of the indirect perception theory. The justification for dispensing with some of Newton's ideas, some common-sense ideas, and, by inference, indirect perception's ideas, comes from the assumed primacy of events in perception. The license to rethink the division of the environment into time and space and the division of time into moments is granted by philosophy and contemporary physics, both of which have noted the arbitrariness involved in the distinctions.

The Ecological Approach to Events and "Stimuli"

Recall from an earlier section that time has traditionally been sepa- rated from space and defined in terms of nothing but itself. Such absolute time is somehow divisible into units, only one of which encompasses the present. This notion is important because it appears to have heavily influ- enced theories of perception which maintain that perception deals with the present—and, therefore, involves only one moment. It would seem, how- ever, that such a view of time, while it is appropriate to Newtonian physics and to an introspective description of experience, is not appropriate to a theory of knowing.

It is important to realize that we are not abandoning the one "real" or "true" notion of time. Rather, we simply abandon a view that Newton found convenient in his science for one that is convenient in ours. It is important to emphasize that our everyday notions of time are somewhat arbitrary. Our experience, culture, and language foster a particular kind of description of time. Wholly different views of time are fostered both by different cultures (Whorf, 1956) and by different sciences (e.g., relativity theory). Nevertheless, it is difficult to step back from our common theory. The extent to which our notions of time are ingrained in us is evidenced by the difficulties we encounter when we try to understand the theory of relativity. That space-time is "bent" around black holes and that a twin could travel off to a distant star and come back younger than his or her sibling simply boggles the mind.

At issue between the popular theory of time and the reconceptualization required for describing the information for event perception are two important points. The first deals with the parsing of time into past, present, and future, and the second, and more fundamental, issue is whether a concept like *absolute* time has a place in psychology.

First, the ecological approach questions the utility, in psychological theory, of distinctions between past, present, and future. It was claimed earlier that this distinction rests on introspection, on an experience of nowness. While "now" and thus, past, present, and future have psychological reality, it is impossible to specify their objective reality. Put another way, whether some event resides in the past, present, or future cannot be decided by physics because the temporal extent of "now" is based on phenomenal experience.[2]

The past-present-future trichotomy as a qualification attached to information, then, is rejected in ecological theory. This is not to say that perceivers do not have experiences of nowness, only that these experiences should not generate the axioms upon which a theory of knowing is based. The consequences of this rejection, as we saw earlier, are that neither perception itself nor the information whose detection is perception is

---

[2] The acceptance, by psychologists, of this trichotomy has far-reaching consequences. The primary implication is that some of the most central theoretical structures are merely the contents of consciousness elevated to axiom. The reasoning behind this claim is as follows. Part of conscious experience is an impression of nowness. On the basis of that impression perceivers divide up time into three domains: past, present, and future. When the perceivers become theorists of perception, the trichotomy emerges in the theory as dogma, and different classes of cognitive operations are called upon to explain the knowing of events in each domain: memory, perception, and expectation. It is a curious fact that, while experimental psychologists carefully avoid introspection as an experimental method, we allow some of our most fundamental paradigmatic and theoretical distinctions to rest squarely and solely on the shoulders of that introspection.

limited to an instantaneous present. Both should be considered quite separate from the impression of nowness that characterizes everyday experience.

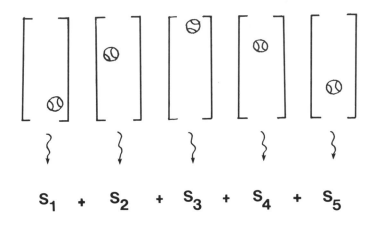

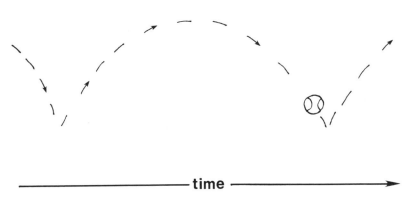

Figure 1-1. The traditional and ecological approaches to events and stimuli. The upper panel is a representation of the traditional view; the event is decomposed into a succession of moments, each described by its own stimulus. For the event to be perceived, the succession of stimuli must somehow be strung back together to reconstitute the dynamic event. In the lower panel, information is over time, and thus, coextensive with the event. The perceiver's task is merely to detect the event as specified by the information.

The second distinction that can be drawn between direct perception and more traditional accounts of time involves the viability of the concept of absolute time. It might be argued that the concept of absolute time has little value in psychology. The main issue here is which of the two concepts, time or change, is more fundamental. Is it the case that absolute time is an empty vessel that change can fill and, if change doesn't occur, time would proceed quite happily on its own? Or is it that change itself permits the existence of time? While it may seem unnecessarily mystical to note that in a static universe there is no time, if time is viewed as an abstraction from change we might well question the value of that abstraction. After all, *change itself* (events in space-time) is of interest to a behaving animal, not absolute time. On this account, the ecological view is that change is what is perceived. Thus, both time and space are needed not only for a description of change but also for a description of information that specifies change. In sum then, the notion of absolute time is given up in favor of space-time on the belief that perceivers do not perceive space and time, but *events* in space-time.

In these formulations, space and time are fused in a continuum of unfolding events. A space-time event need not be partitioned into a succession of nows, each with a perceptual product that must be integrated into an event. The notion of events in space-time allows radical departures from this standard perceptual theory. No longer the victim of an artificially limited present, information can specify or describe an event of essentially unlimited temporal extent. Perception, as the detection of information, is not constrained, either. As the ongoing activity of the registration of meaningful information, perception does not yield discrete products that must be related. Figure 1-1 summarizes these distinctions. In the upper panel, which schematizes traditional theory, the continuum of events is discretized into packets of data. It is left to the perceiver to reconstitute the packets into a continuous event. In the theory of direct perception (lower panel), information is not partitioned; it is coextensive with the event and therefore the event need only be detected, not reconstituted.

ADDITIONAL CONTRASTS

We have singled out Gibson's concept of information as complex structures defined over space *and* time to drive an initial wedge between the ecological movement and traditional psychology and philosophy. But the nature of information and what is or is not done with it constitute only one of several sets of distinctions that can be drawn between the two classes of perceptual theory. There are a number of other emphases and orientations adopted by the theory of direct perception that are at odds with current consensus. In this section we itemize these additional perspectives and thereby complete the philosophical backdrop for the chapters that follow.

While one of the most-discussed and least-resolved problems in the history of philosophy and psychology is the mind-body problem, there is a more fundamental dualism that requires attention: animal-environment dualism (Turvey & Shaw, 1979). Where one stands on this issue will determine, to a large extent, the direction taken on a number of subsidiary questions. The central question is whether an animal and its environment should be thought of as logically independent. More precisely, is the assumption of logical independence justifiable in light of the theoretical problems it creates? Traditional psychology has enforced such a dualism. Not only has psychology implicitly treated animal and world as independent entities, but it has limited investigation almost exclusively to the animal. Research begins with stimuli and ends with motor responses and pays scant attention to the larger context of the environment, i.e., what the stimuli describe and what the responses act upon. To the extent that the environment has entered into the understanding of perception, it has been described as *the* environment, distinct and independent from its inhabitants. The notion that *the* environment is animal-neutral is perhaps the most important manifestation of animal-environment dualism.

In the ecological approach, the dualism of animal and environment is rejected. Because the study of direct perception is the study of an animal knowing its environmental niche, it is suggested that perception must be the study of an animal-environment system (Turvey & Shaw, 1979). Put another way, if the animal is the knower and the environment is the known, a full accounting of knowing (that is, perceiving) cannot be had by analyzing only one. Moreover, it is claimed that the two—the animal and the niche—cannot be disjoined logically since each owes its very identity to the other. An animal is what it is given that its niche is what it is; an animal's wings, gills, snout, or hands describe that animal's environment. Likewise, a complete description of a niche describes the animal that occupies it. For example, if we specify in detail the niche of a fish (its medium, its predators and prey, its nest, etc.), we have in a way described the fish. Thus, just as the structure and functioning of an animal implies the environment, the particulars of the niche imply the structure and activities of its animal. *And it is this niche that the animal knows.* On these accounts it is claimed that there is little sense in saying that an animal knows *the* environment, as if a description of this planet *qua* environment would be the same for worms, birds, fish, dogs, or people. Rather, it seems more sensible to suppose that what an animal can know is as specific to its niche as its body is. As we shall see, the ecological psychology that emerges out of such an assumption is reiterated in several additional emphases embodied in the ecological approach.

One such emphasis of direct perception is on understanding *ordinary* seeing, hearing, and touching, i.e., the animal's knowing of its natural environment. Ecological psychologists are not as concerned with what a perceiver *can* do but with what she or he actually does when perceiving normally. This concern with perception under natural circumstances all but precludes the elegant technologies that are the stock-in-trade of information processing psychologists. These technologies, (e.g., tachistoscopic recognition, masking, and reaction time) are conspicuously artificial, and it is often difficult to ascertain how they relate to ordinary perception.

In contrast, the ecological approach asks what organisms need to know about their environments (e.g., finding a path through a cluttered room or locating a prey) and how it might be known. This results in an almost blanket rejection of questions dealing with objects in isolation, or with things presented very briefly because such situations are virtually non-existent in a natural environment.

Another distinction that can be drawn between theories of indirect and direct perception is the latter's evolutionary perspective. Ecological theories not only assume that organisms *exist in* a rich sea of information about their environments, but also that they *evolved in* a rich sea of information. Consequently, it is supposed that the structure and function of the perceptual systems have become tailored to the available information. It is fair to say that it has been only in the last dozen years or so that evolution has gained even a tenuous foothold in psychology. That half a century of research in animal learning is being rewritten (e.g., Bolles, 1978) with reference to biological constraints on learning, however, bears witness to the indispensability of evolutionary considerations.

Yet another contrast that figures significantly into a comparison of direct and indirect perception is what is meant by the phrase "active perceiver." Both approaches claim that perceivers are *active,* but the meanings of the statements are radically different for the two views. For information processing psychologists, perceivers are active in the "constructivist" sense (see Neisser, 1967); that is, they are active creators (embellishers, elaborators, etc.) of their perceptual experiences. Direct perceptionists, on the other hand, would say that perceivers are active in that they actively explore (look, feel, sniff, taste, and listen to) the contents of their environments. The direct perception approach suggests that perceivers are not passive recipients of information, but active, purposeful obtainers of information. Thus, if information *is* meager, the normal, active perceiver will engage in activities that yield more information.

SUMMARY

Perceptual theories take as their broad objective an explanation of the richness, variety, and accuracy with which human or other animals know their worlds. The ecological approach to this problem, the approach with which this book is concerned, attributes this richness, variety, and accuracy to the richness, variety, and accuracy of the information to the senses. Such a view states, simply, that knowing is the direct detection of that information with no need for such psychological processes as enrichment, inference, or deduction.

We have sketched the foundations of the theory of direct perception by contrasting it with the more traditional approach and, in particular, the current exemplar of that approach, information processing. The traditional approach is called indirect because it supposes that the perceiver makes substantial contributions to perception, usually in the form of memories of prior experience. That such contribution is deemed necessary implies that the input itself is insufficient to specify the perceiver's world.

Traditional psychology's doctrine of insufficient data can be traced to an assumption about how the environment and how stimuli ought to be described—with separable time and space components. An important corollary of this assumption is that time can be parceled into discrete units only one of which—"now"—is of interest to perception. Such time-slices, divorced from a nonexistent past, must contain only meager representations, indeed, of the objects and events in the world. Working on the basis of this assumption, information processing researchers have contrived experiments whose results are used to detail the subprocesses of the act of perceiving.

This entire approach to perception, and by implication, most of current cognitive psychology, is abandoned in adopting an ecological approach. To explain this approach, an emphasis on events was proposed that states, in essence, that the temporal extent of the "stimulus" is to be identified not with the temporal extent of a sensation of "nowness," but with the temporal extent of the *event* that the information specifies. Seams in patterns of energy are information about the beginning and ending of the event in question. Thus, it is not the case that earlier parts of an event are remembered while a later part is perceived; rather, the entire unfolding event is perceived. Moreover, arbitrary limits on how long an event may last are unjustifiable.

Released from the constraint that the input must be characterized as narrow slices, higher-order variables of stimulation emerge. Patterns of stimulation in space *and* time are, by this analysis, the dimensions of the stimulation that permit knowledge of the world. Research and theory in the direct perception approach, in turn, begin the search for information, defined as patterns that specify an environment to an animal.

Finally, there are additional contrasts that set ecological psychology apart from other approaches. Because the study of perception is the study of an animal knowing its environment, the unit of analysis must, by the nature of the theory, be an animal-environment system. One emphasis flowing from this orientation is on evolution—the history, so to speak, of the animal-environment system. A second emphasis is on the concern with perception under natural conditions, that is, an animal knowing *its own* environment. In addition, the animal is seen as an investigator, not simply an inhabitant, of its world.

The contrasts drawn in this chapter are revealing about both theoretical approaches, for a theory is known not only by the questions it asks, but by the questions it does not ask. The two approaches ask wholly different questions. Indeed, there is so little common ground that arguments between proponents of each approach are often exercises in futility or, at best, exercises in frustration. Answers cannot be compared because the questions are different. Questions cannot be compared because the underlying metatheories are different. However, the metatheories—for example, of time—*can* be compared, and such a comparison is what we have in fact outlined in this chapter.

OVERVIEW OF THE BOOK

In this final section, we present an overview of the ecological approach and, thereby, an outline of the chapters that follow.

It is essential, first, to understand Gibson's usage of the term, *information.* Information is the structured light, sound, or other medium that specifies objects, places, and events to an animal. As such, information is a bi-directional arrow, one arrow pointing to the environment and the other pointing to the animal; it is a bridge connecting the knower and the known. Chapter 2 examines the environment side of the bridge and attempts to explain how higher-order patterns of stimulation are invariantly tied to objects and events. We approach *invariants* from three disciplines: psychology, physics, and mathematics.

The second determiner of the nature of information—the animal, or perceiver—is considered in Chapter 3. The primary aim of this chapter is to explain *affordances.* Gibson's idea of affordance is that what the animal perceives are the acts or behaviors that are afforded or permitted by an object, place, or event.

Chapter 4 addresses the *detection of information.* Here we provide a metaphorical description of what might be occurring in the brain when an animal is knowing. Admittedly, the psychobiology of direct perception is the least well-articulated part of the theory. Detection is dealt with on an intuitive level and, perforce, is not described in terms of anatomy and physiology. Our primary goal is to explain what a biological machine that can support knowing might be like. In Chapter 4, we also examine the role of experience in the improvement of knowing. Our concern with improvement in perceiving is not limited to ontogenetic experience, but includes evolutionary "experience" as well. The improvement in knowing emerges in the forms of genetic preattunement to "universal" information and the education of attention to information about the "local" environment.

Chapters 2 through 4 offer, in sum, the ecological approach to the psychology of perceiving. In Chapter 5, attention is turned to the philosophical stance of the ecological approach. The ascription of perception to an animal-environment system, rather than merely to an animal, has several implications: It invites a new species of realism, termed ecological realism; it suggests a reconceptualization of the relationships among the natural sciences; and it offers a framework for investigating the nature of knowing as an activity defined over that animal-environment system.

Because the ecological approach is presented as a new approach to the psychology of perceiving, it should foster new questions, give rise to new types of answers, and encourage attention to topics not usually considered to be directly relevant to perception. Chapter 6 summarizes three areas of investigation motivated by the ecological approach that illustrate such change.

As a final discourse, Chapter 7 summarizes the approach and points out some of the work that still must be done. The Appendix answers some of the questions frequently directed toward the approach and rebuts some criticisms frequently levied against it.

Information
and the
Environment

Chapter 1 provided the foundation for an explanation of Gibson's notion of information. The two major principles that apply to this chapter's discussion of information are (1) the richness and accuracy of perception are due to the richness and accuracy of the information available to perceptual systems, and (2) such information cannot be measured with the traditional variables of physics.

Because the concept of information is of extraordinary theoretical richness, it will be clarified a little at a time, first through a discussion of *invariants* in this chapter, and later by an explication of *affordances*. The latter is a bold new concept which represents Gibson's most revolutionary departure from traditional psychology and philosophy.

INVARIANTS

The viability of a theory of direct perception depends on a demonstration that the energy patterns stimulating the senses contain a specification of the environment. To argue that the sensory input need not be embellished is to argue that, at some level, the light to an eye, the pressure waves to an ear, or the pattern of pressures on the skin are uniquely and invariantly tied to their sources in the environment. The specification is sought in *in-*

variants, patterns of stimulation over time and/or space that are left unchanged by certain transformations. In this chapter we consider the concept of invariant: first, as it relates to "perceptual constancy"; second, as it relates to the laws of physics; and third, as it is quantified and described mathematically. As we shall see, invariants give us only limited insight into the notion of information; a full understanding of information will require a consideration of the animal.

Invariants and Perceptual Constancy

To provide intuitive guidance as to the nature of an invariant and how the concept relates to more traditional accounts of the problem of perception, the concepts of invariant and perceptual constancy can be considered together. We make this juxtaposition of invariant and perceptual constancy with some hesitancy because we do not want to portray the ecological approach as merely an alternative set of answers to traditional questions; it often asks questions of its own. Nor do we want to imply that the importance of the concept of invariant lies solely in its power to solve constancy problems. Nevertheless, some examples of perceptual constancy should serve to usher in the notion of invariance.

"Perceptual constancy" labels phenomena in which the perceived properties of objects remain the same even though there is significant change in the proximal stimulus (e.g., the retinal image or sound waves to the ear). If one itemizes the properties of an object and seeks a basis for each property in variables of stimulation that seemingly ought to provide that basis, one often comes up empty-handed. Consider three such properties: size, brightness,[1] and shape. Size constancy is illustrated by the fact that our perception of the size of an object remains constant in spite of the increase in visual angle which accompanies its approach; one sees an object of constant size even with a changing image size. Likewise, brightness remains constant even though the amount of light reflected off that object changes; coal does not look lighter when brought into sunlight nor paper darker when brought into shade. Nor does the perceived shape of an object, such as a table, change even though the forms on the retina change from one perspective to another.

How is one to explain these constancies? Returning to the contrast between direct and mediational theory, we expect that the mediational approach would see constancies, at least in part, as an achievement of the

---

[1] For consistency, we should use the phrase "reflectance constancy" or "albedo constancy," but "brightness constancy" is the phrase most commonly found in the literature.

nervous system—a correction, as it were, for the changing character of the input. The ecological approach, on the other hand, seeks a basis for perceptual constancies not in corrective mechanisms in the perceiver but in properties of the stimulation whose own constancy or invariance accompanies the persistent properties of objects (e.g., size). For example, the ecological psychologist would not look to the *amount* of light in a patch of the visual field to be the basis of perceived brightness. Rather, it is in the complex relationships among patches that a basis for perceptual constancy is sought. The task for the experimenter is to determine which of these relationships are specific to surface brightness, which are specific to intensity of illumination, and which are specific to the inclination of the surface relative to the source of illumination. Brightness, illumination, and inclination all affect the lightness of a patch, so it must be in some more complex structure that these properties are to be distinctively specified. And these higher-order variables of stimulation provide us with a first approximation to the idea of an invariant as follows: Amid change in some variables of stimulation, there are constant or invariant patterns that provide the basis for perceptual constancy.

But how might we identify the invariant patterns of light to which the perceptual constancies correspond? Brightness, size, and shape are, of course, constant properties of the objects as well as of our perceptions. The search for invariants, then, is the search for the bridge of light between object and perceiver. To ask about invariants for brightness, size, and shape is to ask how these properties are specific—related one-to-one—to the structured light arriving to the eye. We will refer back to these perceptual constancies as we develop principles of sufficient power to capture the invariants on which they are based.

Invariants and Ecological Physics

As a preface to the discussion of what constant properties in the light might be like, a description of how light gets structured is useful. Most of the light detected by perceivers is reflected light (except in such cases as seeing traffic signals and neon signs or reckoning the time by gazing at the sun). Reflected light gets its structure from the process of reflection. That is, radiant light from a source such as the sun is modified by reflection. The particular structures yielded by such modification are due to the surfaces which the light strikes. A lump of coal, a paper, a mirror, and a box each reflect light differently. Figure 2-1 illustrates some of the causes and consequences of this scatter-reflection of light. First, note that some surfaces (e.g., paper) reflect far more light than they absorb; for others (e.g., coal) the converse is true. Second, the angle of incidence of the light illuminates some faces or facets of surfaces more than others. Third, some surfaces (mirrors) don't scatter the light at all while others (paper) scatter it dramatically.

The patterns of dotted lines in Figure 2-1, then, represent a crude picture of the structure of the ambient light specifying a collection of objects on a table. While the structure depicted in our figure may appear complex, it is but a small fraction of the complexity of structure that would normally be present. Our picture shows only two dimensions. Nothing is moving. It ignores the fact that reflection and absorption vary as a function of wavelength. Only three incident rays on each object are shown. And, finally, incident light is shown from only one direction; normally, objects are illuminated not only directly by the radiant source, but also indirectly by light scattered in the atmosphere or reflected from other surfaces.

This analysis would, in Gibson's (1961) terms, fall under the heading of *ecological optics.* Ecological optics is the physics of light relevant to an animal in its environment. A physicist's analysis of light, as particle or wave, traveling at the limiting speed of the universe, bent by gravity, measured in angstroms and photons, is of little use to those of us who wish to describe the structure of light important to an animal. While it might not be immediately obvious how this structure might be quantified or precisely described, it is easy to appreciate the idea that light is structured. Moreover, the structure is locally predictable; that is, physics could, in principle, provide a point by point accounting of reflection and ab-

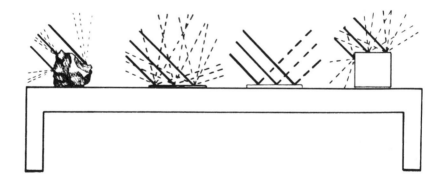

Figure 2-1. Some of the ways in which light may be structured by scatter-reflection by various substances and surfaces—a lump of coal, matte white paper, a mirror, and a box. The solid lines represent incident light; the dotted lines, reflected light.

sorption. That each local point behaves lawfully requires that the global optical structure is lawful (organized) as well. This means, simply, that the correspondence between the structured light and the surface composition, size, shape, position, and other characteristics of the object or place are derivable from the laws of physics.

Let us now consider an entire room filled with structured light. This global structure is, for reasons described above, a precise specifier of the room and its contents. Obviously a perceiver cannot intercept all the individual rays that constitute this structure. Rather, the activity of a perceiver is characterized as *sampling the global structure*. (This sampling is not to be confused with time-slice sampling described in Chapter 1.) Because the various samples that an observer might make are samples of the same thing—the global structure of the light—it is conjectured that the samples are in some way equivalent.

The notions that invariant structures exist, can be sampled, and that the samples can be in some way equivalent are nicely illustrated by holograms and their properties. Holograms are specially created photographic plates that capture on film the kind of optical structure we have been describing. It is not important for present purposes to understand the intricacies of the optical interference that is recorded on film; more important are general properties of holograms. We will, therefore, describe their preparation only briefly and concentrate on the properties relevant to understanding the structure of light and its sampling.

Figure 2-2 schematizes how structured light is captured on a holographic plate. The reflected light (broken lines in Figure 2-2) and the reference beam (solid lines) set up patterns of interference which are recorded on film. The pattern of interference fringes on the film embodies the optical structure. We know that the optical structure is captured because if one looks through the film (under appropriate illumination) one can see a three-dimensional "image" of the original object. The information is so complete that the hologram might be taken for the object itself. But unlike a slide or negative, if the film is inspected no image can be seen. A holographic plate captures more information than a camera can and does so in a different way—without images.

Thus, holography illustrates three important ideas: First, optical structure can specify objects and their layout. Second, optical structure can be registered without reference to images (cf. Chapter 1). A third feature of holograms that guides an understanding of optical structure relates to the claim that such structure is somehow equivalent at various locations (i.e., that a room has *an* optical structure that can be sampled from many station points). If a hologram is cut into little pieces, *each of the pieces will be sufficient* to provide a three-dimensional image of the

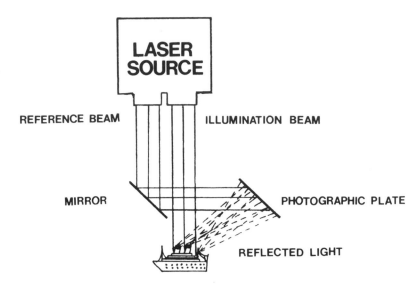

Figure 2-2. A schematic of the equipment and arrangement needed to produce a hologram.

whole object (e.g., the boat in Figure 2-2). These bits of hologram, then, are samples of the structured light.

A perceiver, like a hologram, samples optical structure. A perceiver gets one sample, while stationary, by opening one eye. A more elaborate sample is had merely by moving or by opening the other eye. Thus, ambiguity in a single sample can be dissolved with exploration; it need not, as indirect perceptionists might hypothesize, be rendered unambiguous by processes going on inside an animal.

Different samples of the light structured by one object constitute an "equivalence class." The various samples of global structure are not, of course, identical. If they were, a perceiver would be provided no information about her or his position in the world. Thus, a sample not only carries information about the objects and places in the room, but also about the position of the perceiver.

The notion of samples of *the* optical structure of a room provides, we hope, a strong intuitive description of the invariants that specify the layout of the room and its contents. Such invariants are the basis of constant perception in spite of changes in position and perspective. Various positions and perspectives, again, are samples of the same invariant structure.

By the same token, the light structured by the piece of coal is a sample of a larger equivalence class, that of light structured by any piece of coal. The modulation of light by coal is characteristic of its irregular, multifaceted, achromatic, and absorbent surface. Thus, there exists an invariant light structure specifying coal. Again, not all samples of this structure are identical; individual samples specify the shape of the particular piece under observation. Nevertheless, at some level of description, there exist invariants that specify the substance. And it is in such invariants that the basis of one of the perceptual constancies referred to earlier, brightness constancy, must be provided.

The notion of equivalence classes is generalized to equivalence classes of shapes and even functions. For example, a cube of gray marble presumably structures light in a way that is the same at some level of description as that structured by a cube of meat. All objects that can be sat upon presumably structure light in a way in which an even higher-order invariant would have to be called upon to describe.

In the foregoing examples of invariants, the description of higher-order patterns has been limited to those which show no change over time. That is, they are structures in the light which, despite changes in some variables (e.g., illumination), remain invariant.

Another important type of invariant is a *pattern over time.* Invariant patterns over time refer to constant patterns of change—that is, manners or styles of change. Perhaps this notion is best explained by way of example. A melody is a simple example of an invariant pattern in time; a melody is a pattern over time—not a particular collection of notes nor a particular musical instrument. One invariant for a melody happens to be a set of ratios of times and fundamental frequencies; as an example, given some arbitrary initial frequency, F, the second and third notes of the children's song, Three Blind Mice, will be $.891F$ and $.794F$ with the third note lasting twice as long as the first two, which are of equal duration. What we have done in specifying the ratios of frequencies and durations is to describe a pattern over time. In whatever key and tempo the song is played, the first three notes will always bear these relationships.

The invariants described above are structural properties of proximal stimuli that are shared by objects that, at some level of description, can be considered the same (e.g., the light reflected by two pieces of coal or the acoustic pattern of a song played by cello or harmonica). As such, these invariants are referred to as *structural invariants.* These properties remain constant even though there are other properties that change. One piece of coal does structure light somewhat differently from the next; the acoustic pattern of a melody played on a cello is different from that played on a harmonica. Notice that in these two examples, invariants are properties shared by the energy patterns structured by two or more different objects. As illustrated in some of our earlier examples, it is also the case that the energy patterns structured by single objects can remain invariant while the object undergoes some transformation. These latter structural invariants are more interesting and important than those in the coal and melody examples because these invariants and the transformations associated with them are central to understanding the information that specifies *events*.

As noted in Chapter 1, an emphasis on events is one of the central themes of the ecological approach. If we define events as changes in objects or collections of objects, structural invariants are those properties that specify the object or collection participating in the event.

But what about the change occurring in the object? How is it specified in the stimulation? To answer this question, one must look to *transformational invariants*. A transformational invariant is the style of change in the proximal stimulus that specifies the change occurring in or to the object (sliding, spinning, growing, walking, rupturing, stretching, etc.). Thus, if an event is something happening to something, the "something happening" is presumed to be specified by transformational invariants while the "something" that it is happening to is presumed to be described by structural invariants (Shaw, McIntyre, & Mace, 1974; Pittenger & Shaw, 1975a).

Let us examine transformational invariants by considering how a style of change in a stimulus can specify dynamic characteristics of an event. The Doppler effect in physics provides such an example.

A brief lesson from ecological acoustics will provide us with the basis of the Doppler shift. When an object vibrates, it sends out waves of compression and rarefaction of air molecules—high and low pressure, respectively. When the object and listener are stationary, these pressure waves are heard as a constant pitch or set of pitches. The closer the wave fronts are together, that is, the shorter the wavelength, the higher the pitch. Additionally, the further the listener is from the source, the lower the amplitude of the pressure wave (amounts of compression and rarefaction), and the less loud will be the sound.

A stationary, vibrating object structures the sound simply as a set of equidistant and concentric circles (spheres) moving away from the object. If, however, the vibrating object is moving, the pressure waves become structured in an interesting manner; the object tends to "catch up" with parts of its pressure waves and move away from other parts. Figure 2-3 depicts this situation. An invariant relation between the velocity of the object and this pattern of sound waves is derivable in a simple way from the laws of physics.

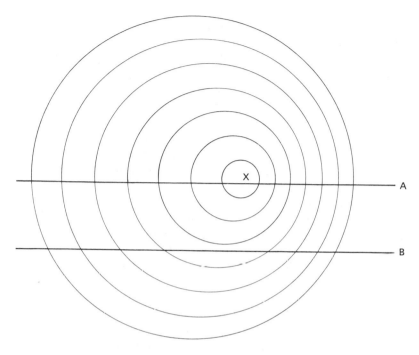

Figure 2-3. The acoustic pattern emitted by a vibrating object moving from left to right. Lines *A* and *B* represent the positions of two stationary observers as the object moves by. Notice the different patterns on each observer line.

If a stationary listener is brought into the picture, the noisy object will, of course, be moving relative to the perceiver. The perceiver will, in consequence, be stimulated by a particular *pattern* of changes in intensity and pitch depending on the distance to the object and its direction of motion relative to the perceiver. On the two horizontal lines in Figure 2-3 are represented the patterns of stimulation available to a perceiver as the object passes by. If the object is almost on a collision course, as with perceiver *A*, the sound pattern at this location will be constant pitch/increasing amplitude, followed by a rapid downward transition in pitch, followed by a constant pitch of decreasing amplitude. The pattern for a second perceiver who is further removed from the object's path is similar, differing primarily in its less-abrupt pitch transition. It is important to note that these patterns are essentially unique to the situations described. (Just how specific the pattern is to the distance and velocity of the object is beyond the scope of this book, but the above analysis captures only the most obvious aspects of the event that are conveyed by the patterns of change associated with the Doppler effect.)

In any case, one can see that it is the pattern of change of amplitude and frequency that constitutes the invariant. The particular amplitudes and frequencies, as long as they are audible, are quite irrelevant. That is, the sounds over which the pattern is wrought can be anything: car horn, flapping wings, or airplane engine. (The identity of the moving object is specified by structural invariants.) It is the pattern of change that is constant or invariant for a particular velocity and distance. As such, transformational invariants underlie a new category of perceptual constancy: *change constancy* (Mark, 1979).

The examples presented above are not meant to imply that transformational invariants are limited to auditory input; they are equally relevant to vision. One of the most elegant demonstrations of the importance of transformations for vision was presented by Johansson (1973). Figure 2-4 depicts a series of lights which are viewed by observers. The lights are attached to a human's major joints—shoulder, elbow, wrist, hip, knee, and ankle. The human is dressed in black and photographed in the dark so only the points of light are visible. If these lights are viewed while stationary, an observer reports some random arrangement of lights. If the person to whom the lights are attached begins walking, hopping, doing sit-ups, or another familiar activity, the observer will immediately and unmistakably see a person engaging in that activity. The manner in which the lights change relative to each other in time and space specifies the event. If the lights stop moving, they return to what appears to be a random assemblage.

What makes Johansson's experiment of further importance is that his stimuli separate "human forms" from invariants specifying humans moving. It is a relatively commonplace assumption that the perception of an object is based on an analysis of forms or images on the retina. Johansson's results are proof that the perception of shape or form (e.g., of a human body) need not be based on shapes or forms on the retina. Even a style of change among lights, as he has shown, is sufficient to carry information about shape.[2]

Johansson's demonstration has a further meaning for us in that it clearly embodies the event orientation discussed in Chapter 1. The gist of that discussion was that events are extended in space and time and, there-

---

[2] Some more recent research indicates that even more detailed information is available. For example, perceivers have demonstrated the ability to detect the sex and even the identity of a walking individual to whom lights are attached (Cutting & Koslowski, 1977; Koslowski & Cutting, 1977).

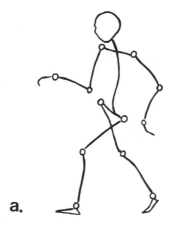

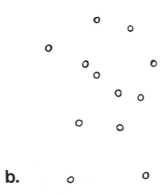

Figure 2-4. Lights viewed by observers in Johansson's demonstration are attached to a human's major joints (*a*). While stationary, the arrangement appears random (*b*). If the "target" walks, however, it is immediately identified as a person walking.

fore, the patterns that specify those events are spatially and temporally extended. Johansson's stimuli are instances of patterns in which a discrete time slice offers no information at all; recall that when individual patterns were observed, the lights were seen as a random assemblage.

If transformational invariants have temporal extent, it is necessary to ask whether there is some upper limit on how long that extent can be. We certainly do not want to impose some arbitrary limits that are consistent with our notions about how long "now" lasts; such an imposition is unjustifiable given our emphasis on events. Rather, the duration of a transformation is tied to the duration of the event which it specifies. Thus, the upper limit would be set by the duration of a psychologically salient event. In Chapter 6, we will examine some research suggesting that salient transformations can last a lifetime.

Invariant as a Geometric Concept

The notion of invariance has been approached from two angles. The first was to suggest that invariants provide a basis in the stimulation for perceptual constancies. The second was to describe invariants as structures or transformations that are straightforward consequences of the laws of physics. While these approaches offer some intuitive appreciation for the existence and origin of invariants, they are not sufficiently explicit. We must ask how invariants are described and quantified. The domain of this question is that of mathematics and, in particular, geometry. The geometrical analysis of invariants presented here has two central aims: (1) to make the definition of an invariant precise, and (2) to exemplify the ecological approach to searching for invariants, or, more precisely, searching for the geometries appropriate for describing the invariants that support perception. The vehicle for the second aim will be that of shape perception. In describing the search for the invariants that specify shape, we shall identify a basis for what is known traditionally as *shape constancy.*

This analysis is presented to assure the reader that invariance is not merely a panacea for constancy problems. Invariants are not simply identified with perceptual constancies and vice versa. Rather, the notion of an invariant is firmly rooted in mathematics, and proponents of direct perception use the term in a wholly proper way. In this section we give a rudimentary explanation of that assertion and illustrate how the mathematical approach might guide inquiry.

An invariant is defined as a constant pattern, usually amid change in other variables of stimulation. As implied above, the branch of mathematics that seems best suited to a description and a quantification of variance and invariance is geometry. But the concepts needed here must go beyond familiar geometry so we will discuss a number of different geometries. While an elaboration of one geometry might be sufficient for fulfilling our first aim—to provide a mathematical description of an invariant—our second aim requires more than that. The notion of "searching for an invariant" underscores the ecological conviction that, *at some level of analysis, there necessarily exists information that is specific to its source* (Turvey, Shaw, & Mace, 1978). The job of ecological scientists is to find that level; for certain questions one geometry might be appropriate, while for other questions another is needed.

To understand the notion of different geometries, consider two ways in which geometries can be defined. First, one can begin with a set of assumptions or axioms (e.g., all right angles are equal) and from them deduce the geometry. Second, a geometry can be distinguished by identifying the group of transformations under which its theorems remain true. This latter way of describing a geometry, first formulated by Klein in his Erlangen program in 1872, is the one that is of interest to us.

To reiterate, the second way to define a geometry is to define the group of transformations that leave invariant certain properties of a space. This approach will be drawn upon as we provide a thorough description of what an invariant is and show how the search for an invariant to support shape perception might proceed. The particular analysis given here is drawn from the work of Shaw and his associates (Shaw, McIntyre, & Mace, 1974; Shaw & Pittenger, 1977).

The first question is, in what geometry can a precise description of the invariants that support shape perception be found? That is, under the transformations (changes) of which geometry is information about shape preserved? There are many geometries that might be evaluated in this regard and we shall present several organized in a hierarchy ranging from the most restricted to the most liberal invariant.

The most familiar concept is, of course, the Euclidean geometry taught in secondary school. In Euclidean geometry, any objects that are metrically equivalent—that is, have the same measurements—are said to have the same shape.[3]

The shape invariant in Euclidean geometry may be summarized as a distance relationship wherein the distance between two points on the transformed object is equal to the distance between two corresponding points on the original object (Figure 2-5). The transformations that preserve distance (therefore allowable in Euclidean geometry) are rotation, translation, and reflection. Any combination of these transformations can be

---

[3] The term *shape* in geometry is, obviously, somewhat different from the way the word is commonly used. In geometry there is no such thing as absolute shape; the shape of something is relative to the geometry. Thus, in different geometries different classes of shapes will be said to be the same.

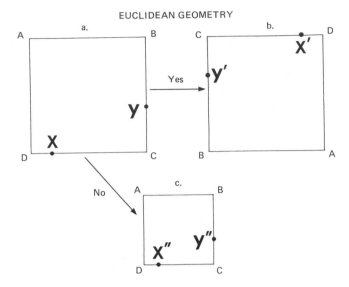

Figure 2-5. A 180° rotation transforms the square in (*a*) to the square in (*b*). In Euclidean geometry, these figures have the same shape—i.e., side *AB* remains parallel to side *CD*, angle *ABC* is still 90°, and the distance from *x* to *y* [denoted $d(x, y)$] is the same as from *x'* to *y'* [$d(x', y')$]. The square shown in (*c*) is not metrically equivalent—the distance from *x"* to *y"* [$d(x", y")$] is less than $d(x, y)$ and, hence, in Euclidean geometry, (*a*) and (*c*) are not the same shape.

applied to a rigid object and its rigid properties (its shape) will stay the same.

There are, however, classes of shapes that seem perceptually equivalent, but which, in Euclidean geometry, are of different shapes. For example, the image of an object viewed at close range vs. at a distance are, in some sense, equivalent though their absolute measurements differ. A photograph illustrates this point simply. If a basketball were photographed from distances of 3, 6, and 10 feet, the size of the image in the picture would depend on the viewing distance. Therefore, shapes of this sort cannot be described fully by absolute measurement—magnifications and reductions require a less restrictive invariant. Some property is preserved in size transformations, but it is necessary to turn to similarity geometry to describe it. In similarity geometry, shape is defined by a ratio of similitude—transformed distances are constant multiples of original distances (Figure 2-6). When distances between parts of a figure remain proportional, the shapes are the same. The domain of equivalent shapes is thereby expanded.

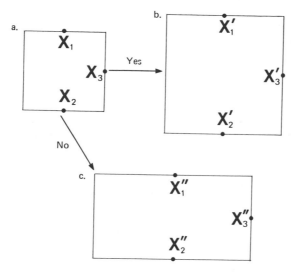

Figure 2-6. Square (*b*) is magnified to two times square (*a*). In similarity geometry, these are equivalent shapes—i.e., $d(x_1, x_2) \times k = d(x_1{}', x_2{}')$ for all *x*'s. Shape (*c*) is not equivalent because the distance proportion is not maintained $[d(x_1, x_2) = d(x_1{}'', x_2{}'')$, while $d(x_2, x_3) \times k = d(x_2{}'', x_3{}'')$; i.e., one distance is changed while another is not].

While similarity geometry is appropriate for this class of perceptually equivalent shapes, other shapes that are different in similarity geometry might, nevertheless, be considered perceptually equivalent. For example, a pencil retains its characteristic "pencil-shape" though it may be sharpened down to a little stump. Similarity geometry fails here because it is limited to uniform, overall size transformations, not those applied to only one dimension.

Stretching or compression in only one direction at a time, as when a square becomes a rectangle, or transforming the angles of a figure, as when a square becomes a nonrectangular rhombus, are not allowable in either Euclidean or similarity geometry. But such transformations still preserve certain properties and these can be explained with reference to affine geometry. The relationship is described most simply as the equation:

$$\frac{X_1 - X_2}{X_2 - X_3} = \frac{X_1{}' - X_2{}'}{X_2{}' - X_3{}'}$$

where the *X*s are the coordinates of three collinear points. Absolute distances are no longer proportional. The invariant is now described as the

33

ratio between two adjacent segments on a given line (Figure 2-7). If the transformation preserves that ratio, the shapes are equivalent.

It should be clear that when an operation is introduced that destroys the invariants of a given geometry, a different geometry must be called upon to provide a description of the new invariants. The new geometries to which we resort can be characterized as progressively "weaker" in that, with fewer and broader invariants, they give rise to progressively wider equivalence classes. Obviously, a very unrestricted geometry is needed to account for all the shapes that can be judged perceptually equivalent (e.g., a football viewed from different perspectives, varieties of apples, Tudor architecture). Mathematically, the description becomes increasingly abstract and complex.

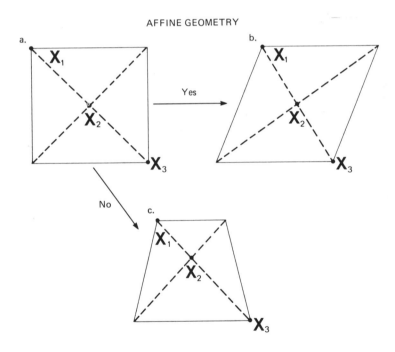

Figure 2-7. A square (*a*) becomes a rhombus (*b*) under a "shear" transformation, which changes the angles of an object. The ratio of $x_1 - x_2$ to $x_2 - x_3$ for three collinear points remains the same such that, in affine geometry, the shapes are the same. The trapezoid (*c*) is a projection of (*a*), but does not preserve the ratio (i.e., is not an affine-equivalent shape).

A common class of shape invariants is that provided by polar projection. These shapes are distinguished by the great distortion of metric relationships. For example, the circular shape of the mouth of a glass is projected on the retina as an ellipse. Parallel railroad tracks appear to meet at the horizon. The corner of a room where two walls meet the ceiling contains three 90° angles that projectively total 360° (Figure 2-8). In projective geometry, shape can no longer be defined as simple measurements or proportions; shape is equivalent to a cross-ratio of the form

$$\frac{(X_1-X_4)(X_3-X_2)}{(X_1-X_3)(X_3-X_4)} = \frac{(X_1'-X_4')(X_3'-X_2')}{(X_1'-X_3')(X_3'-X_4')}$$

where Xs are again collinear (Figure 2-9). One need not understand the computations involved to note the level of abstractness necessary to describe the invariants that would provide a basis for the shape constancy of a simple rigid object.

We have yet to come to terms with the class of elastic shapes such as living, growing things, smiling faces, and bending fingers. The invariants

Figure 2-8. The three 90° angles of a corner project to a sum of 360°.

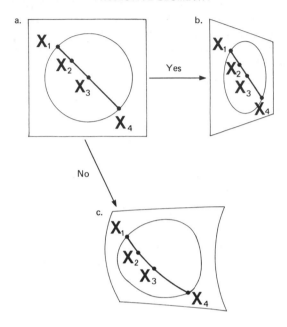

Figure 2-9. A circle (*a*), when rotated about the *y*-axis, is projected as an ellipse (*b*). The cross-ratio referred to in the text describes the invariant preserved in this transformation. The topological transformation induced by bending the paper on which the circle is drawn yields a figure (*c*) in which the cross-ratios are different.

that enable us to know a plant, for example, at various stages of growth must be very abstract indeed. To capture this most liberal concept of shape, invariants must be sought in the weakest geometry, topology. Among the properties preserved in topology are connectivity, closed curves, and linear and cyclic order. Invariants are based on qualitative rather than quantitative properties. The invariants are fewer in number, but more subtle in nature. The abstractness of topological invariants points toward the abstractness of the perceptual information underlying their perceptual constancy.

We have described at some length the concept of invariant, using an analysis of the invariants upon which the perception of shape might be based. But the importance of properties of an invariant as a geometric concept extend beyond shape perception to event perception in general.

These properties can be summarized as follows: An invariant must be described with reference to a transformation or a set of transformations; it is of little use to say that something is invariant without specifying the transformations over which it is invariant. An invariant, together with the group of transformations over which it is invariant, define a geometry. Thus, one task for the perceptionist who seeks to describe information is to find the geometry in which the information resides.

Relating these principles to issues raised in the earlier part of the chapter, and again using the vehicle of shape perception, will make the synthesis more concrete. Two classes of invariants, structural and transformational, have been described. Structural invariants were patterns that remained constant while something else changed. In contrast, transformational invariants were styles of change that remained constant while applied to any number of structures. The term structural invariant is exemplified by geometric shape—those properties that are left unchanged. Similarly, transformational invariants correspond to those operations that leave certain structures invariant.

As an example, consider the structured light schematized in Figure 2-1 and an observer walking toward the assemblage of objects on the table. Some patterns of retinal stimulation are invariant with respect to the transformations that are engendered by walking forward. They can specify the sizes, shapes, and relative positions of the room and its contents. One such invariant would be the cross-ratios of the projections of distances among the objects. And, the transformations in the optic array wrought by the approach of the perceiver correspond to the speed and direction of the perceiver's approach, her or his height relative to the table, and sundry other information about the perceiver's motion.

Taken together, structural and transformational invariants provide the minimal description of a perceptual event—a style of change wrought over an object or object complex. They determine what has been called the *information space* (Shaw & Pittenger, 1977) of the perceptual world; they comprise the geometry for perception.

ENVIRONMENT, INFORMATION, AND ANIMALS

A description of the relation between the environment and the structure of light and sound provides one facet of the concept of information—that is, *information-about*. These patterns of energy describe objects, places, and events in the environment. However, there is a second and equally important facet of information that information-about does not touch upon. This second facet of information is *information-for* and the object of the preposition *for* is the animal. Information is the bridge between an animal and its environment and cannot be usefully described without a specification of *both*.

The structure of the optic array provides human beings with information about the position of objects relative to each other. It is understood that if human beings were not biologically sensitive to that optical structure, it would make little sense to characterize the optical structure as information. Implicit in the concept of information, then, are both the perceiver and the perceived.

If a small mammal is hiding in a room, the heat it radiates will identify its location. That is, the thermal structure of the room specifies the location of the animal. This energy pattern is not information to human beings because biologically we are not equipped to detect that information. Lice, or as a better example, rattlesnakes *are* sensitive to such information. It is said that rattlesnakes and related pit vipers can detect temperature changes on the order of $.002°C$. Their "pits" are directional, temperature-gradient sensing devices that permit them to detect invariants specifying the direction of the warm-blooded creatures upon which they prey. Such thermal structure, therefore, is information to some animals but not others.

In like manner, ultraviolet radiation provides a "nectar guide" to flowers. Again, this is not information to humans or pit vipers because they are not sensitive to such energy patterns; honeybees, on the other hand, are sensitive to this ultraviolet radiation and, therefore, such radiation does represent information to them. It should be noted that in each of these examples the invariants that the organisms detect specify very *salient* aspects of the environment; humans need to know the layout of surfaces, pit vipers need to know the locations of mammals, and bees need to know the location of nectar. Later we shall return to notions of salience and relevance when we examine the idea that the meaning of a place, object or event is to be understood in terms of what behaviors a place, object or event affords an animal.

To summarize, a failure to consider both parts of information—information *about* an environment *for* an animal—is to miss the very essence of the concept of information.

Information and Perceptual Systems

In this chapter, we have begun a consideration of Gibson's idea of information but, as noted, information is not independent from the animal that is being informed. The role of the animal in a description of information is due not only to the fact that the animal must have appropriately attuned perceptual systems, but also to the fact that a large portion of the input is *obtained information*. That is, the animal acts in such a way as to make information available. The classes of exploratory activities that the animal uses to investigate, therefore, are one set of determinants of the classes of information available to that animal.

To elucidate the notion of obtained information, Gibson (1966) suggests that senses ought to be considered as *perceptual systems*. Briefly stated, a perceptual system is a set of organs, including receptors, which can attend to or explore the environment and detect certain classes of information. Gibson (1966) identified five such perceptual systems: the basic orienting system, the auditory system, the haptic system, the taste-smell system, and the visual system.

Included in each of these perceptual systems is one or more exploratory activities that yield information above and beyond that which is imposed upon the organism. Consider, for example, the texture of cloth. As the cloth is held in a perceiver's hand, crude information about its texture is available. If the perceiver engages in the exploratory activities of feeling (rubbing, fingering, touching) more detailed information about its texture is yielded. In this example, the perceptual system is the haptic system, the primary organ is the hand (including muscles, joints, and skin) and the mode of attention is feeling. The new information includes the patterns over time of deformation of the skin, skin-to-cloth friction, etc.

The most obvious cases of exploration-induced information arise in the visual system. Head and/or body movements, for example, induce transformations in the optic array (patterns of light arriving at the eye) that are reliable specifiers of the relative positions of objects and surfaces in the field of view (motion perspective).

Whether the exploratory activity is sniffing, feeling, hefting, or neck craning, all appear to reveal additional invariants, additional information, to the perceiver. Tying this idea together with those in preceding sections of this chapter, we are led to the following conclusions: Energy patterns that are invariant with respect to relevant transformations and that specify the environment are not, by themselves, equivalent to information; *the animal must be specified*. Moreover, even a complete inventory of those invariant structures must be based on an equally complete inventory of the consequences of each of the exploratory (and performatory) activities in which an animal can engage. In sum, animal and environment are inexorably brought together in Gibson's notion of information.

SUMMARY

Information is a dual concept whose components can be described as information-about and information-for. In this chapter we have dealt primarily with information-about.

Much of the notion of information-about is expressed by the concept of invariant. From a psychological point of view, invariants are those higher-order patterns of stimulation that underlie perceptual constancies, or, more generally, the persistent properties of the environment that an animal is said to know. From the perspective of ecological physics, invariants come from the lawful relations between objects, places, and events in the environment (part of which is other animals) and the structure or manner of change of patterns of light, sound, skin deformation, joint configuration, and so on.

Finally, geometry provided the tools to describe invariants more explicitly. Invariants are, quite simply, properties that tolerate certain transformations without changing. Invariants, together with the allowable transformations, constitute the geometry for perception or the information space. Information space, as structures and transformations, provides the basis for describing events—changes wrought over objects. Structures and transformations can both be invariant. Structural invariants are properties that are constant with respect to certain transformations while transformational invariants are those styles of change common to a class of transformations that leave certain structures invariant.

Invariant structures in light and sound not only specify objects, places, and events in the environment but also the activities of the organism (e.g., speed and direction of locomotion by the optical transformations at the eyes). Thus, invariants are, by virtue of the laws that support them, information about the environment and an animal's relation to it.

While an appreciation of invariants in patterns of energy and all the events that such invariants specify is necessary for an appreciation of information, it is not sufficient. This is true trivially in that invariants are not "information" to an animal that does not have the biological machinery (or prosthesis) to detect them. There exists a far more compelling set of arguments for the inclusion of the animal and the notion of information-for, arguments to which we now turn.

3

Information
and the
Animal

Traditionally, information and, more generally, stimuli have been thought to reside wholly in the environment. Descriptions of what is perceived, therefore, are usually couched exclusively in the language of the environment; the animal that might detect that information has been seen as almost irrelevant. When, in the ecological framework, the unit of analysis is taken to be an animal-environment *ecosystem* (Shaw & Bransford, 1977), information is part of that system and cannot be sensibly divorced from the animal. Information is defined over the animal and the objects, places, and events in the environment that the animal knows.

Two reasons for the need to study information with reference to the animal were pointed out earlier. First, because different kinds of information require specialized biological systems in order to be detected, the particular animal must be considered in any designation of information. Second, much of the information that an animal receives is a consequence of the explorations in which the animal engages (e.g., movement yields information through parallax). But there is a third and more fundamental sense in which information must be considered in the context of an animal. It can be seen in the concept of *affordances*.

AFFORDANCES

Affordances are the acts or behaviors permitted by objects, places, and events. "The affordances of the environment are what it *offers* animals, what it *provides* or *furnishes,* either for good or ill" (Gibson, 1979). As examples, chairs, benches, and stools afford sitting on; an object with a handle affords grasping to animals with hands; a cliff affords avoidance; a bottle affords "drinking from" and, alternatively, throwing. Clearly, at its simplest, it could be said that an affordance is what the environment *means* to a perceiver. That a bottle affords grasping says that when one perceives a bottle, he or she *knows* that it can be held in the hands.

This is the innovation of affordances. That chairs afford sitting and cliffs afford avoiding is news to no one; but for Gibson, *it is the affordance that is perceived.* In other words, an animal perceives what behaviors can be entered into with respect to the environment. When perception is interpreted in this way, we would say that humans do not perceive chairs, pencils, and doughnuts; they perceive places to sit, objects with which to write, and things to eat. To say that affordances are perceived means that information specifying these affordances is available in the stimulation and can be detected by a properly attuned perceptual system. To detect affordances is, quite simply, to detect meaning.

This last notion puts in bold relief the need for including the animal in the notion of information. The reason is this: Different animals engage in very different behaviors. The potential purposive behaviors are called its *effectivities* (Shaw & McIntyre, 1974; after von Neumann, 1966). Whether an animal flies, swims, walks, or slithers; whether it pecks, nibbles, sucks, or licks; whether it smokes, watches television, or mugs old people will "determine" the affordances it can detect. Because information specifies *behaviors* that are afforded and because different animals have different sets of effectivities, *affordances belong to animal-environment systems and nothing less.*

We begin this chapter, then, by examining how animals and environments join together to form systems. This joining is both characterized and permitted by compatibilities between aspects of the animal and aspects of the environment. Next, we examine the relationship between perceiving and acting, which that compatibility implies. The nature of this relationship is important because the theory of affordances claims that perceptions are written in the language of actions (seeing that something may be eaten, lifted, or sat upon). The third section of the chapter extends these analyses to include the human-made environment in all its gadgetry. In the fourth and final section of this chapter, we examine some experiments and phenomena that seem to indicate that affordances represent a reasonable framework in which to discuss behavior.

Ecosystems, Compatibility, and Personal Information

A full understanding of the statement that information about affordances exists only in the union of animal and environment requires that we first understand the nature of the union. It is necessary to explore and emphasize the compatibilities of animal and niche, and in doing so, build the case that information about affordances is "personal"; it is unique to particular animal-environment units.

Affordances, like survival itself, rest completely on a compatibility of animal and environment. Shaw, Turvey, and Mace (in press) schematize Gibson's notion of affordance: "A situation or event X affords action Y for animal Z on occasion O if certain relevant compatibilities between X and Z obtain." (An effectivity is schematized similarly: "An animal Z can effect action Y on an environmental situation or event X if certain relevant mutual compatibilities between X and Z obtain.") For example, a wall affords walking to an animal if and only if properties of the animal are compatible with properties of the environment (for example, if the area of an animal's feet is sufficient to cause an adhesive force to balance the downward force created by the effects of gravity on the animal's mass; such a balance is true of flies, but not humans). The animal and environment fit together like interlocking pieces of a puzzle, each shaped by the other.

One is not likely to forget that the animal fits into the environment—a concept that will be considered in greater detail later—but, as emphasized in Chapter 1, it is also the case that the environment fits around the animal. Thus, it is not only to the animal that we look for a reflection of the environment; we also look to the environment for a reflection of its animals. This is illustrated in several ways. Consider, for example, the way certain flowers have evolved so as to increase the probability that they will be pollinated by nectar-gathering bees (see Figure 3-1). That environments complement their animals is implicit in the very concept of ecological niche.[1] Certain environmental features combine to form a niche suitable to a particular species. For example, a damp area hidden from the

---

[1] The term niche was popularized in ecology literature by Charles Elton (1927) who used it to describe the functional role of an animal in a community. Although the term has become the subject of some controversy because of its ever-widening usage, it is still maintained as a concept separate from mere habitat or geographical location (Whittaker, Levin, & Root, 1973).

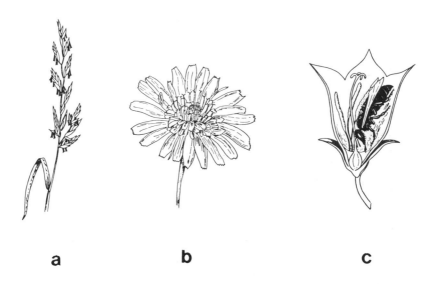

a   **b**   **c**

Figure 3-1. Flowers of wind-pollinated plants (*a*) are distinctly different from insect-pollinated plants (*b*). The location of the nectar requires the bee to contact the pollen (*c*). (From von Frisch, 1971; reprinted with permission)

sun, such as a cave or basement, is favorable for arachnids (spiders, scorpions, ticks), which are endangered if they dry out. But a niche is more than a location for the animals; it reflects and supports their way of life. An animal requires a particular kind of environment and a particular environment will support only certain kinds of animals. Each implies the other.

Support for a particular way of life means that *the niche complements the variety of actions a species must perform;* it provides the trees to climb and the bugs to eat. And that is what is meant by seeing affordances: seeing the trees to climb and the bugs to eat.

That an animal detects the affordances of an environment means that information is *for* a species or *for* an individual. Adopting an evolutionary perspective should help to make this point clear. But in this analysis we are not interested in the possible mechanisms of evolution. Our intent is only to show the evolutionary underpinnings of the view that information is personal.

It must be supposed that organisms evolved in environments rich in structured light and sound, and air- and water-borne chemicals. Moreover, in order to survive, their perceptual systems had to be adapted to their environments. Through the course of evolution, the anatomy and physiology of the animal became tailored to *information* as much as they became tailored to the more obvious aspects of the environment. As examples, the eye of a fish is as suited to underwater information as its fins are suited to underwater locomotion; human eyes are as suited to terrestrial information (witness our problem with "depth" perception under water) as our legs and feet are suited to terrestrial locomotion. From perception to digestion, evolutionary successes evolved to deal with environments in ways important to their survival (e.g., in reproducing, locating food sources, and evading predators). We must assume that selection pressures acted as much on perceptual systems as they did on fins, wings, and skin. Pressures to pick up *useful* aspects of the environment qualified those aspects as information for that animal.

Information is thereby depicted to some degree as "personal," as opposed to a detached list of qualities that could serve all organisms equally well. For example, a catalog of the properties of a tree stump might include its shape and size, its texture, the wavelengths of light various parts reflect, moisture content or chemical composition in general, its position relative to other objects, and so on. But which of these properties permit a human to sit on it, or a termite to feed on it, or a bird to find bugs on it, or a rabbit to make a burrow under it? Qualities such as reflectance and size are certainly quantifiable, but they do not constitute useful, personal information. They are based on variables borrowed from traditional physics, and the only systems that were ever designed specifically to detect such variables are instruments designed by physicists! There is no valid reason to suppose that evolution distributed this same roster of detectable qualities to animals with such vastly different informational needs.

Whether the stump affords sitting, eating, finding insects, or nesting-under depends on the animal's effectivities. The stump does not afford nesting or eating to a human, nor does it afford sitting (on buttocks with vertical torso) to birds, termites, and rabbits—their bodies cannot assume that anatomical configuration. Thus, the information that specifies affordances is personal to the animal who perceives it.

In evolution, then, an animal or species that was sensitive to the appropriate affordances would have the best chance of survival. But an animal that had trouble detecting the edibility of food, for example, would fast become extinct. And, because every species does not share the same predators, food, or habitat, information is defined for a particular animal with respect to a particular environment. Just as species do not share the same predators, food, or habitat, neither need they be sensitive to the same kinds of information; evolution tailored them to the information available in their particular environments. This principle is illustrated by some examples discussed in Chapter 2. Recall the discussion of three types of structured energy: light, heat, and the ultraviolet nectar guide. The claim was that for structured energy to qualify as information, the animal must be able to detect it. As these examples are pressed, we can see that more than biological transduction is involved. Namely, for structured energy to qualify as information, an animal not only must have an ability to detect that information, it must also have a way to *use* it. Thus, thermal radiation is information to pit vipers not because they have exquisitely sensitive temperature-gradient sensing devices, but because such information affords a class of behaviors: approaching and striking a prey. (Note that it is not temperature per se that the snake perceives. Rather, the direction of attack is detected. "Temperature" is a nonpersonal quality like the color and shape of the stump mentioned earlier.) In like manner, the ultraviolet nectar guide is not information to a honeybee because it is sensitive to ultraviolet radiation, but because the nectar guide affords approach to and collection of nectar. Put in these terms, structured energy is information only if it can have consequences sooner or later on the acts that an animal executes. The affordance is specific to a particular object-animal system in terms of both perception and action.

One might infer from the above that all members of the same species share the same list of affordances, but this is not the case for several reasons. Consider the problem of body-scale. The same object can afford different things for different-sized animals. While a box may afford climbing-into for a child, most adults would probably treat that same box as a storage vessel. Similarly, a large stick may afford grasping for an adult, but not for a child whose small hand will not fit around a large object. Sensitivity to body-scaled information has been demonstrated in the praying mantis which will attack prey items of a diameter optimal for the angle of opening of its foreleg "pincher" (Figure 3-2a); items that are either larger or smaller than optimum are attacked with less frequency (Figure 3-2b from Holling, 1964; in Pianka, 1974). The objects that afford attack are just those objects with which a mantis of a particular size can deal effectively. An affordance, then, is with regard to a particular animal as it relates to a specific object or layout of surfaces.

In summary, perception is the detection of useful information. Useful information, in turn, is seen as structured energy (e.g., sound), which permits the animal to act, in an adaptive way, in and upon its environment. This is the kind of information that is taken as the object of ordinary seeing and hearing, where useful behaviors are the goal. That is, in knowing its natural environment, an animal does not merely register visual events: The useful aspect of seeing prey is that they may be eaten. Therefore, affordances are spoken of in active terms—something affords acting upon. Useful information is more than that needed to name or identify objects; it specifies what those objects mean to us as perceivers, what we can do with them.

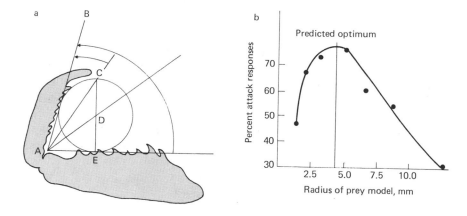

Figure 3-2. Schematic of Holling's geometric analysis of a praying mantis' foreleg. The optimal diameter, *D,* of a prey item was calculated for a mantis of a particular size. At right, a plot of the percentage of attack responses to prey items of various diameters. (After Holling, 1964; with permission)

For the species, one must look to evolutionary pressure to pick up useful information. A species evolves to deal with its environment in ways that will insure survival. Similarly, an individual animal learns to deal with its *particular* environment. These adaptations involve both a selection for certain anatomical attributes compatible with the environment *and,* as will be discussed in Chapter 4, an increased sensitivity to relevant aspects of the environment. Species become physically and perceptually attuned to their environments through evolution and experience.

THE RELATION BETWEEN PERCEIVING AND ACTING

As noted earlier, affordances write perception in the language of action. This is simply to say that the detection of information tailors perceivers' actions to their environments. The concept of affordance brings perception and action together in a way that denies traditional distinctions, such as sensory-motor and stimulus-response. A conjoint treatment of perceiving and acting is mandated by the idea that the properties of each are to be rationalized by the other. After all, what *is* the point of seeing, hearing, and so on? For perception to be valuable, it must be manifested in appropriate and effective actions on the environment. And, in turn, for actions to be appropriate and effective they must be constrained by accurate perception of the environment.

This dual assertion provides the basis for demanding a consideration of activity in perceptual theory (and a consideration of perception in action theory). Because actions are with reference to the environment, the information that specifies this environment must provide a basis for activity. Therefore, perceptual theories must be developed to allow perception to constrain action appropriately. To elaborate, we shall briefly describe the arguments in support of this assertion made by Turvey and his colleagues (Turvey, 1977; Fitch & Turvey, 1978; Fowler & Turvey, 1978). The details of how an ecological psychologist comes to terms with what an act is, how it is executed, and how concepts in perception should be fitted into concepts in action will be addressed in Chapter 6.

The successful control of activity requires the availability of certain kinds of information. As noted earlier, the actor must be provided with information of adaptive significance. When we spoke of affordances, we referred primarily to "large" behaviors that an animal may enter into with respect to the environment. In order to deal with environments in ways important to their survival, perceiving animals must detect, in the optic array, properties that permit or invite those behaviors (e.g., locating food sources, evading predators, and reproducing). This is the notion of *useful information* discussed earlier. It is also the case, however, that adaptive behavior requires information that somehow will tailor individual aspects of the behavior to the particular object or place in the environment. That is to say, the acting animal must have a specification of "tuning" parameters that adapt the *details* of motor activities to the situation at hand. While both level and sloping ground may afford walking, the manner in which that gait is executed must be geared to the slope of the surface. Thus, the domain of the perception-action interrelationship includes not only global aspects (a ball affords throwing) but also minute ones (a baseball affords throwing in a different way from a whiffle ball).

In order to understand the kinds of variables that are of concern in the control of activity, consider the relationship between the act of "approaching" and its informational support. In order to approach some particular object—for example, a tree across an open field—one must act in such a way as to keep that object at the center of optical expansion (Figure 3-3). An expanding optic array specifies approach while the rate of expansion specifies the imminence of arrival. To avoid collision with the tree, the actor will have to slow down and eventually stop as the tree fills 180° of visual angle.

In the context of this example, the mutual compatibility of perception and action can now be explained in more detail. The activity called "approaching" requires two bases of support—an informational one wherein the optic array must permit guidance of the activity, and an

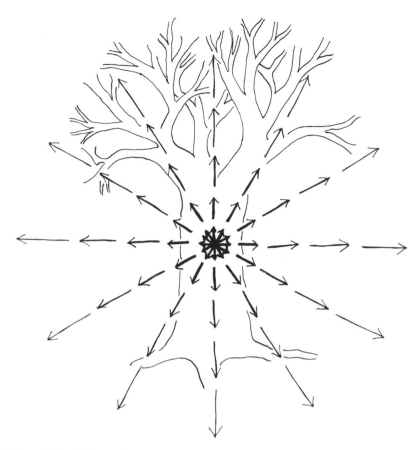

Figure 3-3. Schematic of the optical expansion specifying approach.

anatomical one wherein a collection of muscles and joints permits the execution of the activity. Thus, the argument for the conjoint investigation of perception and action is the argument that the perceptual and actional must fit together or must be mutually compatible for adaptive activity to be possible. To describe information (optical expansion) for an act (approaching) is to imply a muscular organization that the information constrains. To describe the muscular coordination of an act is to imply some sort of energy pattern that can constrain it. By such an analysis, information and the existence (and coordination) of the muscle collective are coimplicative.

Given this coimplicative relationship, "control" is not something that exists *in* the animal as a consequence of perception. It cannot be said that the optics change first and the act is in response to that. During an activity, the actor and the optic array are continually changing. What is usually taken as evidence of control is merely a necessary consequence of the natural fit between perception and action (Fitch & Turvey, 1978).

Because information is taken to be closely related to the concept of a muscular collective, it is important to understand the nature of such a collective and how that collective is constrained by information. If the arguments in the preceding paragraphs are correct, the fit between the action and perception systems should also be manifested in the organization of muscles into these functional collectives. That is to say, a group of muscles that are not necessarily mechanically or anatomically linked are constrained to act as a unit for a particular activity. For example, in skilled sharpshooters, there is a correlation between movement in the shoulder and movement in the wrist which contributes to less scatter around the center of a target (Arutyunyan, Gurfinkel, & Mirskii, 1978; Figure 3-4a). That is, movement in one joint is compensated for by movement in the

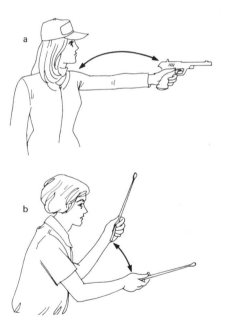

Figure 3-4. *A:* In aiming a gun, the wrist and shoulder of the same arm have a reciprocal influence. *B:* In drumming, the two wrists are mutually constraining.

other joint; the two joints have a reciprocal influence. In a bilaterally rhythmic activity such as drumming, however, that same wrist joint is coupled instead with the wrist of the opposite arm (Figure 3-4b) so that only certain combinations of rhythms are easily achieved (e.g., a 1:1 or 2:1 beat [von Holst, 1973]). The activities of the two wrists are mutually constraining.

The muscles and joints involved in these collectives are not merely constrained by each other; the collectives themselves are also constrained to take advantage of certain invariants and thereby elevate those invariants to the status of information for the particular animal engaged in the particular activity. The organization of the musculature "sets up" perception by accepting only certain kinds of information and at just those times when it will be used most effectively in the act. In other words, not only the form but also the regularity of an act depends on functional constraints on the musculature. The nature of the organization of the collective of muscles needed for a behavior makes said collective susceptible to the kind of information such that, when it is available, regulation is a natural consequence of the dynamics of the system. Therefore, regulation or control is not accomplished by a device extrinsic to the system.

The idea that action sets up perception means that the organization of the action system can constrain the form and timing of its own regulation. This notion is, perhaps, best conveyed metaphorically and, to that end, we borrow a clock metaphor from Kugler, Kelso, & Turvey (1980).

Based on three simple parts—an energy source, an oscillating component, and device which links them—a clock is a self-maintaining periodic mechanism whose periodicity is due to the dynamics of its structure. Figure 3-5 illustrates how this works in the common pendulum clock. In our example, the pendulum (p) serves as the oscillating component, and the hanging weight (w) as the source of energy. The device that correlates the operations of p and w is called the escapement ($e_w + e_p$). The escapement is composed of two parts, a wheel with teeth (e_w) and a pallet or bar (e_p) with two projections which alternately engage the teeth of the wheel as the pallet rocks in "seesaw" fashion. At the equilibrium position of the pendulum—i.e., where its velocity is greatest—a tooth escapes from the pallet [which is linked to the pendulum via the crutch (c)], allowing the weight to fall a short distance. The kinetic energy of the weight is thereby delivered, by impulses through the escapement, to the pendulum, thus keeping the latter in regular vibration and, thus, periodically allowing a tooth to escape from the pallet. A suitable arrangement of other gears and wheels links this mechanism to the hands of the clock allowing them to revolve periodically (for example, once every hour).

The important aspect of this operation is that the timing relation-

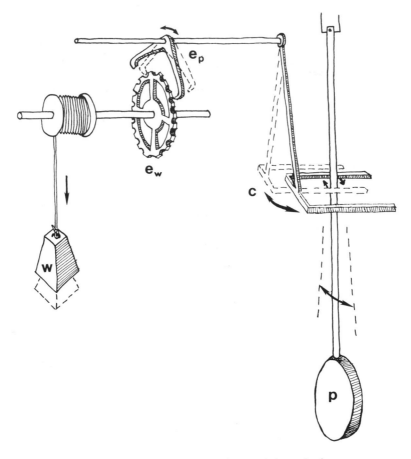

Figure 3-5. A diagram of a pendulum clock.

ships depend not on time but on the nature of the organization of the system. Although the power source is continuously available—the weight has potential energy—it is tapped according to the position and velocity of the parts. Notice that the escape occurs and delivers energy to the pendulum in a position where it will least interfere with that oscillator's free swing and still take advantage of its greatest kinetic energy (i.e., at equilibrium). There is no separate monitoring device that says when to inject power; the dynamics of the oscillator tap the power selectively, at those states where it will do the most good.

To bring this metaphor into the realm of action, let us now draw parallels between the activity of a clock and a simple act, the swing of a

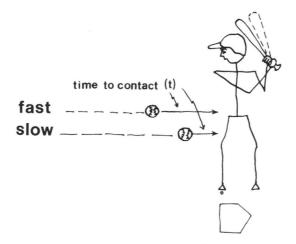

Figure 3-6. Schematic of the timing relationships between the pitch and swing.

baseball bat.[2] In baseball batting, the step and the swing are done with reference to the pitch, and, as with the clock, the interjection of information is selective. Although the start of the step is correlated with the release of the pitch, the speed of opening of the batter's stance (from start to finish of the step) and, therefore, the start of the swing, depends on the speed of the pitch (Hubbard & Seng, 1954; Figure 3-6). The duration of the swing is thereby left invariant; that is to say, for most batters the swing will start a constant amount of time before the ball is hit. Optical information specifying the imminence with which the pitch will cross the plate must be available while the ball is in flight: The swing is too tightly linked to the velocity of the ball for it to be otherwise. The information is continuously available for regulation of the act, but it is selectively percolated through the act so as not to interfere with the integrity of certain parameters (e.g., duration of the swing)[3] but still take advantage of the functional constraints on the musculature (the organization that allows swinging the bat). The dynamics of the system in this case allow the batter to time the

[2] The baseball swing (pitch, step, swing) represents the limiting case of an oscillating system—one period.

[3] It is not altogether clear why this variable and not another (e.g., speed of the step) remains constant. It has been speculated that it might contribute to better bat control (a faster swing might lessen the batter's ability to maintain a level swing relative to the plane of flight of the ball) or power (a very slow swing would provide very little power). Most likely, it is an optimization over several variables of this type (Fitch & Turvey, 1978).

swing to that information that will specify the location of the ball. That is, the relevant information is not about absolute time, but time-to-contact (body-scaled information that relates the ball to the batter). A separate monitoring device is not needed, therefore, to say when it is time to start the swing. Regulation is a consequence of the fit between the optic array and activity.

The foregoing is fundamental to theories of perception and action and will be treated more thoroughly in Chapter 6. For now, the essence of this analysis is that in order to allow for the control of activity, perceptual theories must come to terms with the kind of information that activity requires. First, this means that the transforming optic array is specific to the event. As with the example of approaching, the flow of optical texture specifies what is happening (walking toward) and what is about to happen (imminence of collision). Beyond this, the actor requires that the information be in a usable form. This means that it must be specific to the animal (body-scaled) and specific to the animal's particular environment. Perceptual information is specific to the event and compatible with the level of regulation involved in activity (Fitch & Turvey, 1978).

In summary, the perceiving animal and the acting animal are one and the same, and the duties of each are complementary descriptions of the same event. The action system (effectivity structure) and the environment (affordance structure) are in a relationship of mutual constraint.

AFFORDANCES IN THE HUMAN-MADE ENVIRONMENT

We have limited the discussion to the evolutionary-biological aspects of affordances, especially with regard to the natural environment and lower animals whose goals extend little beyond survival. People, however, have created a more complex environment for themselves by altering nature and expanding the range of their goals.

What we call the human-made (formerly, man-made) environment is the result of various alterations people have made on the world. These range from primitive weapons and tools to sophisticated instruments such as microscopes and radar. The cultural environment is separated from the natural environment for pedagogic purposes only; both comprise *the* environment, with one merely a modification of the other. Nonetheless, it is of interest to examine the human-made environment as it relates to the issues raised earlier.

The world has been selectively changed to suit the needs of people. Technology makes pleasant things more available and difficult jobs easier.

The net effect of such alterations is to change the affordances of the environment (Gibson, 1979). In seeking to tailor the world to human needs and desires, people have altered what the world has to offer. If a sharp rock affords chopping or cutting, then an axe or a knife affords doing so more efficiently. The manufactured tool is, in a sense, a refinement of the affordances of the natural environment. That is, it is specifically tailored to do a limited class of jobs well.

The need for such efficiency can be traced ultimately to survival purposes. Just as prehistoric hunters would have had better success with crafted weapons instead of rocks or sticks, modern survival is at least made easier with technological advances. Needless to say, compatibility is not ignored in such developments; tool designs generally display optimal compatibility with human physical characteristics. On these accounts, it seems reasonable to suppose that manufactured objects differ only in degree from natural objects. Thus, as with naturally occurring objects, it is the affordances of these artifacts that are perceived.

Instruments such as telescopes, thermometers, and Geiger counters serve a different purpose. This raises a different set of questions. The purpose of such devices is to make available information that is not normally available. In a sense, they are an extension of our perceptual systems, just as tools are extensions of our action systems. Instruments permit a wider range of exploratory activities and, in so doing, make available a greater number and kind of affordances. For example, to determine whether or not a bone is broken, one could rely on vision or touch alone. This method, however, would not reveal small breaks or hairline fractures. An x-ray of the bone, on the other hand, would reveal facts not available to unaided senses.

One issue that should be considered is whether the detection of fractures by x-ray, of mitochondria by microscope, or of nebulae by telescope, are to be considered direct or indirect. Gibson (1979) has labeled them indirect, but we take strong exception to this label. We do not think he means that detection of the properties that instruments reveal requires epistemic mediation of the sort described in Chapter 1. Thus, the only sense in which such perception is indirect is that equipment exists between the distal object (broken bone, mitochondrion, or nebula) and the perceiver. In our view, that a machine intervenes is no different from the "intervention" of light between a distal object and perceiver. In both cases, what is important is that there exists an invariant relation between the distal object, place, or event and detectable information about it. Thus, that a limb affords setting is directly detectable through x-rays.

In summary, the human-made environment serves to change the affordances of the environment to suit the goals of human beings. Two broad classes of alterations were discussed: objects used in some activity and devices employed to obtain information. Both are ego-extenders, or extensions of self. One resides on the perceptual end and permits the detection of more and different classes of information, and the other resides on the action end, permitting more powerful, faster, more delicate and more effective actions.

AFFORDANCES AND CONSTRAINTS ON LEARNING

The idea that perceiving is detecting what behaviors are afforded by objects, events, and places in the environment is a radical departure from traditional psychological theory. Indeed, to some, it may seem outlandish. In order to demonstrate the reasonableness of the concept, this section presents experiments with an affordance interpretation. The research described here is usually described in learning texts as "biological constraints on learning." For present purposes, however, the concern is not with what this research says about learning, but with what it says about perception. From an ecological perspective, the research indicates that animals perceive affordances.

Before proceeding to particular experiments and their implications about perception, let us set the stage for this research by describing the issues in learning that it addresses. A tacit assumption that pervaded much learning theory and research for the 50 years following Pavlov was what Seligman (1970) has called the "equivalence of associability assumption." This implicit doctrine suggests that any associations between stimuli or between stimuli and responses are equally learnable. This assumption has been seriously questioned in recent years as a function of the accumulating evidence that some things cannot be learned, other things can be learned with consummate ease, while others fall somewhere in between. In other words, there are natural constraints on what can be learned.

From the ecological perspective on perception, the inability to learn a particular response in the presence of a particular stimulus is due to the fact that the response is not afforded by the stimulus situation. In describing the following experiments, the basis for this claim is made clear.

The first experiment to be considered concerns discrimination learning and was reported by Lawicka (1964, cited by Seligman, 1970). Lawicka assessed the difficulty of learning four pairs of discriminations. The four conditions were the factorial combinations of two stimulus conditions and two response conditions. The first response condition was a go/stay differentiation (advance upon hearing tone 1; stay upon hearing tone 2). The second was a left/right differentiation (turn left upon hearing tone 1; turn right for tone 2). One stimulus condition had the two tones (one high, one low) emanating from one centrally located speaker. The second stimulus condition had two tones of the same frequency, one emanating from a speaker on the left and the other emanating from a speaker on the right. Four groups of dogs were used in the four combinations of stimulus and response conditions (go/stay to high/low tones; go/stay to left/right tones; go-left/go-right to high/low tones; and go-left/go-right to left/right tones).

Lawicka observed that there were substantial differences among the conditions in the animals' abilities to learn. Little difficulty was observed both when the animals had to turn left or right to speakers placed on the left and right and when the go/stay response was signaled by a high and low tone. However, the animals found it difficult to learn to go or stay as a function of the location of the speaker and to learn to go left or right as a function of whether the tone was high or low. Performance in the "learnable" conditions demonstrates unequivocally that the signals can be discriminated and the responses can be learned. Why, then, do the animals have difficulty in the "unlearnable" conditions?

The concept of affordance provides a convenient account of this differential performance. An analysis in terms of affordances would claim that the two stimulus pairs—high/low and left/right—have different affordances. By this analysis, high and low tones from the same speaker do not afford (to dogs) going left or right. Nor are stay vs. approach behaviors afforded by a spatial characteristic (position) of the source of a sound. Thus, the difficulty observed in these two conditions is not that the dogs cannot *learn* the appropriate behaviors, but that the "correct" behaviors are not afforded by information.

Bolles (1975) describes an experiment, carried out in his laboratory by Duncan, which has similar implications. The task in this experiment was avoidance learning. A rat was placed in a box 20 inches square. In order to avoid a shock, the animal simply had to move at least 6 inches. Any activity that succeeded in moving the animal that far would either terminate a shock that had started or prevent one that had not started. Strangely, the animals simply could not learn to avoid the shock in a plain box. But when Duncan put a stripe across the center of the box, the rats were able to learn the avoidance behavior!

That the rats could avoid the shock in the presence of the stripe tells us that the rats can certainly learn the response of moving to avoid a shock. Why, then, couldn't they learn it in the absence of the stripe? If one thinks in terms of affordances, the answer is fairly clear. The reason that rats could not learn without the stripe is that they could not see a portion of the box that afforded running to. We suggest that when the stripe was present, the animals detected the "other" side of the stripe as a place that might (and did) afford escape. But without the stripe to define "the other side of the box," no escape was afforded. Thus, we might say that the animal could not learn the response because it could not see that other locations in the box invited escape.

The affordance interpretation offers an interesting and eminently sensible account of these and related animal experiments. (It seems, for example, far more parsimonious than Bolles's idea that the rats in Duncan's experiment learned a "rather complex abstraction" [1975, p. 196] .) Not only does the explanation of these experiments benefit from the theory of affordances, the theory of affordances itself benefits from the experiments, for they suggest ways in which aspects of affordances can be put to experimental test.

Another very different observation in psychology may evidence affordances in humans. This observation is *functional fixedness* (Duncker, 1945). The textbook case of functional fixedness is a problem-solving experiment reported by Maier (1933). A subject is brought into a room that has two strings suspended from the ceiling and a pair of pliers lying on the desk. The subject's task is to tie the strings together, but they are so far apart that the subject cannot reach one while holding on to the other (even while using the pliers to extend his or her reach). Remembering that one could use the pliers, how can the problem be solved?

Many people experience difficulty with this problem. The solution is to tie the pliers to one string, swing the resulting pendulum, run over, grab the other string, and catch the pliers-pendulum. An analysis of subjects' difficulty in terms of affordances suggests that the subject may detect that the pliers afford pinching, crushing, holding objects, and even extending reach, but none of these affordances aid in solving the problem. The subject sees those uses and they do not help. Functional fixedness—seeing an object as having a fixed function—says simply that one does not see the intrinsic properties of objects (e.g., weight), but, rather, one sees their uses.[4]

A consideration of this problem-solving difficulty in humans together with the animal research cited earlier not only lends credence to the concept of affordance but also provides some insight into how affordances might be experimentally studied.

SUMMARY

In Chapters 2 and 3, Gibson's notion of information was presented. In Chapter 2, the environment side of information was examined; we asked how patterns of light and sound might reliably specify the environment. In

---

[4]One might ask why the affordance is not seen. The response concerns attention and detection, concepts that will be addressed in Chapter 4.

Chapter 3, the animal side of information was of central concern. It was claimed that structured light and sound cannot be considered to be *information* unless they can inform the animal in some useful way. In turn, the theory of affordances supposes that useful information is that which permits an animal to act in an appropriate or adaptive way in and upon its environment.

Such an analysis asserts that animals do not detect the intrinsic properties of objects (size, weight, structure), nor do they detect the metrics of energy that might interest a physicist (amplitude, duration, wavelength). Rather, they detect invariants or collections of invariants that specify the behaviors afforded by the object, place, or event. An analysis of information in terms of affordances, therefore, includes both the animal and the environment.

Animal and environment taken together form an *ecosystem*. The ecosystem is marked by a harmony of animals and environments, wherein animals have evolved to (and learned to) meet the requirements of the environment and the environment meets the needs of its animals. The animal's task is to detect information that is *useful* to the performance of its effectivities. The environment's "task" is to provide that information and, as seen in Chapter 2, it usually does so generously. In this view, information is seen as personal to the animal or, perhaps more accurately, particular to the ecosystem. This characterization applies to both the natural environment and to the technological environment in which we now live.

To say that perceiving is detecting the behaviors the environment affords requires an understanding of the relation between perception and action. At issue is how information for an act constrains a muscular organization that is compatible with that kind of information. We described an account wherein coordination arises from the natural fit between animal and environment and is not something that perception imposes on an action system. This relationship requires that perceptual theories come to terms with the kind of information that activity requires and, similarly, that action theories must be concerned with the kind of information to which animals are sensitive.

While the notion of affordances makes sense on an intuitive level, it was necessary to make explicit some experimental work that illustrates the concept. Research indicating biological constraints on animal learning and phenomena such as functional fixedness in humans provide what might be considered as the beginnings of that experimental support.

But information about affordances is still just information. We must still ask how it is selected and detected. In the next chapter these questions are addressed.

4

Detection of Information

We follow Shaw's and McIntyre's (1974) intuition that perceiving or knowing may be fully understood with reference to three questions: what is perceived, how is it perceived, and who is perceiving it. The two preceding chapters described at some length the information available to the animal. As such, those chapters were concerned with *what* is perceived. Notice, however, that the three questions—what, how, and who—are not clearly distinct from one another. It was impossible to describe *what* is being perceived (affordances) without reference to the biology and psychology (intent) of the animal. In spite of the dovetailing of what, how, and who, these latter two classes of questions deserve more detailed discussion. The first question, how, involves the biology of knowing: How might living tissue be knowing tissue? The second, who, involves purely psychological issues: How might needs, intentions, desires, and feelings be manifested in perception of and action upon the world. In this chapter, we turn our attention to these issues and ask *how* perception is done and *who* is doing it.

BIOLOGY OF KNOWING

Preliminaries

The inattention to physiological considerations that currently marks the ecological movement is due more to a first-things-first attitude than to a lack of interest in neural function or a notion that the study of the nervous system is peripheral to the study of knowing. After all, it seems premature for the ecological psychologist to theorize on how perceptual systems detect information without knowing exactly what that information is. Primary effort has been expended in studying information at the expense of several subdisciplines that are long-standing residents of the perceptionist's bailiwick.

Despite this inattention, some approaches to physiology that are implicit in the direct perception approach can be discerned. Spelling out these attitudes toward brain is the aim of this section. The ideas presented here should not be seen as any kind of a theory of neural function, but as an ecological approach to identifying the purpose of that function. That is, an ecological approach seeks to describe what nervous systems *do*.

Perhaps the most overriding bias that is nested in the ecological approach is an emphasis on what the brain *does* rather than what it *has*. A commonplace understanding—and one that is justly attributed to physiological psychologists—is that the brain, or mind, contains things. While the list of contents would certainly vary, a fairly representative enumeration would include knowledge, perceptions, experiences, and memories. Perhaps some would prefer to say that the brain gives rise to these contents or that there are structures or dynamics that correspond to these psychological entities, but these are all tokens of the same view. The alternative approach to the brain suggests that the brain does things: knows, perceives, experiences, and remembers, with "contents" explicitly omitted. In brief, ecological psychologists prefer to talk about knowing as something that the organism does rather than knowledge as something the organism has.

The distinction between knowing and knowledge may appear to be a superficial one, but abandoning knowledge in favor of knowing drastically alters the types of questions one might ask about brain. The selection of noun or verb determines, in part, the way particular concepts emerge in theory. By way of analogy, it has been said that a noun-verb distinction influenced progress in understanding heat. Many languages, including English, foster an understanding of heat as something an object or collection of molecules has. But from modern physics, heat is understood as something molecules do—namely, move. The noun "heat" is quite convenient for our everyday understanding of the environment, but it is not convenient—and may detract from—a scientific understanding. In like manner, it may be the case that while "knowledge" provides a convenient description of phenomenal experience, its inclusion in our scientific vocabulary may insidiously structure the questions that are asked. In fact, classifying knowledge as a "thing-in-the-brain" puts one automatically outside of the theory of ecological psychology. Nowhere is this point more obvious than in learning. A belief in "knowledge" leads one to believe that the role of experience is an increase in knowledge: a storage, literal or abstract, of experience. A belief in "knowing," on the other hand, treats experience as leading to an increased ability to know. Traditionally, psychologists have opted for the former interpretation, while proponents of direct perception opt for the latter.

A second orientation toward the biology of knowing that is implicit in ecological theory is that knowing is an activity of the organism not merely an activity of the brain. Put another way, we might ask what it is about an animal that supports or permits knowing of an environment. When phrased in this way, the nervous system is but one of several systems that permits knowing. Again, this may seem to be a gratuitous comment, but the sentiment it expresses has far-reaching theoretical consequences. On this analysis, perception is not considered as an achievement of the brain wrought out of the deliverances of the senses. It is not the brain that knows or perceives but the animal. The biological support for the detection of affordances rests not only in the brain but in the skin, muscles, bones, and tendons. Therefore, in the ecological approach, we ask what it is about an animal that permits knowing an environment. Both of these points—that animals, not brains, know and that they know rather than have knowledge—should become clearer as we consider the resonance model.

The Resonance Model

Gibson (1966) has suggested a radio metaphor for perception that is very revealing. The radio metaphor captures the essence of an information-detecting machine. It is also a useful metaphor with which to contrast direct perception with the more usual storage or library metaphor of brain, for in radios, a record is not stored, while in libraries it is.

A radio station broadcasts information, or rather, radio transmission structures a particular band-width of electromagnetic radiation in characteristic ways. A carrier wave is the particular radio frequency that is used by a station (and none other in the vicinity) to carry information. The process by which information is "attached" to the carrier wave is called modulation. For present purposes one need not understand the electronics of modulation; one need only appreciate that some characteristic of the carrier frequency (amplitude, frequency, or duration, depending on mode of transmission [AM, FM]) is structured so as to be formally equivalent, at some level of description, to the acoustic structure of the announcer's voice, for example. Modulation, then, structures the carrier wave into information, and this structure is, in turn, projected into space by the transmitting antenna. The result is not unlike dropping various-sized pebbles into a pond. The waves that carry information about the pebbles, though very different from radio waves, radiate outward from the source, or point of impact.

The reception or detection of radio waves is based on principles of resonance. A mechanical example illustrates resonance in a simple way. Imagine that one wants to keep a simple pendulum moving by rhythmic pushes with a finger. For the motion of the pendulum to be sustained, the pushes must be properly timed. If the pushes are properly timed, the pendulum resonates, that is, it responds in a relatively large way to the oscillatory force provided by the pushes. *Tuning* is accomplished by arranging the two vibrations to be the same or nearly the same. In the pendulum example, one could tune the oscillating force by adjusting the push rate or tune the pendulum by lengthening it, shortening it, or changing the mass of the bob.

In radio reception, resonance of electrical current is the method by which a frequency-sensitive circuit selects a particular signal. Given that many frequencies (stations) reach a receiver from the antenna, proper tuning of the receiver causes a current in it to resonate in response to one of the incoming signals, and not others.

The parallels to the theory of direct perception are fairly obvious. In the case of vision, electromagnetic radiation (light) is modulated by reflection (see Chapter 2). This is one way in which the environment "broadcasts" information; the structuring of acoustic patterns is another. The peripheral sensory organs, like the receiving antenna, must be transparent to the carrier frequency; that is, both must let the signal pass through. Finally, the information must be "tuned in." For some types of information, animals are genetically preattuned; for others, some effort must be expended to tune them in. Examples of the former include detection of the direction of gravity, detection of the sounds of human speech, and detection of the location of an event by eye or ear. Abilities that are manifested by infants, then, can be taken as approximate evidence for genetic preattunement. The latter category of tuning, the one that requires effort, may involve exploration (rubbing a surface is tuning in texture, moving around an object may be tuning in shape) and/or learning (detecting the semantic content of speech, detecting velocity while driving a car). In any case, the tuning, if successful, results in resonation to the information.

Taking these notions together with the concept of affordances leads to the following illustration. A pencil lying on the table broadcasts its structure by modulating the light in special ways. If we imagine that a perceiver is looking for something with which to write, he or she is tuned in or prepared to resonate to information specifying the affordance of writing. When the pencil comes into view, the perceptual system resonates to the information—which is to say, the affordance is detected.

A simple radio metaphor of the kind outlined above is only a partial metaphor for perceiving. It fails on two accounts. First, it deals only with the perceiving end of the perceiving-acting continuum. The second, but less problematic, difficulty is that a radio needs some external agent to tune in a channel. That is, someone must push the buttons. By contrast, a perceptual system is a self-tuning device. A simple feedback system that governs tuning, not unlike some current receivers that scan for strong or stereo broadcasts, would certainly suffice for simple visual systems. More complex systems would be needed to reflect the dynamic self-tuning of a human visual system.

Despite these and other failings of the radio analogy, it does describe, in an approximate way, the class of machine to which a perceptual system belongs. Again, the account of brain provided by the radio analogy is very different from the account that currently enjoys wide acceptance in the psychological community.

Detection, Storage, and the Radio Analogy

An electrical engineer would be puzzled if she were asked to indicate where, inside a radio, the station WCAT "is." She knows that the station is not *in* the radio, but simply that a state-configuration of the machine permits the response of the radio to the broadcasting station. On the other hand, asking a similar question of a computer scientist would produce very different consequences. If he were queried about where in a computer information is for a certain social security number, he might be able to supply the address in the computer's memory or, better yet, point out the chip on which that information resides.

At issue here is whether a neurophysiologist, when interrogated about where in the brain the knowledge of pencil is, will be more like the radio engineer or more like the computer scientist. We propose that his or her response would be more like that of the computer engineer. The neurophysiologist might not want to speculate as to *where* the knowledge is or even *what* it is in the language of neurons, but he or she probably has the firm conviction that it is in there somewhere. Those of us who embrace the ecological view would prefer the radio answer.

Computation vs. Detection

It is important to emphasize that, in Gibson's theory, resonance is to higher-order variables of stimulation, to information. It is supposed that a perceptual system directly registers these variables; it does not calculate them. In this section, a distinction is drawn between *computing* higher-order variables and *detecting* higher-order variables. This distinction is important for understanding both the ecological position and how that position relates to the more typical theory.

Most traditional psychologists might accept the notion of resonance, if it were limited to lower-order variables of stimulation. We doubt, for example, that anyone would reject the statement that red cones "resonate" best to a wavelength of 570 millimicrons. But strong objections would probably be raised to the claim that resonance is to much higher-order variables of stimulation than wavelength. The source of the objection to resonance to information is an implicit doctrine that higher-order variables must be *calculated* from more elementary variables. Thus, if a neurophysiologist demonstrates that the nervous system trades in fairly abstract mathematical currency, traditional theory would ask how the brain computes the fancy mathematical description. It would attempt to itemize the variables that are computed along the way. The story of how higher-order variables emerge in nervous tissue would have receptors detecting light followed by a concatenation of computations. "Simple cells" compute edges and lines; "complex cells" compute these less restrictively along with movement; and "hyper-complex" cells compute (retinal) size and direction-specific movement. Each successive array of features provides a more salient description of the light to an eye. Even a more pontifical cell—in monkey cortex, a cell that responds preferentially to the presence of a monkey's hand—has been suggested (Gross, Rocha-Miranda, & Bender, 1972).

The ecological alternative to this position is that the invariants specifying salient dimensions of the environment are *detected,* not computed. The idea that fancy properties can be detected without the intercession of elementary and intermediary variables may seem at first to flout common sense, but the conceptual difficulty is, perhaps, simply due to the absence of a common sense metaphor. Recently, however, Runeson (1977) has presented such a metaphor for perceptual systems. He likens a perceptual system to a real-world device that registers a higher-order property without computation.

To introduce Runeson's metaphor, a mathematical problem may be useful. Imagine that the task at hand is to measure the area of a certain rectangle. Area is taken to be the higher-order variable, while lengths of sides are lower-order variables. The question is, quite simply, whether the

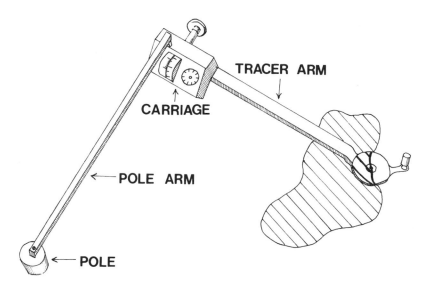

Figure 4-1. A polar planimeter (Lasico, Model 702).

lengths of two sides must be measured and multiplied for us to know the area, or can the area itself be measured?

As those familiar with drafting know, there exists an area-measuring device that neither measures length nor multiplies. This device is the polar planimeter, and it is shown in Figure 4-1. (As the figure implies, the planimeter can measure the area of any planar surface. For purposes of simplicity, however, we shall limit our discussion to rectangles.)

In order to measure area, the dial is first set to zero. The pole is planted at some arbitrary spot, and the end of the free arm is traced around the perimeter of the figure. A wheel under the carriage turns and skids, and its turns are registered on the dial. The value read off the dial is the area of the figure (in millimeters squared, divided by 10 for the particular planimeter sketched in Figure 4-1).

What makes the planimeter an especially interesting "fancy property" detector is that it does not perform well at all in measuring the "lower level" property of length. This fact, of course, returns us to the original premise: Detecting higher-order properties need not entail detecting lower-order properties and doing computations.

Pressing the planimeter metaphor further provides some insight into the conceptual muddle that arises when an investigator confuses detecting higher-order properties with computing higher-order properties from lower ones. The following discussion describes an attempt to study the planimeter while holding fast to the assumption that measuring area *necessarily entails* measuring length.

One would most likely begin the study of the planimeter by verifying its accuracy as an area-measuring device. One would conclude that it does a superb job measuring this higher-order property. Next, its accuracy in measuring the lower-order property, length, must be assessed. Given an appropriate makeshift contrivance, the device could be made to measure length, but it would not do that job well. Now, if one holds to the assumption that measuring area entails measuring length, a wonderful puzzle at once arises: How can the planimeter accurately measure area if it cannot accurately measure length? The only solution could be that somehow the device itself corrects or embellishes the inaccurate input (length) into an accurate output (area). But this is surely an absurd solution and, in fact, it was the original assumption that was erroneous.

The parallels of this story to the psychology of perception are easily seen. The assumption that the detection of higher-order properties of stimulation necessarily entails the detection of lower-order properties demands an evaluation of a perceptual system's response to these lower-order variables. That such jobs are not done well immediately raises the question: How are the fancy properties of the environment known so well if the constitutive parts are registered inaccurately? Again, the device itself, in this case the nervous system, must be called upon to bridge the gap with some creative achievement.

The alternative to this puzzle is that perceptual systems register higher-order variables directly, as the planimeter does. When called upon to measure variables that they were not "designed" to measure, both do so inaccurately. The difference is that it seems ludicrous to attribute creative achievments to the device pictured in Figure 4-1, while it is easy to attribute creative achievements to devices like nervous systems, which are already shrouded in mystery.

One final intuition about perceptual systems can be garnered from the planimeter analogy. An act of information registration—tracing the perimeter—that takes a substantial amount of time may contain no discernible steps. Area is measured when the act is complete, and being part way around the perimeter is not equivalent to having measured part of the area. It is the whole act that registers information. Thus, if perceptual systems behave like planimeters, the fact that perception takes time need imply neither that it has steps nor that it is some sort of cumulative process.[1]

[1] Like the earlier radio analogy, the polar planimeter also has limitations for perceiving. As will be seen in the next chapter, the ecological approach asserts that perception is neither a process of measuring environmental properties nor of producing an end-product (percept).

To reiterate, the theory of direct perception considers perceiving to be the detection (direct registration) of information. In response to this, it was claimed that a biological account of perception should describe how a biological machine might be a detector of information. Two metaphors supplied a crude model of how information is detected. The first was the radio, in which there is a resonation to broadcast information. The second was the polar planimeter which registers, but does not "calculate," higher-order properties. These metaphors were contrasted with the more commonly accepted view of a perceptual system as a computer—namely, a device that calculates, stores, and retrieves information.

ATTENTION: THE CONTROL OF DETECTION

It is certainly the case that ecological psychologists have concentrated their efforts on an explication of the concept of information. This emphasis, taken together with their claim that the variety and accuracy of perception is attributable to the variety and accuracy of information, has led some to the view that Gibson's approach is more a theory of stimulus than a theory of perception. We have heard more than one respected authority state with some seriousness that either the animal plays no role in Gibson's theory or, if it does, its head is filled with cotton.

If these charges were true, the ecological theory could give us no accounting of why or how different people perceive the same objects, places, and events differently. It has been argued that if all the information necessary for perception is in the input, then all perceivers should see the same object the same way. If individual perceivers add nothing to the input, there is no way for experiences to differ. The same argument questions how one person can perceive an object differently on different occasions.

While these reproofs may seem logical, they are not justified. The solution to the puzzle of perceptual variety is found in the statement that different perceivers can detect *different information.* Remember that what the information is depends, in part, on the animal, insofar as it is defined with reference to a particular animal. But, more important, even if all the information were identical, different perceivers can *attend* to different invariants. Several examples of this were provided in the discussion of affordances. For example, there is information specifying that a bottle may be drunk from or that it may be thrown. Because different perceivers are apt to select information for any number of reasons, variety of perceptions is to be expected. It is also supposed that the same perceiver can detect different information on different occasions. Note that the source of the variety of experience does not reside in the perceiver's head, but in the variety of stimulation; the perceiver merely chooses from an array of possibilities. Gibson calls this procedure by which inputs are selected *attention.*

In the broadest possible terms, attention concerns the means by which some things are perceived and others are not. Beyond that, the meaning of attention in psychology spills into so many subsidiary denotations, connotations, and theoretical constructs that it is unfortunate that Gibson used that particular term in his theory. A better summary of Gibson's ideas on this matter is captured by the phrase *the control of detection.* We begin with a brief discussion of attention as it is generally treated in psychology. We then explain Gibson's use of the term especially as it might be interpreted as "control of detection" and end with a contrast of the two notions.

Selective attention, as studied in information processing theory, began with an attempt to understand the "cocktail-party phenomenon" or how one might carry on a conversation amid the din of a crowded party. Even though sensory systems are overloaded with several linguistic inputs, a perceiver is easily able to select one and reject others. In the quarter century that followed Cherry's (1953) note of that ability, researchers have attempted to determine how inputs (usually linguistic) are selected or rejected, what is known about rejected messages, and where in the flow of information is the selection or rejection made. The process may be characterized as a general weeding out of inputs.

The above formulation of *attention* stands in bold contrast to the interpretation put forth by Gibson and his colleagues and that we have termed *control of detection.* Recall that in Gibson's theory, detection is the means by which information in the environment is picked up. Control of detection, then, is simply a constraint on what information will be picked up. By attention, Gibson means that perceivers select from all the available information.

Exploratory activities are an attentional procedure of this type. In exploration, perceivers actively investigate their environments, usually with some purpose. For example, one might heft a rock to see if it is the right size for throwing. Or one could sniff a suspect carton of potato salad to see if it still affords eating. By exploring appropriate parts or details of the environment, the information that can be detected is controlled. Clearly, to characterize these activities as a rejection of certain inputs is not accurate; rather, they constitute a *selection* of inputs. Exploration (attention) is not an unconscious sifting-through and subsequent rejection of most inputs: It is a directed control of what will be detected.

That detection is directed or purposeful harks back to Chapter 3 and the notion of affordance. Recall that an affordance relates the environment to an actor-perceiver in terms of what uses that animal has for it—to throw or to eat, for example. In order to do the animal any good, the information specifying the affordance must be detected. Attention as exploratory activity reveals affordances to an animal. By hefting the rock, a person can perceive whether or not it is throwable.

Of course, not all forms of attention are as obvious as the exploration described above. For example, someone who is looking for his or her keys might behave to an outside observer precisely like someone who is looking for a matchbook. In such a case, it can be supposed that it is a brain configuration that distinguishes the would-be driver from the would-be smoker. It would be desirable to be specific about how such brain configurations might be described; unfortunately, at this time it can only be suggested that the term "brain configurations" means whatever it is about the brain that serves the same function as the interleaved metal plates (variable condensers) in old-fashioned radios.

Nor is it the case that one must be searching for something in order to detect it. While much of exploration and attention is controlled by intention, it is also true that they are at the beck and call of the environment. Because some portions of the array are more structured than others, those portions will arouse attention:

> ... interesting structures in the array, and interesting bits of structure, particularly motions, *draw* the foveas toward them. (Gibson, 1966, p. 260)

Shaw and McIntyre (1974) have characterized areas that contain more information as having higher *attensity.* This concept can best be understood with reference to intensity. With physical variables of light, sound, or force, intensity describes the magnitude of the variable, how much of it there is. So, too, can attensity be considered a measure of strength; it is, in a sense, a measure of the attraction that an area of information has for a perceiver. Areas of high attensity are more likely to be detected; low attensity portions may go unnoticed. *Imprinting* provides an extreme example of this; certain optical transformations have tremendous attensity for the newly hatched gosling.

The control that a perceiver has over the input is not limited to specifying the location in space at which the interesting event is occurring. In addition, a perceiver might control the scope of the attended space. As an example of this, Gibson (1966) asks us to consider a pilot viewing the array of instruments on his panel. The panel as a unit is the object of attention. Presumably, the pilot can detect whether the panel in toto specifies that the plane is, for example, in the appropriate configuration for landing. Changes in the panel's *Gestalt,* in turn, afford some compensatory adjustment. Attending to one instrument at the expense of others might be

disastrous. From this example, we can draw the conclusion that the perceiver controls the *unit* of detection. Attention may cover a large region or
small region depending on the intent (and ability) of the perceiver.

We have presented the notion of attention as the control of detection. Whether attention is the result of active, purposeful explorations
or regular (exploratory) fixations, detection is still directed toward certain
aspects of the environment over others. Clearly, this is one answer to the
question addressed by a concept of attention—namely, what is the means
by which some things are perceived and others are not?

The difference between this and information processing accounts of
attention is that, in the latter, inputs are *rejected,* while in the former,
inputs simply go undetected. To use an analogy, in information processing
models, attention may be likened to a secretary; he or she answers the
phone for the boss and lets some calls through while rejecting others. This
approximates the standard filtering model of attention. In the ecological
view, *the executive places the calls*—that is, the *algorist* (Shaw & McIntyre,
1974) controls the detection of information.

The Algorist

When we liken the control of attention to an executive placing phone
calls, we must confront the problem of *who* controls the detection of
information. To say that detection is controlled is to imply that it is
controlled by an *agent.* In this section, we consider the problems associated with talk of cognitive executives and, in particular, how to retain both
a notion of agent and our scientific integrity.

Over the centuries, psychological thought has been laced with internal agents of one sort or another. Such an agent has many aliases: homunculus, the ghost in the machine, executive, mind, soul, and will, to
name a few. He or she is usually seen as the last step in perception, the first
step in action, the searcher of memory, and the maker of decisions. Calling
upon homunculi in order to explain those aspects of cognition that cannot
otherwise be explained is, of course, no solution at all: The problem is
simply shifted to another level. One is left with trying to explain how the
homunculus perceives, acts, searches, and decides. Unfortunately, it is easy
to endow these characters with magical powers or to make them immune,
as it were, to natural law. As happy as our grandparents might be with
such mentalism, it is obviously not the cloth from which good psychological theory is cut.

On these accounts, any psychological theory that speaks of agents is
likely to raise eyebrows. Theorists who cannot live without an executive
can stay on relatively firm metaphysical footing by operationalizing the

executive into computerese wherein an executive *program* selects and uses subroutines according to strict algorithms. Because we have used the term agent in this book without a retreat to a concept of executive program, we are obliged to describe an ecological approach to the concept agent and, thereby, attempt to persuade the reader that an agent need be neither a metaphysical spook nor a last hold-out of mentalism.

We shall describe an approach to the problem of "knowing agent" that seeks to gain scientific credibility. The ideas summarized here are those of Shaw and his colleagues (e.g., Shaw & McIntyre, 1974). As noted earlier, at the heart of Shaw's and McIntyre's thesis is the notion that knowing is a complex interplay of what is, how it is known, and who knows it. Moreover, a complete accounting of knowing cannot be had without answering all three questions. The aims of their paper are to justify these assertions and, in doing so, to provide a rigorous definition of an algorist or knowing agent.

The first issue is whether or not an agent or algorist is extraneous to a theory that can, in principle or fact, accurately and completely describe both the algorithms (in this case, the rules and procedures specifying *how* a biological machine detects information) and the data (invariant energy structures) upon which those algorithms operate. That is to say, would a complete accounting of information and the biological routines that detect that information constitute a full accounting of *perception*? Shaw and McIntyre think not. In brief, they claim that the notion of algorist is presupposed by the concepts of information and algorithm.

The reasoning behind this claim is best conveyed, again, by an analogy. Imagine that it is basketball, rather than perception, that we seek to understand. The "what" is the equipment (ball, court, and basket). The "how" is the set of algorithms (players must dribble the ball, for points to be scored the ball must pass through the hoop). The "who" is the collection of players. It is obvious that the game cannot be sensibly described without the inclusion of all three. But it is also the case that the who, what, and how must fit together. Each serves to constrain what the others can be. The rules must fit together with the equipment (dribbling could not be a rule if a medicine ball were used). The equipment must fit the players (balls cannot be so big or heavy that they cannot be used by players). And, the rules must fit the players (the rules cannot be so long and complex that a player cannot learn them). Thus, it is not only the case that the game cannot be understood without reference to who, what, and how, but also none of the three alone (players, rules, equipment) can be understood without reference to the other two. Each constrains what the others can be and each is itself constrained by the nature of the others.

With respect to perception, then, it is suggested that perception must be understood with reference to who, how, and what. Moreover, a full accounting of any of these bases of perception (the algoristic, the algorithmic, and the informational) must embody the fact that that basis is constrained by the other two.

If these assertions have a ring of familiarity, it is because just such an approach was used in Chapters 2 and 3 to define information. Recall the claim that invariants can be accorded the status of information if and only if the invariant could be detected by the biological system *and* served some useful purpose (for example, directing attack). Information—the *what* of perception—is constrained both by algorithmic considerations (how transduction is done) and algoristic considerations (the goals of the animal).

By the same token, the algorithmic bases of perception are constrained both by the informational and algoristic bases. As an example of the former, the biological procedures by which "location" perception is done are constrained by the nature of the available information. The algorithms of location perception by bats, who use structured sound, and people, who use structured light, must be very different indeed. For an example of the algoristic constraints on algorithms we seek a case in which the particular detection procedures are determined, in part, by the needs of the animal. Say, for example, that some invariant specifies a salient dimension of the environment and that any of three algorithms for its detection could be instantiated in neural tissue. Assume, further, that one algorithm requires 600 neurons and takes 200 milliseconds; another requires 400 neurons and takes 80 milliseconds; the third requires 200 neurons and takes 200 milliseconds. Obviously, something must "choose" which to develop. What is it, then, that provides the degrees of constraint that make one potential algorithm into the one actualized in tissue? The question is an algoristic question because there is nothing in an algorithm *itself* that makes it best (e.g., most cost-effective). And, there is nothing in an invariant that makes one of the three algorithms best. Therefore, there must be something nonalgorithmic and noninformational that constrains the choice. The constraint falls to the algorist.

All in all, then, the first approximation to an algorist is the nonalgorithmic and noninformational constraints on perception. It is somewhat unsatisfying, however, to label "the algoristic basis" whatever is left over when the informational and biological constraints have been teased out. For a more direct approach, we quote Shaw & McIntyre (1974):

> ... the task of cognitive psychology is not so much to describe what behaviors man might emit, nor even what stimulus conditions might evoke them, but to determine what is the nature of man that requires and supports the need and purpose of such activities— whether they be physical or mental. (p. 307)

The algorist, then, is not something or someone inside an animal. Rather, the algorist is better thought of as those aspects of the animal—the whole animal—that render certain algorithms cost-effective, certain environmental objects useful, behaviors as intentional, and so on. As examples, the algorist is (animal has) a certain behavioral repertoire, and that repertoire shapes the affordances of its environment; the algorist is (animal has) certain drives that make certain objects into goal objects. The ecological claim is simply that the animal term must be included if perception and action are to be understood.

Recalling the statement on affordances in Chapter 3, it is possible to dissolve further the mystery of the concept of agent or algorist. At that time we quoted Shaw, Turvey, & Mace (in press): "A situation or event X affords action Y for animal Z on occasion O if certain relevant compatibilities between X and Z obtain." Animal Z and occasion O represent the algorist. To say that "object X affords action Y" is to say nothing at all: Anything could have any affordance at any time. Clearly, the animal must be acknowledged. But acknowledgment of animal variables need not put theory outside of science, as was assumed to be the case in the heyday of behaviorism.

This analysis suggests that goals and intentions do not emerge in full form out of a stockpot of mentalism. Rather, goals, intentions, and effectivities have evolved as the general and particular expressions of the dynamic symmetry of animal and environment. The general expression of that symmetry is that an animal must maintain contact with the environment to survive. The temporary manifestation of that symmetry is that an animal's psychological states and behaviors must be symmetrical with environmental states, fear and escape in the presence of a predator, desire and copulation in the presence of a mate, for example. Fears and desires do not well out of consciousness (or subconsciousness) any more than knowing (innate or acquired) does. All three are the children of evolution that are reared by the local environment. Discussing them and including them in theory are no less scientific than talking about liver cells.

We have addressed the issue of the propriety and meaning of the concept of algorist. Loosely conceived, the algoristic basis of perception is the intention or set of intentions that limits both the information that is detected and the biological procedures used to detect that information. To claim that perception and action are purposive is not to invite rampant mentalism in psychology, it is only to claim, as have many others (e.g., Dewey & Bentley, 1949; Kantor, 1920), that the who—knowing, intending, and feeling—should be accorded the same metaphysical footing as retinae, brains, and acoustic information. The who, what, and how are reflections of each other. All three, in turn, constitute a minimal description of an animal-environment system.

In sum, a consideration of the algorist is deemed an integral part of understanding perceiving and acting. It is argued that such consideration is not only a legitimate domain of scientific inquiry—i.e., nonmentalistic—but that any attempt to understand perception and action that ignores the algorist will, in dealing only with algorithms and environment, leave a gap that mentalism eases in to fill. As we shall emphasize in Chapter 7, identifying and elaborating these algoristic issues will have high priority in ecological theory in the years to come.

LEARNING

Learning, just like perception, is drastically altered when cast in the ecological mold. As with more traditional approaches to learning, it still seeks to understand the nonmaturational sources of the improvement in responses that accompany experience. However, the particulars of the definition of learning that emerge out of ecological thinking are quite different from the particulars of typical cognitive theory. To grasp Gibson's idea of learning, we must divest ourselves of many assumptions that are the legacy of this theory. We must adopt a different attitude toward the process of learning. In particular. we must dispense with the concept of memory.[2]

Evolution and Memory

As claimed above and in the first chapter, memory does not have a place in the ecological approach to perception that is presented here. For obvious reasons, this "omission" has been the most difficult notion for more traditional psychologists to accept. It is made more palatable by thinking about learning in a way that relates *ontogeny* (the development of the individual) to *phylogeny* (the evolutionary development of a species). In particular, we suggest that the consequences of learning should be viewed in the same way that the consequences of evolution are viewed.

There would probably be broad agreement with the statement that phylogenetic and ontogenetic development both lead to an improved ability for species and animals to know salient dimensions of their environments. While some authors have drawn token parallels between these two types of development (for example, random variation and natural selection are akin to trial and error learning), the languages with which evolution and learning

---

[2]This is not to dispense with the phenomena of remembering or recognizing. Memory is a theoretical construct called on to explain the phenomena. The ecological approach seeks an alternative account of the phenomena that does not require the storage or retrieval of information.

are usually described are quite distinct. This difference persists even though both evolution and learning concern how the past influences the present.

The primary distinction rests on memory. Scientists never view the evolutionary consequences of experience as the amassing of memories while they rarely view the consequences of an animal's personal history as anything *but* the amassing of memories (e.g., associations). Lurking at the back of this traditional thinking is the idea that evolution produces a new machine, while experience produces new parts that are used by the old machine. It is not at all clear from an ecological perspective why phylogeny and ontogeny are usually treated so differently, but whatever the sources of this dichotomous thinking, the differences run very deep.

The split between concepts in learning and concepts in evolution can be easily seen in the rather bizarre account that emerges if evolution is described in the terms that are usually used to describe learning. Such a description might proceed as follows. The animal would be thought of as *the* primordial creature upon whom eons have laid and overlaid structures and functions. The random mutations that occurred in its progenitors and that were selected for would be conceived of as writing on the originally clear slate of the earliest life form. And somehow the "original animal" uses these writings, these anatomical and physiological improvements, to cope with the present environment. As such, the animal brings its ancestry to bear on daily dealings with the environment. *It is still the same animal,* but, thanks to evolution, it has appropriate perceptual and behavioral skills at its disposal.

The formula for evolution, when created in the spirit of the formula for learning, then, might read as follows: primordial creature + natural selection = primordial creature + anatomical/physiological improvements. But surely no one conceives of a human as an amoeba with many fancy accessories.

While the formula for evolution given in the last paragraph seems quite strange, the consequences of *personal* experience are described with just such concepts. "Animal + experience (learning) = animal + knowledge" sounds perfectly reasonable. It proposes that knowledge is laid down in the organism and that *the* organism uses the knowledge in dealing with the environment. The schism between thoughts on evolution and thoughts on learning could not be more obvious.

What happens, on the other hand, if we try to write the story of learning in the language of evolution? Implicit in ecological thinking is just such an idea: We should conceive of the role of experience in the same way that we conceive of the role of evolution. Both lead to a new animal that is better able to cope with its environment.

If the consequences of learning are described in the same way as the consequences of evolution, the resultant formulation, unlike its counterpart above, is not at all bizarre. In fact, it makes good sense. If it is assumed that evolution leads to a *new* biological machine that is better suited anatomically and physiologically to the environment than its predecessors or extinct cousins, we might also assume that personal experiences lead to a new machine that is better suited to its particular, personal environment. It is better able to detect the environment's affordances. In this analysis, the consequence of personal experience is *not* that the old animal has new knowledge, but that *it is a new animal that knows better.*

When evolution and experience are characterized in these terms, the necessity of proposing memory storage is less apparent. Consider, for example, how difficult it would be to include something like memory in evolution. The changes wrought by evolution certainly are not memories. If an organism's ontogeny is treated the same way as its phylogeny, the concept of memory becomes equally inconvenient. Just as our perceptual systems are tailored to environmental information by evolution, so are they tailored by experience. And just as we do not need a vessel in which *ancient* history is brought to bear on the present, we do not need a vessel (memory) in which *recent* history is brought to bear. Plainly and simply, experience changes the animal.

Genetic Preattunement and Preparation

Animals have evolved in and grow up in a world that is rich in structured energy. Some of these energy patterns are of great ecological significance to the animal; some are completely unimportant. The task for the perception theorist is to understand how an animal comes to be able to detect the energy distributions that *are* of ecological significance. As noted earlier, there appear to be two routes to this sensitivity, two routes by which animals come to know their environments. They are evolution and learning. The following discussions of both of these factors reflect the view that experience, both evolutionary and personal, leads to an improvement in knowing; neither leads to an accumulation of knowledge.

Some energy distributions are of such ecological significance and are so universally distributed that evolution has yielded pre-wired nervous systems to detect them. A species is *genetically preattuned* to them; no learning is involved. One example of genetic preattunement in "lower" animals is the frog's entire visual system, which seems prewired to detect bugs (edibility), two classes of predators (escape), and borders (direction of escape) (Lettvin, Maturana, McCulloch, & Pitts, 1958). It is probably safe to say that such information is universal for frogs; as far as we know, all frogs eat insects, live near water, and so on.

One should not infer from the above examples that it is only among infrahumans that genetic preattunement is evident. Humans, too, share such abilities. Unhealthful things, like rotting human bodies, missiles approaching the eyes, and very hot objects touching the skin, are among those things so unpleasant to the senses that they afford escaping from. Healthful things, like tasty morsels on the back of the tongue or a nursing infant, afford (in a compelling way) swallowing or milk secretion (the let-down reflex).

Obviously, such genetic preattunement rests on the universal availability of information. All appropriate members of a species (note that some are limited to one sex and to one condition [lactation]) anywhere, and at any time, share the need and have the ability to detect that information. To say that the information is universal means that it spans all the animal-environment systems into which members of a species enter.

It should be recognized, however, that there exists other information that *is* unique to the particular animal-environment unit. This information is *local,* and examples of it include that which specifies who one's mother is, where the watering hole is, or where one's nest (hole, home) is. Certainly these are local, rather than universal, because all members of a species do not share the same mother, watering hole, or nest. Because they are local, genetic preattunement to such information is impossible. In such cases, however, it seems that there is often genetic preparation for the *types* of energy patterns that constitute such information. Put another way, evolution may *prepare* an animal to learn about its local habitat.

That animals need not start from scratch, so to speak, in learning the details of their local environments is evidenced in many ways. Imprinting in geese is one such example and it concerns the means by which a newly hatched gosling learns who its mother is. In brief, the first larger thing a gosling sees move during the interval shortly following birth will become the gosling's mother; the gosling will follow this "mother" and stay close to her when danger is near. It may be a telephone, it may be a turtle, or it may be an ethologist, but most often, it will indeed be the gosling's mother. In effect, evolution has said to the gosling, "I can prewire you to follow your mother, stay close in times of distress, make this response when you want to be fed, but you will have to learn for yourself who she is. One hint: She will be specified by the first wiping-out, unwiping, and shearing of a particular visual angle of optical texture."

Another example of genetic preparation can be seen in human language. Obviously evolution cannot build in or preprogram the ability to detect the ecological significance of spoken words; words vary from language to language. However, evolution has yielded a peripheral organ that is especially sensitive to the frequency range of speech. Moreover, evolution has resulted in neural circuitry to detect components of speech that *are* universal. For example, voicing (the phonetic feature that distinguishes /ba/ from /pa/, /da/ from /ta/, and /ga/ from /ka/) is, for all purposes, universal. To be sure, infants demonstrate the ability to detect voicing (Eimas, Siqueland, Jusczyk, & Vigorito, 1971). Thus, nature says to the human infant, "I cannot build into you the ability to detect the meaning of spoken utterances, but I will give you the ability to detect the universal invariants that lawfully join together to constitute the higher-order invariants that embody meaning."[3]

Additional evidence for genetic preparation is to be found in biological constraints, discussed in Chapter 3. It was claimed that biological constraints on learning implied that animals perceive affordances. The consequence of that claim on the present discussion is fairly clear. Biological constraints on learning suggest that not only has evolution prepared us to detect certain kinds of energy distributions, but it has dictated the kinds of behaviors that might be afforded by those distributions. Clearly, the particulars have to be learned, but it does not seem unreasonable to assert that genetic preparation serves not only to provide sensitivity to the classes of energy structures that constitute local invariants, but also ties them together, at least loosely, with the actions they might afford.

To summarize, ecologically significant invariants come in two varieties: universal and local. Universal invariants span animal-environment systems into which members of a species enter. Local invariants may be unique to a particular animal-environment system. For the most part, it is expected that there should be genetic preattunement (as evidenced by reflexes or fixed action patterns) to universal information. However, the animal must learn to detect local invariants. Even though learning is needed, evolution often gives animals a generous head-start in terms of the *kinds* of energy structures to which they should be sensitive and the behaviors afforded by those structures.

The Education of Attention

We now come to learning itself. The reader is asked to bear in mind the attitude toward learning, developed earlier: Experience does not give an "old" animal new knowledge. Rather, like evolution, it yields a new animal that knows better.

[3]No doubt developmental psycholinguists who ally themselves with the "nativist" camp (e.g., McNeill, 1970) would claim that children are preattuned to detect invariants of much higher-order—for example, that collections (phonemes) of the invariants described in the text (features) can join into collections (words) that are themselves invariant, which can in turn enter into invariant (grammatical) relations with other collections, and so on. These higher-order invariants are the so-called *linguistic universals*.

Building on the principles of genetic preattunement and preparation, the task for learning becomes the education of attention to those invariants and collections thereof (that are themselves invariant) that specify the affordances of the local environment. Local information, like universal information, can specify permanent or transient objects, places, and events in the local environment. It is for the fledgling perceiver to learn to detect them. And, because "attention" is that which controls detection, learning becomes *the education of attention* (Gibson, 1966).

Referring back to the language of the radio metaphor might help to clarify these thoughts. Places, events, and objects broadcast structured distributions of energy. Some of these distributions are of such significance and are so universally available that perceivers need not tune them in; their perceptual systems are preattuned to such distributions. Other "frequencies," while within the sensitivity range of our metaphorical radio, are not automatically tuned in; perceivers must learn to tune them in. That is, perceivers must learn to put their perceptual systems in the appropriate resonant state-configuration. As examples, rubbing a surface with the fingers is being in an appropriate state-configuration for detecting texture, hefting is the state-configuration for detecting weight.

Of course, not all "tunings in" are so obvious to an outside observer as the examples cited above. As noted earlier, a person looking for keys might behave much the same as a person looking for matches. What distinguishes them on the inside is that the two have different neural state-configurations—each tuned, so to speak, to information specifying the sought-after object.

The education of attention can manifest itself in many ways. The domain covered by the phrase *education of attention* is far broader than what has been called *perceptual learning*. Indeed, we would claim that all learning can be understood as the education of attention. In this context, however, this assertion will remain unproven, for we shall describe learning in a very broad and general way.

The ecological psychologist's emphasis on the confluence of perception and action spills inevitably into learning. The ramification of this emphasis is that all learning concerns the education of attention to information that adapts motor activity to environmental conditions. This approach blurs to some degree the distinction between perceptual learning and the acquisition of a motor skill. It does not deny that some learning relies more on perceptual differentiation—for example, learning to detect information that distinguishes two "identical" twins—but such differentiation would be unnecessary if one did not somehow act differently toward the twins. Similarly, some distinctly stylized and precise motor skill, such as the long jump, is not simply a matter of learning to coordinate muscular activity. Lee, Lishman, & Thompson (1976) have shown that the last few steps are modified so that the board is accurately reached. Such modification, of course, could not be accomplished by an actor blind to the optic array.

In sum, then, learning can be seen as education of attention to the invariants that will appropriately motivate and/or constrain activity. As an example, what does one need to learn in order to find a place to sit down when tired? First, the would-be sitter has to have learned to detect information specifying that something may be sat upon. In our culture, that information is defined by a rather large class of geometrically equivalent shapes of a fairly narrow size-range. Further, the perceiver must learn to approach the object that affords sitting.[4] As described in Chapter 3, approaching requires that the to-be-arrived-at object is the center of optical expansion. The point from which the optic array expands is the place at which a traveler will arrive if locomotion continues. Learning how to walk toward something is, then, learning what properties of the optic array should be constraining motor activity. In the present case, it is learning to keep the desired location at the center of optical expansion.

Although there is much more that could be said, we shall leave to others the task of elaborating the ecological approach to learning (Johnston & Turvey, 1980). To summarize the essence of such an approach, one could say that if perception is taken as knowing the environment, learning is how we improve at doing so. To a species, the improvement is to be understood with reference to evolution. To an individual, the improvement is to be understood with reference to personal experience, which might include communication from others. Moreover, evolutionary learning and personal learning are thought to operate in an analogous manner. Both serve to make animals better able to detect the affordances conveyed by ecologically significant energy patterns. Evolution results in preattunement to these affordances, and learning results in the education of attention to them.

SUMMARY

In Chapters 2 and 3, we presented an ecological version of the concept of information. In Chapter 4, we turned our attention to the selection and detection of that information. Issues relating to selection and detection engender questions above and beyond those required to define ecological information. Those questions are *how* is information detected by biological

[4] In retrospect, it is not certain that this is a learned skill. Animals may well be genetically preattuned to optical information specifying approach. But it suits the purposes of pedagogy to assume that it is learned.

machines and *who,* in terms of an intentioned algorist, is controlling the detection.

With respect to the first question, how is information detected, the ecological approach has several orientations. One such orientation emphasizes *doing* rather than *having.* In particular, *knowing* rather than *having knowledge* is stressed. A second orientation is that knowing is something done by an organism, not just a brain. Given these orientations toward perceiving, we asked what class of device might serve as a metaphor for a biological knowing machine. The digital computer, which generally serves as the electronic metaphor, was rejected because in it information is stored, retrieved, and compared. Instead, the radio was selected, because that metaphor emphasizes the detection, rather than storage, of information. Clearly, the radio analogy misses many essential aspects of a perceptual system, but it seems to us to be a better first approximation than a computer. The most obvious applicability of the radio analogy is seen in the notion of resonance: Biological systems resonate, as do radios, to information that the environment "broadcasts."

It was claimed that the higher-order variables of stimulation that constitute information are simply registered, rather than computed. Following Runeson (1977), the polar planimeter was offered as a simple mechanical analogue of a perceptual system. The planimeter is an area-detecting device that neither detects lower-level properties nor computes area. The planimeter demonstrates, therefore, that rudimentary variables are not logically entailed in the registration of complex ones.

Which of many informational invariants will be registered or "tuned in" is governed by attention. Attention was thereby characterized as the *control of detection,* the tuning in or resonation to some part of the information available to the senses. This view of attention was contrasted with the more common interpretation of attention as a means by which inputs are rejected.

To say that attention is controlled implies that it is controlled by some sort of agent. In describing such an agent in a scientifically acceptable way, we presented Shaw's and McIntyre's claim that a description of perception in terms of algorithms and information is not an exhaustive description of perception. Nor is it the case that algorithms and information can themselves be understood without reference to algoristic considerations. What information is detected and how that information is detected are constrained by the needs and intentions of the animal. The algorist neither constructs information nor dictates algorithms; it merely constrains what they will be while itself being constrained by them. The long term constraints are probably due to the purpose of life itself; the short-term constraints aim at maintaining symmetry between animal and environment

so that the psychological states of an animal—its knowing, feeling, and de-
siring—are at once symmetrical with the facts, threats, and offerings of the
environment.

After considering the algorist, attention turned to learning. Most
cognitive approaches to learning maintain that learning involves the collection and storage of information. Experience writes on an animal's slate
and the animal uses that slate in its moment to moment dealings with the
world. In contrast, the ecological approach supposes that the consequence
of experience is an improved ability to know. As such, learning can be
likened to evolution; both serve to make the animal and species, respectively, better able to detect ecologically significant objects, places, and events.
Neither the functions of evolution, nor, by extension, the functions of
learning, should be thought of as "giving the animal knowledge" or "writing on its slate."

The consequence of evolutionary learning was seen as the preattunement of perceptual systems to ecologically significant, universal
information. Learning, in turn, was seen as the education of attention.
Animals, through some structural change in their nervous systems, become
able to *resonate* to information offered by the environment. These considerations of learning, coupled with the idea of affordances, provide an
approach that applies not just to perceptual learning, but to learning in
general.

To broaden this summary further, we can distill these first four
chapters into a few general statements. The study of perception is the study
of a process in an animal-environment system. Information is the glue that
holds the system together; it keeps the animal in contact with the environment. Thus, information is to be understood with respect to both the
animal-environment relationship that it specifies and the animal to whom
that relationship is specified. The unitary nature of animal and environment, when taken together with the interweaving of perceiving and acting,
leads to the claim that animals are born to detect and learn to detect the
affordances of their environments.

5

Philosophical Implications of Animal-Environment Synergy

The view that the system to which the phenomena of perception are to be ascribed is the animal-environment system has been contrasted with the implicit doctrine in psychology—and science and philosophy, in general—that animal and environment are different theoretical domains, each independently understandable. We have examined how the assumption of animal-environment synergy restructures perceptual theory; we now turn our attention to its broader implications. In particular, we shall examine the philosophical stance that is invited by the forfeiture of animal-environment dualism. The philosophical consequences of animal-environment mutuality or synergy are far-reaching, and whatever changes this attitude fosters in psychology may represent the most important contribution of the ecological movement.

This chapter presents the three strong undercurrents of the approach. First, it is claimed that the ecological approach assumes *realism*, a realism that is markedly different from the traditional realism cultivated by animal-environment dualism.[1] Next, certain issues in the *philosophy of science*

[1] A theory of direct perception must suppose realism while a theory of indirect perception may suppose realism. The distinction between direct realism and indirect realism concerns the relationship of the perceiver to the environment during perception. To rephrase arguments made in Chapter 1, the indirect realist supposes that something (a retinal image, a sense datum, or a representation) stands between the

are addressed—in particular, those that consider how the sciences of physics biology, and psychology relate to one another. Finally, it is claimed that the ecological approach partakes of *empiricism,* but unlike traditional empiricism, the ecological form does not ignore evolution.

REALISM

Realism is the philosophical position that there are perceivable objects and events whose existence does not depend on being perceived or thought about. Put another way, realism claims that a real world exists and does not rely for its existence on being experienced. Moreover, a realist would claim that this "objective reality" is known, at least in part. Perhaps a picture of realism can be painted more boldly by using idealism as contrast.

Idealism holds that the properties of objects owe their existence, at least in part, to being perceived. Whatever we know of the "real world" is framed by our ideas. As examples, the idealist would claim that redness is not a characteristic of objects, but of experience. Similarly, smoothness is a property of a sensation or an idea. Such characteristics, it might be claimed, exist *because* they are perceived.

While arguments between realists and idealists might appear to be intellectual games to the nonphilosopher or trivial to special scientists such as physicists, biologists, or psychologists,[2] they are neither. The special sciences presuppose the conclusions of metaphysics; they begin where metaphysics leaves off. For example, a physicist presupposes that atoms exist; an idealistically inclined metaphysician might propose that atoms

---

environment and the perception. The direct realist, in contrast, claims no such intermediaries. As realisms, however, both schools claim that perceivers know environmental objects and events; they divide primarily on the issue of whether that knowledge is inferential. We should note, however, that Shaw and his colleagues (Shaw & Bransford, 1977; Shaw, Turvey, & Mace, in press) have questioned the cogency of the argument that perceptual realism *can* reasonably be indirect, because, as Locke pointed out, there is no way to guarantee that the representation stands for a real object:

> It is evident the mind knows not things immediately, but only by the intervention of the ideas it has of them. Our knowledge therefore, is real, only so far as there is conformity between our ideas and the reality of things. But what shall be here the criterion? How shall the mind, when it perceives its own ideas, know that they agree with things themselves. (Locke, Book IV, Chap. 3, Sec. 3)

[2] To keep our discussion simple, we treat the sciences throughout this chapter as if they had well-defined boundaries. In particular, we treat them in terms of their conventional subject matters as disciplines. However, we recognize and applaud those attempts by contemporary physical biologists to identify physical principles or strategies that are scale- (or in the present context, discipline-) independent.

exist because of the physicist's concept of matter. A biologist might seek to explain the functioning of an organ, while his counterpart in metaphysics might puzzle over what it means to claim that something has a function.

If we grant the claim that the special sciences rest on metaphysical assumptions, the metaphysical choices that one makes, either implicitly or explicitly, are far from trivial. If the metaphysical assumptions are faulty, the sciences that are built upon them will, sooner or later, have to be abandoned. (One would hope that they would be abandoned, but bad metaphysics is considerably harder to detect than bad science.)

For the scientist, the choice between realism and idealism is an easy one: realism. Most scientists assume that what they are studying is real and objective. They are realists. For the psychologist, choice of philosophy is fuzzier. As a scientist, the psychologist feels it necessary to assume that psychological entities (for example, knowledge, desires, or personality attributes) have a status independent of their recognition by scientists. Thus, the psychologist as scientist must be a realist. Nevertheless, perceptual theorists have tended to argue that the perceiver is not directly acquainted with the environment as such, but with a surrogate for that environment. The latter position, of course, means that psychologists do sometimes adopt idealist attitudes. It is the ecological position that psychologists should maintain a complete commitment to realism. By the ecological view, any forfeiture of realism is a forfeiture of science.

If it is correct to assert that psychology should be a science and that science demands realism, it follows that psychology should demand realism. This does not mean that psychologists should ignore the phenomena that seem to require idealism, but rather that realism should only be abandoned if a thorough attempt at it fails. To follow this argument, we shall examine some often-raised arguments against realism and demonstrate that they are rooted in animal-environment dualism. In abandoning animal-environment dualism, it is suggested that the "barriers to realism" (Shaw, Turvey, & Mace, in press) are abandoned, too.

Psychologists question realism on two grounds. The first is the observation of the supposed nonveridicality of perception. There are a variety of situations in which our experiences of the world seem to be simply inaccurate; what we perceive appears different from what is there. If nonveridicality is a fact, a serious commitment to realism is unjustified. The second barrier to realism arises from the observation that different individuals experience the same objects and events of the environment differently. The same person will even experience objects differently on different occasions. And, the difference in experience is presumably even greater among different species. If *A* and *B* are two different experiences of object

C, so the argument goes, and *A* and *B* are contrary experiences, both *A* and *B* cannot be true experiences (knowledge) of *C.* If one wishes to make a serious commitment to realism—and the ecological approach does—the first order of business is to remove the preceding two objections or barriers to realism.

Veridicality

One assertion that is often used to undermine direct realism and realism in general is the claim that perception can be nonveridical. Two forms that this argument takes will be addressed. The first concerns our perceptual response to physical energy and has been summarized as follows:

> If [perception] were primarily veridical, the organism would consist of a set of property analyzers and there would be a property-by-property monotonic transform for those properties which are processed. For example, light would be analyzed spectrally, taste would classify molecules in a way comprehensible to a chemist, loudness would not vary with wavelength. [But perception is clearly nonveridical;] e.g., there is an infinity of different physical configurations mapping onto any color experience. . . . The structure of experience is altogether of a different order from that of physical reality.
>
> [In addition,] edges are enhanced, gradients suppressed or exaggerated; "constancies" can be significantly altered by experience. . . . Not only is organismic mind a non-veridical reflector of ambient energy, it doesn't know what is going on out there and it doesn't want to know. (Kaufman, 1978 pp. 3.17 and 3.53)

Our response to this kind of argument does not dispute the facts cited (e.g., perceived loudness is a nonmonotonic function of sound pressure level and does vary with wavelength). What we do take issue with is the way "veridicality" is implicitly defined—in terms of the response to a certain metric of energy (e.g., wavelength). Perception is nonveridical only if nonveridical is taken to mean that experience or behavior does not reflect the nuances of physical energy that can be discerned by a physicist who chooses to describe that energy in terms of classic (and animal-neutral) variables. But such a definition of veridicality hardly suits an animal who needs to know survival-related characteristics of its environment.

The story of color perception illustrates this point nicely. The property of the optic array that corresponds to our experience of color is not wavelength; the visual system does not analyze light spectrally. But to assert that because the analysis is not spectral, the structure of experience is "altogether of a different order from that of physical reality" arbitrarily accords to wavelength the status of premier descriptor of reality. The simple fact is that the wavelength of a shaft of light to the eye is not an informative dimension of energy; it varies along with changes in the radiant energy. Thus, if an eye were to analyze light spectrally, the color of objects would vary and, perforce, color could not be a property that contributes to the detection of objects.

As Land (e.g., 1977) has demonstrated, the wavelengths of a shaft of light are not uniquely related to a particular color experience. Identical stimulation bordered by a different collection of wavelengths can lead to a wholly different perceived color. This is not to say that there is *nothing* in the optic array that is uniquely related to a perceiver's experience of color. Quite the contrary, it turns out that there is a property to which color experience corresponds—a property that *is* invariant with respect to the transformations induced by changes in illumination. It is a set of ratios of "scaled integrated reflectances" on three axes of lightness (long-, middle-, and short-wave) and the products of three integrals. One need not understand the details of the invariant supporting color vision, however, to appreciate the main point that has been elegantly illustrated by Land:

> . . . many people viewing some of our experiments for the first time will identify something as being red or green but will then ask, as if their eyes are being fooled, "What color is it really?" The answer is that the eye is not being fooled. It is functioning exactly as it must with involuntary reliability to see constant colors in a world illuminated by shifting and unpredictable fluxes of radiant energy. (1977, p. 108)

It is nonsense, therefore, to suggest that spectrometers react veridically while eyes do not; both respond veridically to the dimensions which they were either evolved or designed to detect. The idea that one dimension—wavelength—is reality and the other is not cannot be justified.

The logic of the assertion of the nonveridicality of perception appears to rest on the assumption that finding a variable, any variable, of stimulation that is not precisely mirrored in experience is *in and of itself* proof that perception is nonveridical. From our perspective, the judgment of whether or not perception is veridical—a judgment of profound philosophical import—should not be based on so meager an observation. The main argument from Gibson's second book is that information should not be thought of as that which stimulates receptors, but that which stimulates perceptual systems. Therefore, we should not search for variables such as wavelength that stimulate receptors, but rather, we should consider the senses as perceptual systems and seek variables of stimulation (as Land has done for color) at that grain of analysis. Moreover, even at the coarser grain, the energy patterns stimulating our perceptual systems exist at many different levels of complexity. Some energy patterns may be variant at one level of description (e.g., in one geometry) and invariant at another level (e.g., in some other geometry). Finding a variable of stimulation that is not registered does not demonstrate nonveridicality; it only means that we have failed to identify information that a perceptual system detects. The conclusion of nonveridicality must be based on a cogent demonstration that there is no variable at any grain of analysis that describes the stimulation in a way commensurate with perception.

The second argument that is used to question realism concerns error. This argument runs as follows: If perception is direct and the world is as we see it, then we should not make mistakes: Direct realism implies errorless perception. Although cases of erroneous perception evidenced by behavioral mistakes appear to occur, we intend to show that the labels "error" and "mistake" are not justified. First, an effort will be made to establish a broad criterion for veridical (nonerroneous) perception through the concept of appropriate and useful action. Next, we describe several categories of "erroneous perception or action" and hold each up against the criterion of appropriate and useful.

In the preceding part of this section, it was claimed that veridical perception should not be taken to mean the monotonic transduction of an arbitrary metric of energy. If we take seriously the claim in Chapter 3 that the purpose of perception is to constrain appropriate and effective action, then perhaps the sphere of action provides the best test of veridicality. That is, the test of the veridicality of perception should be on the appropriateness and effectiveness of the actions it constrains. Veridical perception is demonstrated, therefore, when the actions of the actor-perceiver are mutually compatible with the affordances of the situation. Recall that useful, adaptive information is said to specify affordances—what a particular animal can do with respect to a particular object or layout of surfaces on a particular occasion. For actions to fit with affordances does not require that the animal be apprised of the positions of all the atoms constituting the situation or the spectral absorption of the surfaces, or even all the affordances that the situation might offer. Rather, it merely requires that said animal perceive enough to do something appropriate and effective. That is, in order to act effectively in a situation, an animal need not notice all, or even most, of its affordances; veridical perception entails detecting those affordances that are appropriate to the percipient on that occasion.

This view of veridicality calls for a definition of truth-about-the-environment that is not metaphysical (always and for everyone) but pragmatic (useful for a particular someone on a given occasion). In other words, what

Shaw, Turvey, & Mace (in press) call ecological knowledge must capture reality sufficiently to motivate useful action by a particular (species of) animal; it does not demand an egalitarian consensus as to the facts of the world. Of course, this implies that what is pragmatically true for one species may differ from what is pragmatically true for another species. Nor must ecological knowledge for one individual be the same as ecological knowledge for another individual. Moreover, useful knowledge for the same individual may differ from occasion to occasion. On this account, effective action as constrained by ecological knowledge should be the only criterion for judging the veridicality of perception.

Even if we admit effective action as our criterion for veridicality, there are some situations wherein an animal's behavior seems to conflict with what is true about the environment. Organisms seem to act inappropriately, presumably because of misconceptions of what is "really there."

Although there is considerable overlap, one can discern five such sets of circumstances to which the label "in error" has been attached to perception. We shall enumerate those circumstances and assert that the label "in error" is inappropriate.[3]

Case 1: Inadequate Information.   In this case and the next, it is proposed that there is a *failure to perceive* rather than an error in perception. The two cases are, respectively, failure of an energy medium to embody adequate information about environmental properties and a failure to detect available and adequate information. Examples of inadequate information might include blurring of optical structure by fog, the masking of a whisper next to a waterfall, or the various restrictions (e.g., tachistoscopic exposures, Maxwellian peepholes) applied by perception researchers. In these cases, we recognize perception as a source for successful action to be incomplete rather than in error. What is known is "correctly" known, but for whatever reason, what is known is not enough for felicitous activities, given the environmental circumstances and the animal's intent.

Case 2: Undetected Adequate Information.   Here, knowledge of the environment is also incomplete but the reasons reside more on the animal side of the system than the environment side. As examples (and expla-

---

[3]We omit from this enumeration experiences and activities associated with lesions of the nervous system, drugs, electrical stimulation, and sleep. They include alexia, hallucinations, grand mal seizures, dreams, etc. The rationale for this omission is that these phenomena, while perhaps falling under the headings of "experiences" or "things that animals do," do not fall under the headings of perception and action. The notion that they are somehow intrinsic to an understanding of perception (e.g., Pribram, 1977) seems no more cogent to us than the claim that an upset stomach is intrinsic to the understanding of digestion.

nations) we include the inability to detect well-articulated optical structure under conditions of very dim illumination (due to insensitivity of the visual system) or the inability of a toddler to detect the write-with ability of a pencil (his or her attention is not yet educated to information about this affordance). In these cases, invariant energy patterns are adequate, but they can go undetected. Again, however, perception as such is more incomplete than incorrect.

Because the above cases are based on actual insufficiencies in information or the perceptual apparatus, it is easy to see that calling them erroneous perception is unjustified. In the next three cases, however, the label "in error" derives from certain theoretical biases which are usually brought to bear in describing the situations. But in these cases, too, we show that it is inappropriate to say that the perceiver has erred.

Case 3: Illusions. Here we would include such phenomena as geometrical illusions and apparent movement. Illusions might be defined as situations in which the scientist's measurement of the "stimulus" does not correspond to the perceiver's reports about the "stimulus." According to tradition, the perceiver is "in error," but we would claim that the *scientist is in error*—that is, he or she is measuring the wrong thing.

Consider, for example, Gibson's description of the Müller-Lyer figure (Figure 5-1):

> But the information for length of line, I have argued, is not simply length of line. To suppose so is to confuse the picture considered as a surface with the optical information to the eye. A line drawn on paper is not a stimulus. The stimulus information for the length of line is altered by combining it with other lines. (Gibson, 1966, p.313)

A similar analysis can be provided for illusions of movement. *Apparent motion* labels phenomena in which a perceiver is presented with a succession of discrete and stationary stimuli and perceives continuous movement. For example, in a motion picture there is no motion; each frame is a static image. Nevertheless, movement is seen. As in the Müller-Lyer case, our understanding of the phenomenon must be based on a clear conceptual separation of the thing itself (the succession of static frames) and the information it embodies. Thus, it is claimed that while there is no motion in a motion picture there is information about motion. The successive order of images specifies a dynamic event.

Therefore, the importance of illusions is in the distinctions they enforce between traditional metrics for describing the environment and ecologically motivated metrics for describing the environment. Indeed,

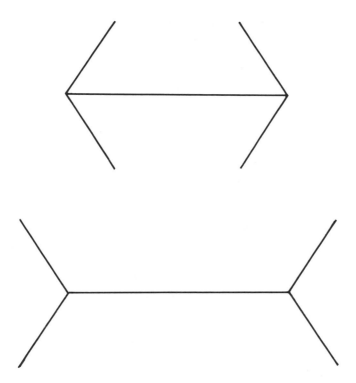

Figure 5-1. The Müller-Lyer Figure. The horizontal segments are the same length.

ecometrics has materialized as the science of measuring the information to which perception refers (Shaw & Cutting, in press).

In geometrical illusions and apparent motion, then, the disparity between some measure of the "stimulus" and a perceiver's report is due to a confusion on the part of the measurer, between things and information. As in our earlier argument for ecological information instead of arbitrary measures of physical energy, the perception is not in error.

Case 4: Inappropriate Use of the Human Perspective. This case comes about when an observer tries to explain an event in which she or he has not participated. This is especially troublesome when the event involves nonhuman species. As examples, when a frog lashes out at a rapidly moving dark spot that is not a bug, or a gosling follows the first moving object it encounters even if that object is not its mother, or a hermit crab investigates a sea anemone when the crab is in need of a shell, we are tempted to say that they have all made perceptual errors. But it is only our human perspective that requires this evaluation.

For frogs, small, dark, erratically and rapidly moving objects typically afford eating. The appropriate action for such an affordance is to attack. To say that the frog errs when it attacks the decoy is to assume that "decoy vs. insect" is a possible or meaningful perceptual distinction for a frog simply because it is meaningful for us. But in the ecological niche in which they have evolved, frogs are not required to make such distinctions. Given the optical information that frogs have evolved to detect, the frog's action is correct. That it is "unsuccessful" in the contrived world of experiments does not deny the ecological appropriateness of the response.

Our account of the gosling example would follow the same lines: In its natural environment, the first moving, relatively larger object usually is its mother so the gosling, too, is acting on pragmatic knowledge at the species level. It should not be expected to entertain the possibility that "mother" might be an impostor just because humans know that being aware of that possibility would be useful in this laboratory setting. For its natural surrounds, the gosling, just like the frog, has taken the appropriate action.

But what of the hermit crab that appears to be making a mistake while it is in its own niche? A crab that has lost its shell seems to approach the apparently hollow body of a sea anemone in order to enter it. We call this an error if we assume that the crab perceives the anemone to afford climbing inside: Because a crab could never enter an anemone, it must be acting erroneously. If the anemone is merely an object that affords investigating, however, the crab's action is appropriate. Any object of a certain size, shape, texture, and so on would have the same affordance. Investigating objects that afford any degree of access will eventually allow the crab to find a protective covering. (An effective action need not be the final action.) The anemone (or, for that matter, an actual protective shell) is *no more than an object to be investigated.* We cannot assume that a hermit crab can or should distinguish anemones from shells; what it can do is explore its environment in appropriate and effective ways.

Case 5: Arbitrary Limits on the Scope of Perception. In this category, the label "in error" is applied by someone who, for purposes of theory, limits the definition of perception to that referring to information about the physical properties of the environment available in a brief interval, within one sense modality, and to a perceiver whose exploratory activities are limited. The theoretical issues here involve what kind of information is available to perceivers, the amount of time over which perception can be said to occur, the number of sense modalities to which a perception refers, and the importance of exploration to perception. For each of these issues, the ecological approach adopts the less conventional stance: Perceiving is an ongoing activity, not limited to a definite interval, which may involve many perceptual systems and significant exploration. And, because information is what it is by virtue of the fact that animals are active, it cannot be defined in an animal-neutral way. In what follows, it is claimed that the label "in error" only makes sense with reference to the restrictive definition of perception, and, moreover, the restrictive definition is unjustified.

To those for whom perception must "tell all" in one brief glance (or touch, sniff, etc.) or must guide the animal to some *ultimate* consummatory behavior, perception can be in error. This description, however, presupposes that perception is accomplished in an instant. More generally, it assumes that perception has a single, definite endpoint—the percept— which must stand or fall on its own, and that there are qualitatively distinct and logically independent percepts (visual ones, tactile ones, etc.). But if, as we have elaborated in Chapter 1, the domain of perception is continually unfolding ecological events, the label "in error" is, again, inappropriate. *In the ecological view, the purpose of perception is not to produce an end-product (such as a percept), but to constrain actions in such a way as to continuously reveal useful aspects of the environment.* Perception cannot be in error because no one moment in that event must stand as the last word on pragmatic truth.

Thus, we are fooled by a hologram only until we try to touch it. An optical shimmer on the desert looks like water only until we get close enough to see that it is a mirage.

But what is the perceiver-actor doing while such "extended" perception is going on—for example, when an optical shimmer is thought to be water? She or he is behaving appropriately with regard to what information is available. Insofar as an action *contributes to* "bringing about a change in the existential circumstances of the agent (e.g., reaching a desired goal)," that action is appropriate (Shaw et al., in press). It need not be the final, consummatory behavior. If one wants water in the desert, it is wholly appropriate to investigate optical shimmers. If those shimmers turn out to be (have been?) a mirage, the actor-perceiver has not made a mistake; the fact of the mirage was revealed through perceptually constrained effective actions. The mistake would be to take no action.

In both Case 4 and Case 5, we have identified actions that at first might appear not to be appropriate or useful. On closer examination, however, their appropriateness and utility become more apparent. There remain certain classes of actions, however, whose appropriateness and utility are not as easily rationalized. Clearly, there are misactions that result in the injury or death of the animal. Can these actions, too, be construed as appropriate or, in the end, must one acknowledge that actions, and, perforce, perceptions, can be in error?

Our response to this query comes in two parts. The first is that appropriateness and utility are based on *history*, not outcome. Whether an action should be deemed appropriate should be judged by whether it is appropriate *given the phylogeny and ontogeny of the animal.* Thus, an animal is not misperceiving (or misacting) if it is doing what it is supposed to do (has evolved or learned to do), the apparent "success" of the act aside. The second and more fundamental argument is whether or not perception (or action) can, *in principle,* be in error (or correct, for that matter). This argument, which will be addressed later, concerns the nature of things that can be said to be in error and whether or not perception and action should be counted among them.

To summarize the realist position with respect to error in perception or action, five types of situations were discussed: impoverished information, undetected information, illusions, biased descriptions of "third-party" events, and perception restricted by theoretical assumptions. In all of these, perception has, by various theorists, been called "in error." We claimed that in all of the cases, "in error" is a misnomer because the criteria by which perception is judged are unjustifiable. Perception departs from absolute—and with reference to animal activity, arbitrary—physical metrics, but are we to suppose that because animals' perceptual systems detect variables different from those detected by a physicist's instruments that the former are *in error*? Perception departs from metaphysically perfect truth, which is itself a concept of dubitable worth, but does an animal need to know the quintessence of a substance (its particular chemical and atomic composition) or, more simply, whether or not it can be eaten? An animal's perception departs from what *we* think it should see, but does that mean that frogs should not lash out in the direction of optical displays that embody the invariants to which frogs have evolved to respond?

The conventional criteria referred to above are irrelevant to an organism's survival. Insofar as the purpose of perception lies in its effectiveness in motivating and guiding useful activity, such activity can be the only criterion for the success of perception. And, if we take useful activity as one necessary condition for the continuation of animal life, the existence of life reflects the fact that animals' actions have met and continue to meet the criterion of appropriateness. That birds fly into windows and that people fall down do not mitigate this argument. Such mitigation would make no more sense than deeming the theory of evolution false because we find a run-over squirrel in the road (the squirrel is dead and, therefore, was maladapted; the theory of evolution predicts that animals *are* adapted; therefore the theory of evolution is false).

We have advocated the realist stance and questioned the claim that perception is nonveridical. Assuming that the argument for ecological veridicality is reasonable, it provides a backdrop against which to confront the second and related barrier to realism: that facts of the world are the province of physics, while facts of perception belong to psychology. We shall show how this barrier is built on the assumption of animal-environment dualism, and that there need be no barriers to realism if psychological laws are written over animal-environment systems.

The argument, in a nutshell, is this: An assumed logical independence of animal and environment invites the description of each system, animal and environment, in the different languages of the different sciences. The problem for the realist is the problem of reconciling these two descriptions. The union of animal and environment invites their description in a common vocabulary. Thus, the traditionally defined incommensurability of "mind and world" (or as the ecological view necessarily puts it, of animal and environment) is not created and, therefore, need not be solved. Let us now elaborate these assertions.

DESCRIBING REALITY AND DESCRIBING KNOWLEDGE

The first question one must address is where the two sets of descriptions—of animal and environment—have come from in traditional science. That is, to what disciplines does one turn for the terms needed to describe the world as perceived and acted upon and the terms needed to describe what the contents of the world are *really*? The natural inclination for scientist and nonscientist alike would be to assume that the first question falls under the purview of psychology, while the second falls under the purview of physics. The following exchange illustrates the natural inclination:

Q: What is a pencil?
A: A device with which to write.
Q: But what is it really?
A: A cylinder of graphite surrounded by wood.
Q: And what are they, really?
A: Well, graphite is hexagonally crystalized allotrope of carbon . . . .

The familiarity of that kind of script suggests that "really" has come to mean that which is described by physics; and the smaller the parts, the closer we are to reality. Note that the reliance on physics for describing reality carries with it two assumptions. First, reality is described in animal-neutral terms; what a thing really is does not imply a "to whom." Second,

a traditional form of reductionism is assumed in the sense that the finer
the grain of analysis, the closer to reality is the description (Fodor, 1979).

What is left, then, to the psychologist or philosopher who seeks to
understand the relationship between animals' perceptions and actions and
reality? Must we adopt the physicists' metrics of reality and compare
knowledge to that, or can reality be described and measured at a level
more commensurate with perceiving and acting? This approach, of course,
questions physics' final authority on reality.[4] We have already made a case
for why physics should not have exclusive title to such authority. Now we
must provide some ground rules for determining the scientific domain in
which a particular question of reality should reside. In the end, we intend
to present the conditions under which physics is appropriate and, when it
is not, what is.

The legitimacy of physics, or any branch of science, as a descriptor
of reality should be contingent on two principles. First, the phenomenon
at issue must exist within the grain of analysis investigated by the science.[5]
Second, the reality to be described must reside *wholly within* the system
over which the description is to be written. For example, suppose that a
scientist wants to understand what food "really is." The grain of analysis
at which food exists is the biological, so it cannot, by the first criterion
above, be understood *qua* food at a physical grain of analysis (e.g., as a
swarm of atoms). Neither can some matter be judged as food unless there
is an animal that can ingest it. Thus, by our second criterion, food cannot
be understood in a system that is completely indifferent to animals. Food—
what it really is—resides in animal-environment systems and both animal
terms and environment terms are required for its explication.

Our answer, then, to the question of which science should have authority on reality is the one at whose grain of analysis the to-be-explained
phenomenon exists. Thus, if one's concern is with perceiving and acting,
the science that ought to be describing reality—that is, the environment
that is seen and acted upon—is the one in which perceiving and acting exist:
psychology. Obviously, the psychologist's description of the world as seen
and acted upon *cannot* be indifferent to who is doing the seeing and acting
because the environment affords different acts to different animals. The descriptions of an environment that are relevant to the activities of knowing
must be in terms of the animal doing the knowing. Therefore, we claim
that *the description of the environment that is appropriate to the investigation of perceiving and acting must come from an analysis of an animal-
environment system at a psychological grain.*

---

[4]What is being denied here is the authority of physics either of the cosmic
scale (classical mechanics) or of the microscopic scale (quantum mechanics). Instead,
physics at the *ecological scale* is being pursued.

[5]"Vertical questions," to be described later, are exempt from this.

Incidentally, this is not to imply that physicists cannot justifiably inquire into what is occurring in an animal-environment system when the animal is knowing the environment. One approach, that taken by Iberall (1977) and Bunge (1973, 1978), is to develop a physics that applies across scales (e.g., wherein "psychological particles" follow the same rules as atoms). Another approach would be to describe the animal-environment transaction atomistically.

The latter inquiry might contain statements like "Certain wavelengths of electromagnetic radiation are absorbed, while other wavelengths are reflected by a flat surface of a certain area. The reflected radiation travels through a medium (air) until it arrives at a second medium, where it is slowed and bent toward a line perpendicular to the tangent of the more or less spherical boundary of the medium and . . . . This eventually puts a collection of atoms (of the brain) at new positions, moving at new speeds in new directions." What is interesting about such an analysis is that the term *knowing* need not and *should not* appear. Indeed, one need not even discuss *animal;* all one needs to do is indicate where the atoms are and how they are moving. Even if such a description were possible in principle (although it is not because of the indeterminacy principle, and because the amount of storage that would be needed to represent all the information probably exceeds the capacity of any finite machine), what would we understand of knowing? Little, if anything. Therefore, we must assume that if knowing is explicable by science, then an analysis of elementary particles, for example, is but one of many possible grains of analysis, and of those, it is not the one best-suited to describing the world as the object of an animal's knowledge (assuming that that animal is not a physicist). In short, this argument grants biologists and psychologists license to describe reality.

To extend this analysis, we shall next examine the properties that emerge in these descriptions of reality. As biological and psychological examples, respectively, consider vitamins and edibility. The claim is that a vitamin, as part of reality, can and *must* be described at the biological grain of analysis. If we call upon physics, we are no longer referring to vitamins *qua* vitamins. As part of the environment, vitamins imply an animal whose metabolic processes require the substance, so we must describe this segment of reality with reference to an animal. Further, vitamins are no less real than the molecules, atoms, or particles that constitute them. More important, one should not infer that because a substance is a vitamin for some animals but not others, it is not *really* a vitamin; it really is a vitamin to certain animals. Reality can be—and for certain questions must be—animal-specific. Finally, and perhaps most important of all, for something to be a vitamin, it need not *be used* in metabolic processes: It need only *be able to be so used.*

If a parallel example can be offered for describing the environment as the object of an animal's actions (rather than as it relates to its nutritional needs), we should have a description of the reality to which knowing refers. This description can be outlined by rewriting the preceding paragraph with a few pertinent substitutions. The main substitution, of course, is the psychological for the biological. In particular, *edibility* is substituted for *vitamins*. In doing this, we assert that edibility is a genuine part of reality—a part of reality taken with reference to the action of an animal.

The edibility of food as part of reality can and must be described at a psychological grain of analysis. If we call upon biology, we are no longer referring to edibility *qua* edibility. As part of the environment, edibility of a substance implies an animal that could eat that substance, so we must describe this segment of reality with reference to an animal. Further, edibility is no less real than the food that constitutes it. More important, one should not infer that because some matter is edible for some animals but not for others, it is not *really* edible; it really is edible to some animals. Finally, and perhaps most important of all, for something to be edible does not mean that it is being perceived as edible, it need only be perceivable as edible.

There are several significant aspects of the last paragraph that ought to be highlighted. Obviously the most important is the claim that the environment, taken in reference to an animal's action, has certain properties—*objective and real*—that cannot be inferred from an animal-neutral description. These properties are its affordances, the acts that it permits. Second, a description of environmental properties that is animal-referential is still a part of realism; these properties exist independent of an animal's perception of them. Were their existence dependent on perception, this approach would be idealistic. Thus, on the issue of the animal's contribution to reality, idealists would claim that the animal's *perception* contributes to reality, while we would claim that an animal's *existence* contributes to reality.

The points made above are crucial to the developing argument. To reiterate, the central claim is that while a description of reality that is neutral to animals certainly serves some purposes in science, such a description does not serve the needs of the biologist or the psychologist. The phenomena of interest to biology and psychology exist in animal-environment systems; the environment cannot just be excised and described at the whim of the scientist. The properties of the environment that support living, both at the biological and psychological levels, are specific to animals. Further, if perception and action are what we seek to understand, the properties of the environment relevant to perceiving and acting ought to constitute our description of reality. Those properties of the environment are its affordances.

The foregoing analysis implies a novel organization of the subject matter of science and a new framework for describing the kinds of questions that scientists and philosophers of science ask. We shall contrast that framework with the more customary framework of animal-environment dualism, and distinguish between the kinds of scientific questions invited by the two approaches.

In the top part of Figure 5-2, we schematize the division of scientific labor that accompanies animal-environment dualism, while the bottom part illustrates the division of scientific labor that accompanies the ecological approach. What kinds of questions are encouraged by the dualism shown in the upper part of the figure? To the extent that a to-be-understood phenomenon spans animal and environment, as is most common with biological and psychological phenomena, the dualist asks questions that *span the sciences.* Such questions try to relate concepts in physics, for example, to concepts in psychology. Tokens of these questions are: How can different animals experience the world differently, given that there is only one world and physics describes it? How can physical things (e.g., photons) produce psychological effects (sensations)?

The kinds of questions that are asked by the scientist who organizes subject matter as illustrated in the bottom part of the figure are very different. Indeed, the questions that emerge as legitimate are very limited; for example, the questions presented in the preceding paragraph would be nonsensical. We schematize the kinds of questions that are reasonable in Figure 5-3.[6]

First, any question that remains within grain is deemed legitimate (e.g., how do the molecules of the environment interact with the molecules of the animal?). Similarly, questions that span sciences, but stay within the same system or subsystem, are legitimate (e.g., what is happening in the brain when one sees a pencil? Or, how do molecules interact so as to form a cell wall?). The arrows of Figure 5-3, then, are meant to designate the relationships into which one can justifiably inquire.

We emphasize that vertical questions (for example, how does mind relate to brain?) are very different from horizontal questions (such as, how does idea relate to object? or, how does structured light relate to retinae?). The kinds of relations that can obtain between subsystems (animal and environment) are distinct from the kinds of relations that can obtain between grains of analysis. For example, causal interactions (*A*

---

[6]For the purpose of contrasting the traditional separation between the animal system and the environment system with the ecological alternative, we treat the animal-environment system as *provisionally* separable into two subsystems. We make this provisional separation only for pedagogic purposes and are careful to use the term *subsystem* to remind the reader that the properties of the subsystem are to be rationalized by the larger system.

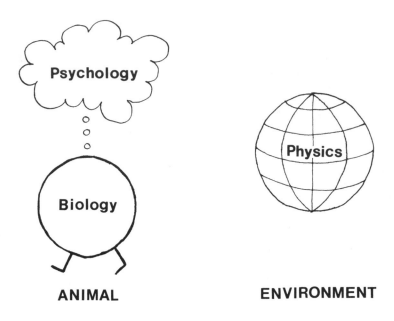

ANIMAL   ENVIRONMENT

**ANIMAL-ENVIRONMENT
SYSTEM**

Figure 5-2. The upper panel shows the division of scientific labor that accompanies animal-environment dualism; biology and psychology study the animal and physics studies the environment. The lower panel portrays the sciences as grains of analysis that can be applied to the animal-environment system.

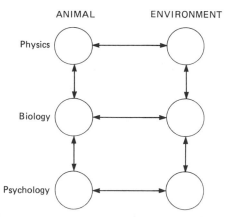

Figure 5-3. A schematic of how grains of analysis relate to one another and to the animal and environment subsystems. The arrows connect the cells whose comparison is meaningful. At the physical grain, animal and environment terms would both include atoms and their positions, mass, and velocity. At a biological grain, the environment consists of nutrients, predators, detectable light, and so on, while the animal consists of cells, organs, etc. The animal at a psychological grain includes effectivities, intentions, and emotions, while the environment at a psychological grain includes affordances, goal objects, and threats. In each of the cells would be the kinds of terms that one would find in an analysis of that sub-system at that grain.

causes B) can only be proposed within the same grain; a molecule can bump into another molecule, and a neuron can stimulate another neuron, but a molecule cannot bump into a cell or an idea. Thus, causal interactions may be sought only in horizontal questions.

In contrast, vertical questions might address two kinds of issues. First, how do phenomena at one level relate to phenomena at another level? For example, how do psychological phenomena relate to their biological counterparts? Or, in particular, what pattern(s) of neural activity are occurring in the nervous system when a walker steps over an obstacle in his or her path? Or, how do phenomena at one level of a science relate to phenomena at another level? As an example of this, one might ask how a property of a large system (such as the temperature of a container of gas) relates to properties of the parts that make up the system (number and velocity of molecules of gas).

Second, vertical questions can ask how *laws* at one grain relate to laws at another grain. Indeed, reductionism has received its greatest support from its ability to derive the gas laws (relating temperature, pressure, and volume) from more elementary laws—those of thermodynamics. To emphasize the general point, the laws that relate grains of analysis—whether they seek to establish relationships between phenomena or to establish relationships between the laws that describe those phenomena—are expected to be answered with a set of principles that are very different indeed from the laws that relate processes inside animals to processes outside animals. Nevertheless, the examination of both vertical and horizontal relationships may be addressed by scientists and philosophers of science.

Diagonal relationships, however, are another matter. In particular, it is argued that diagonal questions propose direct relationships where none exists. They may seek to identify the nature of interactions between entities that cannot interact. Or, they may seek causality in interactions that cannot be causal. In sum, they are conceptual muddles that are rendered seemingly sensible only by a steadfast assumption of the independence of animal and environment. Dissolving the independence of animal and environment dissolves the question. Thus, the absence of arrows crossing both subsystem and grain of analysis in Figure 5-3 is meant to assert that questions that seek to relate them are unreasonable.

We have argued for a commitment to realism on the part of psychologists. We have argued that the barriers to perceptual realism (e.g., non-veridicality) are barriers created by a faulty metaphysical assumption—namely, that environments and animals are logically independent entities that should be described by different sciences. The abandonment of animal-environment dualism sets the stage for a general conception of both what the special sciences are about and how they relate to one another. Our model of the relations among the sciences, in turn, permitted the identification of three kinds of questions: vertical, horizontal, and diagonal. Only vertical and horizontal were considered to be sensible questions, and, even then, they are wholly different species of questions, wherein it is illegitimate to seek causation in vertical relations. Equally illegitimate is the attempt to discern any direct relation for diagonally positioned subsystems.

These comments are crucial to the psychology of perception because psychologists usually seek vertical causation, and, worse, questions in perception are usually of the diagonal variety. We now present two of the most durable questions in psychology and show how they fit into this scheme.

The Mind-body Problem.   While mind-body questions are framed in a variety of ways, one set inquires into the interaction of mental and physical. They ask what are the nature of the effects of mind on body, body on mind, or both. As examples, how do physiological states cause hallucinations, or how do intentions cause muscle contractions? These questions suppose that phenomena at one grain of description can *cause* phenomena at another grain of description. It is asking how a molecule can bump into an idea.

Our rejection of this question is not unlike the reasoning used by Ryle (1949) who proposed that the mind-body problem was a *category mistake*–treating members of different kinds of categories as if they were members of the same category. We would consider the concepts used at different grains of analysis to be in different categories. We argue that only entities at the same grain of analysis can interact in the way that mind and body are presumed to interact. Mind and brain are entities from the psychological and biological grains, respectively.

The Problem of Perception. This second question is one that has been presaged by much of this chapter. It asks how knowledge of the world, as described by psychology, can be related to *the* world, as described by physics. To the extent that they arc different–and they surely are–perceptual theorists are required to propose either that the world of experience is created out of whole cloth by the percipient or, more commonly, that the perceiver *in the act of perception* transforms the physical into the psychological.

Studying the nature and process of that transformation has been and continues to be the preeminent enterprise of scientists of perception. That has been what the discipline is about. Even the titles of the textbooks reflect this question (e.g., Lloyd Kaufman's *Perception: The World Transformed*). One can consult any perception textbook to find particular tokens of this overarching assumption. Gregory (1978), for example, devotes an entire chapter to light, wherein he discusses æther theory, velocity of light (in vacuums and in media), wavelength, and quanta. If these are *the* characteristics of the optical support for vision–what it really is–it is small wonder that something must be called upon to transform it into knowledge of smiling faces, poached eggs, or quarterback sneaks. Forgus and Melamed (1976) make the study of the transformation the explicit purpose of their perception text:

> Our approach to this problem [psychophysical correspondence] will emphasize the increasing disparity between experience and the *distal stimulus* . . . as one proceeds to each successive stage . . . . increasing transformations often involve an active construction of stimuli information . . . . (Forgus and Melamed, 1976, p. 7)

Notice that the very phrasing of the problem dooms realism from the start. The dimensions of the world, including stimuli, are *assumed to be different from*—and impoverished with respect to—the dimensions of knowledge. To the extent that psychologists appear to solve the problem, which we take as unsolvable, they go "over and down" in the diagram of Figure 5-3. (For example, light causes neural firings which causes sensations or perceptions.) But the unwitting "over and down" approach ignores the expectation that different types of interactions or relations are to be found depending on the direction—vertical or horizontal—of the question.

What is left, then, to those of us who adopt the philosophical stance schematized in Figure 5-3? The course is straightforward, if not simple, and has been described throughout this book. The ecological psychologist must begin by describing the environment with reference to an animal. He or she must then ask how that environment is specified by the energy patterns to which the animal's perceptual systems are sensitive. Further, attention must be given to how that information tailors the behaviors of the animal to the facts of the environment and how behaviors make available information about those facts.

EVOLUTIONISM

We have proposed that reuniting animal and environment for theory (they have always been united in nature) yields both a new brand of realism and a different view of the subject matter of the special sciences. The realism is one in which the *real* nature of the environment *can* be described with reference to the effectivities (goal-directed behaviors) of the animal. The different view of the sciences asserts that if knowing is the activity to be investigated, the real world *must* be described with reference to the animal—at a psychological grain of analysis.

We shall now consider at a more fundamental level the relationship between the psychological description of the animal and the psychological description of the environment (see Figure 5-3). What is it that insures the symmetry of these subsystems—both in the long run (for species) and in the short run (for individual animals)? We shall show that the relationship should be viewed in a way very different from that which has dominated traditional philosophical thinking.

Epistemology is the branch of philosophy concerned with the theory of knowledge and is, therefore, the area most relevant to the interests at hand. While epistemologists address themselves to a variety of issues, two are central to the thesis of this section. They concern the nature and the reliability of knowledge. One must suppose that for actions to be appropriate, knowledge is at least pragmatically correct. Thus the epistemologist must lay a basis for behaving in correct knowledge about the world. To the question of how to insure the correspondence of knowledge and reality, traditional philosophy has called on two sources: reason and experience. Rationalism holds that knowledge that is true to the world is derived chiefly through reason rather than sense experience. Empiricism, in contrast, holds that knowledge rests ultimately and necessarily upon sense experience.

The ecological psychologist has two fundamental difficulties with the problem of knowledge as posed by the epistemologist. First, epistemology considers knowledge to be an entity inside an animal. Second, insofar as reliability or truth is an issue, the epistemologist conceives of knowledge as propositions about the world. The assumption that the basis for an animal's appropriate action are things (propositions) inside the head is in stark contrast to the ecological position. The ecological psychologist is concerned with how behaving itself, rather than an hypothesized mental entity underneath it, might be appropriate to the facts of the environment. Additionally, the knowing or behaving is not considered to be propositional or to be based on propositions—or "based on" anything else, for that matter. To deny a propositional status to perception and action will, ultimately, question the appropriateness of terms such as *erroneous, false, incorrect,* and their opposites as qualifiers of actions and perceptions. Denying the validity of these adjectives will provide a final buttress for the realism for which ecological psychologists campaign.

To begin, let us comment on our strategy, especially as it applies to the concept of knowledge. In spite of the gulfs between epistemology and ecological psychology revealed above, our discussion maintains parallels between the two fields as long as possible. We do this for two reasons. First, for those who consider the relationship between things in the head and facts in the world to be a legitimate avenue of inquiry, the ecological alternative will shed light on that hypothesized relation. Additionally, maintaining the parallels permits a clearer discernment of the relationship between ecological philosophy and its traditional counterpart. In this spirit, we will defer to epistemology and couch our discussion in its language—the language of *knowledge.* However, to recognize that we consider "knowledge"—as an entity underlying behaving—to be mythical, the ecological sense of the word "knowledge" will mean *perceptions and actions themselves.* To remind the reader that two meanings of "knowledge" are intended—one for the epistemological and one for the ecological—we will flag the word with quotation marks.

The ecological view is, with significant qualifications, consonant with empiricism and, thereby, opts for experience over reason, but the brand of empiricism to which it subscribes pays close attention to evolution and is called, therefore, *evolutionism* (Shaw & McIntyre, 1974; Shaw & Bransford, 1977; Turvey & Shaw, 1979). Evolutionism is based on the principle that only things that are compatible with one another can coexist.

This principle would translate into epistemology as follows: The pragmatic "knowledge" of the environment that is an animal's actions upon that environment must be symmetrical with the affordances of the environment. In the absence of a compatibility of effectivities and the affordances of the environment, successful reactions to and actions upon the environment and, thus, animal life, would not be possible. As was argued earlier, an animal's actions continue to exist because of their compatibility with the affordances of the niche. Actions, whether based primarily in ontogeny or in philogeny could no more be incompatible with the environment and continue to exist than an anatomical characteristic could be incompatible and coexist. In sum, it could be said that because actions—the expressions of pragmatic "knowledge"—exist, they must be compatible with the affordances of the environment.

Thus, the animal's "knowledge" of the affordances of its niche as specified by the information to the senses must be pragmatically true, where "pragmatically true" means compatible with the environment. The importance of experience (i.e., encounters with the environment) in this scheme is apparent and, as such, it makes evolutionism a species of empiricism. In part, what sets evolutionism apart from empiricism is on *whose* experience knowing is based. Traditional empiricism, it seems, relies solely on the individual animal's experiences; evolutionism, in contrast, would include the experiences of one's progenitors as the ultimate and necessary basis of the ability to know one's niche. Thus, pragmatic "knowledge" is rooted not only in the encounters that an individual animal has with the environment, but also in the encounters (both successful and unsuccessful) by which its progenitors (rather than their relatives) were selected in the evolution of the species. In both phylogeny and ontogeny, to the extent that actions are compatible with what the surrounding substances and surfaces afford, the act (animal) and the niche can continue to coexist. To the extent that the act and the niche are not compatible, they cannot coexist.

With respect to the claim, then, that "knowledge" and niche must be compatible, what can be said to those who insist that perceptions are sometimes true and sometimes false? To speak to this, one must ask how the concept of compatibility relates to the concepts of true and false. First, an advocate of the ecological position would not equate *compatible* and *true*. The ecological claim is *not* that perceptions and actions are correct; they just exist and *to exist is to evidence compatibility*! Moreover, it is argued that perception and action cannot be labeled *correct* or *true*, because in order to be so they would have to belong to a class to which ecological realists think they do not belong: propositions (Shaw, Turvey, & Mace, in press). Propositions are the things that can be true or false, so if one assumes that perceptions and actions can be true or false (correct or incorrect), one necessarily assumes that perceptions and actions are propositions. The ecological stance, in concert with the views of philosophical naturalists (Dewey, Bentley, and Kantor), is that perceptions and actions are not propositions, nor based on propositions, and, therefore, cannot be either correct or incorrect.

In defense of the claim that perceptions and actions are not propositions, we shall raise the suggestion that the same kind of logic that is applied to an animal's anatomical attributes should be applied to its knowings. That is, states of affairs at the psychological grain—"knowledge"—should be treated the same way that states of affairs at the biological grain are treated. The parallels between pragmatic "knowledge" (a psychological state of affairs) and anatomical structure (a biological state of affairs) will figure significantly in our attempt to develop the claim that perception-action does not consist of propositions, true *or* false. We do this by contrasting "the compatibilities of states of affairs" against "truths of propositions" for things in general, for anatomical attributes, and, finally, for pragmatic "knowledge" (perception-action).

As this book is being written, the writer's desk is quite cluttered. That is the state of affairs of the desk. No argument, however clever, can prove that this state of affairs is true or false; it just is. The number and arrangement of items on a desk do not fall into the category of things that can be said to be true or false.

One can ask if the current arrangement is compatible with writing, for example, but that is different from asking whether the arrangement is in error or not in error. The state of affairs of a desk is in no way a proposition about writing; it just is what it is. And if and when that arrangement is put to the test of compatibility—when I try to write—the arrangement will stand or fall on its compatibility with the writing, not on its truth with respect to writing. If clutter and writing are compatible, they can coexist; if they are not compatible, they can not coexist. States of affairs, it is argued, need not be thought of as propositions about other things.

A biological analogy brings us even closer to appreciating the non-propositional status of perceptions and actions. Consider the interlocking canine teeth of carnivores. They are a state of affairs not unlike the desk clutter referred to earlier or the perception and action to be referred to later. The teeth taken as a state of affairs cannot be true or false.[7] What they can be is compatible or incompatible with a certain type of food.[8]

---

[7] This is not to deny the existence of false teeth.

[8] The compatibility described in this example and the last is the limiting case of two things. Normally, for one thing to exist it must coexist with—and thus be compatible with—a host of other things. In the present example, the arrangement of the teeth must also be compatible with the constraints of tooth composition and growth, jaw shape, etc.

One might ask whether such teeth are compatible with eating meat and whether they are compatible with eating grasses. To the extent that they are compatible with the former but not the latter, one would expect that the teeth, or even the whole animal, cannot coexist with an environment not offering animal prey.

The story of the interlocking canines might, however, be phrased as propositions about the world. This would be treating the anatomical characteristics of an animal in much the same way that we usually treat its perceivings-actings-knowings. The proposition is stated in words as, "For the substances that I will eat, this arrangement of teeth is the optimal configuration." This proposition can indeed be true or false. If the animal is called upon to eat meat, the proposition is true; if it is called upon to grind grasses, the proposition is false. Let's assume that the latter turns out to be the case. Does that mean that the *teeth* were, in fact, in error, incorrect, or false? If the answer is yes, then one must also suppose that dinosaurs—even while they were alive—were false, that their anatomical characteristics were false propositions about the future of this planet's climate.

But obviously just because the characteristics of teeth or dinosaurs can be put into the form of propositions doesn't make the things themselves propositions. Making them so invites into the science a host of conceptual difficulties not the least of which is who is making the propositions. The disappearance of anatomical attributes, whole animals, and species as a function of natural selection does not permit one to decide *a posteriori* that they were false. In like manner, it is argued that the disappearance of an action or even of the animal through a fatality, for example, does not render that action or the pragmatic "knowledge" it expresses false. They are merely states of affairs that in time came to be incompatible with the environment.

Of course, the goal here is to put an animal's knowings on the same metaphysical footing as interlocking canines and clutter on a desk. They are all states of affairs that may prove to be incompatible with other states of affairs. While the psychological states of an animal, like its anatomical features, must be compatible with another state of affairs—the facts of the environment taken with reference to the animal—they should not be thought of as propositions about the environment.

Consider the bird that flies into a window. If we try to state in words what the bird knew just before impact, we might say "I can fly there." But again, it is the writer that makes the proposition out of the state of affairs, as was done with the teeth; the state of affairs is not a proposition. And because the principle of compatibility inexorably grinds out coexistence, the state of affairs that is the bird's "knowledge" will coexist briefly with a broken neck, then not at all. Compatible psychological states of affairs in animal and environment can coexist; incompatible ones cannot.

The relationship between compatibility and coexistence may well be an ontological argument of great significance, but we limit its expression here to two claims. First, *evolution* is the term applied to the particular manifestation of compatibility and coexistence that results in animal-environment systems and, thereby, ensures the compatibility of pragmatic "knowledge" and reality at the species level. Second, *learning* is the term applied to the particular manifestation of compatibility and coexistence that results in specific animal-environment systems and, thereby, ensures the compatibility of pragmatic "knowledge" and reality at the level of the individual animal.[9]

Let us now recapitulate the major themes of this section. One problem for epistemology is identifying that which insures that "knowledge" and reality correspond. That correspondence is usually equated with the truth of the "knowledge," and its basis has been sought traditionally in reason and/or sense experience. The ecological position described here, while considering encounters with the environment to be the necessary basis for "knowledge," has appealed to a more general principle—that the coexistence of things evidences their mutual compatibility. This position denies a propositional status to psychological attitudes and considers them as states of affairs that will either cease to exist or continue to exist according to the rule of natural selection; those psychological attitudes manifested in actions must be compatible with the affordances of the environment. The game of evolution has animal-niche compatibility (or at the psychological grain, "knowledge"-fact compatibility) as its only rule.

SUMMARY

In this chapter we have clarified the assumptions that constitute the ecological philosophy. In examining this philosophy, one is struck by the difficulty of finding the right combination of traditional categories in ontology and epistemology in which to fit the approach. By and large, our strategy has been to identify, albeit simplistically, the traditional categories and to impose on those categories whatever changes seem required by the central concepts of the theory. The notion of affordance is the most central of these. Together with the animal-environment system in which it resides, it provided the departure point for the philosophical implications described here.

[9]This approach leaves the problem of mechanism to the theorist.

The first philosophical position with which the ecological approach was identified was realism. Several objections to realism were aired, but each seemed rooted in animal-environment dualism. It was argued that the known does not correspond to a physicist's animal-neutral measurements of the world. Further, that one can single out "a perception," treat it as if it were a proposition, and deem the proposition to be in error jeopardizes only a realism based in animal-environment dualism. A realism written over animal-environment systems considers the environment as a setting for behaviors; thus, its properties are ascertained with reference to the animal doing the behaving. These properties of the environment are its affordances. And while they depend on the animal, they do not depend on its perception.

To claim that reality can be described with reference to an animal's behavior is to deny that physicists have the final authority on describing "the" environment. Psychologists, biologists, and physicists are all invited to describe animal-environment systems—at different grains. This division of scientific labor provided a convenient framework for the description of the kinds of questions that scientists ask. Horizontal questions inquire into the relationships within grain of analysis. Vertical questions seek intergrain relationships: How do phenomena or laws at one grain relate to phenomena and laws at another grain? While both horizontal and vertical questions seem to make scientific sense, the third category—the diagonal—seems to mix apples and oranges. We emphasized this last point because most theories of perception have explicitly asked diagonal questions.

On the assumption that affordances and actions are the entities that must fit with one another for life to persist, we asked what it is that permits or insures the fit. The fit is insured by the law of compatibility, which says that only compatible things can coexist. Actions incompatible with the affordances of the environment could not exist with that environment. Further, the animal side of knowing is not a matter of making propositions about the environment. Knowings are just states of affairs at a psychological grain, and, like states of affairs at a biological grain, they *must* stand in some sort of adaptive relation to the environment.

This formulation of the animal-environment fit plays the role in ecological philosophy that epistemology plays in traditional philosophy. But in epistemology, it is the truth of knowledge (propositions about the world) whose basis is sought. This phrasing makes sense only in the context of two logically independent systems—animal and environment: How can things in the animal correspond to things in the environment? The ecological psychologist would argue that they *must* be compatible for life to persist. But, more important, the ecological psychologist would claim that it is the assumed logical independence of animal and environment that lends apparent legitimacy to the question of how knowledge relates to facts. The untying of animal and environment *creates* the problems that epistemology tries to solve. The ecological position is that animal and environment are the warp and woof of evolution and that they should not be untied in the first place.

6

Applications

The ecological approach as set down by Gibson and as elaborated by other proponents is properly considered a metatheory or set of orienting assumptions. This "paradigm"[1] is taken to be distinctly different from the traditional psychological "paradigm" and, because of that, the ecological approach sets the stage of psychology with a new cast of characters. New theoretical questions replace old questions; to questions that have survived the paradigm shift, answers are often sought in new places; and areas of inquiry that have made only cameo appearances in traditional psychology are brought to center stage.

In this chapter, we will illustrate each of these changes by describing in some detail the application of the ecological approach to three areas. First, we shall consider the new questions that the ecological approach frames about binocular stereopsis. Second, we examine how the ecological approach has yielded new answers to the question of how one perceives a face. Third, issues in the theory of action, which have been long neglected by mainstream psychology, are considered. While any of a number of experimental programs might have served as illustrations, we present those that we are working on and, therefore, know best.

[1]We acknowledge that there would be debate over whether the ecological approach represents a paradigm shift of the kind described by Kuhn (1962). Nevertheless, we have tentatively treated it as one.

BINOCULAR STEREOPSIS

When an ecological psychologist addresses some puzzle in perception, the questions that he or she asks—the questions to which individual theories are to provide experimentally verifiable solutions—are often different from the questions that previous theories tried to answer. Such has been the case with an examination of binocular stereopsis, or seeing three-dimensional structure with two frontally located eyes. This section summarizes a renovation of questions about binocular vision formulated by one of us (CM). This renovation is presented against the backdrop of the questions that traditional accounts of binocular vision have sought to answer.

Animals with eyes positioned on the sides of their heads (rabbits, most birds, some fish, etc.) enjoy a panoramic view; they can see all encroaching predators and, thus, have a maximum possibility of escape. Some species (humans, apes, birds of prey, cats, etc.) have given up this advantage in favor of the advantage that accrues to animals with frontally located eyes. This latter advantage is acute perception of the shapes and positions of objects that, unlike motion perspective, does not require head or body movements. It is this frontal binocularity with which we are concerned.

Binocular vision has been an object of discussion for three millenia. In that time, philosophers, mathematicians, and psychologists have sought explanations for two puzzles in binocular vision. The first is how binocular vision might be stereoscopic or three-dimensional when both of the images are two-dimensional. The second puzzle, the one of primary concern in this section, is how can two separate stimuli, one delivered to each eye, yield a single phenomenal impression? We experience one object in spite of the fact that there are two anatomical images. The most popular solutions to this singleness puzzle have been variants of concepts like fusion and replacement: Either the two images must somehow be united or one must take precedence. The particulars of such a union are debated often while *the need for a union is merely assumed.* But it is this original assumption— that two separate entities must become one and that the product has a property, three-dimensionality, not contained in the input—that a theory of direct perception must question.

Rather than evaluate current accounts of the "fusional" processes, we ask whether single vision is the real issue around which a theory of binocular vision should be built. This skepticism is prompted by the ecological orientation, which denies the need for inference or for the brain to "fix up" the information into perceptions. We will develop two arguments to buttress the position that singleness is a pseudo-issue. The issue of three-dimensionality will be held in abeyance, but in coming to terms with the singleness issue, new light will be cast on the stereoscopy problem as well.

116

In short, we shall show that the questions typically asked about binocular stereoscopy are not sound and offer an ecological alternative to them.

Our critique of traditional theory makes two points. First, singleness does not appear as a problem in theoretical treatments of our other perceptual systems. This is troublesome because every perceptual system has more than one receptor site (i.e., we not only have two eyes, but two ears, two hands [ten fingers], two nostrils and numerous taste buds), but notions of fusion are limited primarily to vision. A second argument is that traditional treatments of binocular perception differ unnecessarily from the treatment of motion perception.

Normal perception is characterized by singleness. When one object exists in the world we typically experience it as one object whether it is by sight, touch, or smell. But in none of these perceptual realms besides vision does it seem necessary to give an account of this phenomenal unity. Indeed, if we force the fusion issue on something like haptic perception, logical absurdities quickly arise. We shall describe a theory of bimanual fusion to demonstrate that this is so.

Imagine grasping a cup with two hands. One cup is experienced despite the presence of two tactile "images," one on each hand. Because of this parallel between the bimanual and binocular cases, we would hope that a theory of perception would treat them the same way. If the haptic theory follows the visual theory, then we must suppose that the images on the skin of the two hands must be conjoined to inform the perceiver that there is only one cup-shaped object. The algorithms for achieving this union must include a detailed account of the actions of dozens of joints and a hundred muscles. And, this account would require additional rules to explain why one knows that there is still one cup when a third tactile image is introduced, as when the cup is also held to the lips. Moreover, if the cup were merely grasped by the fingers, need one wonder about the fusion of images from each separate surface? Or, perhaps, should we inquire into the fusion of inputs from each receptor that is stimulated?

Obviously, the complexity of a fusion theory that would explain "single touch" can easily get out of hand, as it were. We are happy to say that most psychologists would not embrace such a theory. Rather, despite theorists' reluctance to admit the possibility for vision or audition, it is generally agreed that haptic perception is direct. In haptics at least, it is generally accepted that one feels the contents of the environment, not their bodily accompaniments.

Our bizarre tale of bimanual fusion is based on and molded by a "definition of information in terms of the geometry of an *arbitrarily* selected anatomical structure or set of anatomical structures (two hands, one hand, ten fingers, etc.)" (Michaels, 1978). That is, the receptor surface, not the object, has been allowed to dictate what information is. But we question the relevance of such body-surface geometry. For example, consider two methods of determining shape: enveloping an object in the hand and exploring it with a single extended finger. While the image on the hand is of a certain quality, a single finger cannot even be said to have an *image* of the object at any one time. On this account, we would argue that the information for haptic perception cannot be based on the geometry of the receptor surface, for the choice of receptor surface is an arbitrary one.

In response to this, one must assume that information about shape is best defined not in terms of the geometry of the receptor surface but over a complex space-time coordinate system. Simply, the geometry of information is not the same as, nor based on the geometry of the receptor surface. A similar argument will be made later for the geometry of binocular vision—the selection of the surface geometry of one (or two) retina(e) is just as arbitrary.

From the preceding analysis, we draw the following conclusions. First, a notion of fusion is not a necessary adjunct of anatomically distinct inputs. In the example of haptic perception, fusion was shown to be the foundation of an absurd story. Second, we are warned not to mistake the geometry of a receptor surface for the geometry of information. The former imposes unnecessary constraints on the latter.

We now turn to a second argument, using the example of monocular kinetic vision, to reiterate the above conclusions and to provide an intuitive basis for the concept of a *binocular array*. We shall attempt to develop the idea that information in this array, like the monocular kinetic array, comprises transformations.

Consider an observer who, using one eye, fixates some stationary object while a rabbit scampers into and out of view. As noted in Chapter 1, this event could be described as the stimulation of a succession of retinal locations by light reflected by the rabbit; each location is provided with an image of the rabbit at a different time (Figure 6-1). If one claims, as many have (e.g., Neisser, 1967), that each image is a stimulus, a problem of single perception emerges: How might the successive images be integrated so that a single, moving rabbit is produced? In a theory that defines the stimulus in terms of discrete temporal cross-sections, singleness is an achievement of the nervous system.

The "issue" of singleness in motion perception disappears with a redefinition of stimulus. Instead of a series of images from which a single rabbit must be deduced or created, let us say, as did Gibson (1950), that *transformations* of the optic array over time specify that there is one rabbit that is moving. It is the manner of change (i.e., a transformational invariant) that constitutes this monocular kinetic information. Rather than

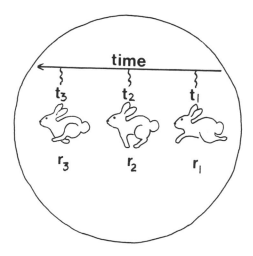

RETINA

Figure 6-1. A schematic "three part" stimulus for the perception of a running rabbit.

a succession of anatomically distinct inputs, Gibson proposed that information is in transformations defined over time. By redefining the information for motion perception, Gibson eliminated the need for a concept such as fusion.

We propose to rethink the information for binocular perception along the same lines used by Gibson for motion perception. Just as Gibson took issue with the idea of discrete retinal snapshots, we will take issue with the supposition that the information has two parts, one to each eye, and that these two parts require fusion. And, just as he found it more useful to consider the information for monocular motion perception to be transformations over a third dimension (time), we might reconsider binocular information in terms of transformations over a third dimension of space. Such a reformulation argues that the information for binocular vision should not be thought of as two anatomically distinct images but as a *single* entity (transformation) defined over two surfaces. Transformations over time describe the successive order of an optic array and so constitute monocular kinetic information. Similarly, transformations over space describe the adjacent order of two arrays and constitute binocular static information—what will be called the *binocular array*.

Neither monocular kinetic nor binocular static information can be done justice by a two-dimensional snapshot characterization of the visual field. A three-dimensional description (two spatial and one temporal dimension for monocular kinetic, three spatial dimensions for binocular static) is needed to capture the richness of both kinds of information. This means, of course, that the geometry of a retina as a two-dimensional Euclidean surface is insufficient.

In sum, single vision is a theoretical problem only if one assumes two stimuli (images). Such an assumption necessarily defines a stimulus in terms of the organ that is stimulated. But the haptic and monocular kinetic metaphors suggest that single perception is not a problem simply because more than one anatomical structure is stimulated; the geometry of information must be kept independent from the geometry of a receptor surface. The *binocular array* has been defined in terms of transformations over two optic arrays and is offered as a new characterization of binocular information. Let us now examine what this binocular array might be like.

We have already argued that the information for binocular stereopsis cannot be described in the Euclidean geometry of retinal images. Rather, we need a geometry that can capture the structures and transformations of information that is defined over two surfaces. Put another way, we seek the transformational and structural invariants that constitute the information space of binocular vision.

Let us characterize the transformation entailed by binocular viewing as a rotation. That is, the view of one eye could be made identical to the other if the visual scene were appropriately rotated. The axis of this rotation is a line perpendicular to the plane defined by the two lines of sight, going through the intersection of those two lines. The amount of rotation is the convergence angle (see Figure 6-2). In other words, the binocular transformation is equivalent in the monocular case to rotating the world around the axis specified.

First, we shall examine the structural properties that are invariant with respect to binocular rotations. These are less interesting than the transformational invariants and, therefore, even though they play an important role, we shall describe them only briefly. To determine structural invariants, we must turn to projective geometry. Each eye receives a different projection of the same surfaces in the visual world. These projections are, of course, projective transformations of the world. To discover the information that is invariant to the two eyes, we need only ask what properties the projective transformation leaves invariant. Recall from Chapter 2 that the invariant property in projection is the cross-ratio of four collinear points. (Assume for the sake of argument that "points" are texture elements.) The role of the structural invariant is to specify the identity of the two projections, one to each eye. Because the cross-ratio is the same for each of the two perspectives, it cannot convey information beyond that available monocularly. But, because it identifies the surface,

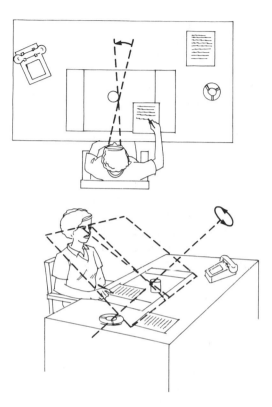

Figure 6-2. Top and side views of the binocular rotation.

it makes possible the detection of the transformation. Without some property shared between the two perspectives the transformation relating them would be indeterminate. Notice that though this structural invariant is necessary to binocular information, it is not part of it: It cannot be *binocular* information because it is the same for the two eyes. For truly binocular information, we must look to transformational invariants.

The styles of change from one perspective to the other can be shown to be exceptionally informative about the environmental objects under scrutiny. While the mathematics are too complex for inclusion in this summary, we can outline the properties that this information specifies.

First, it can be shown that the transformational invariants specify the amount of rotation, which is invariantly tied to the distance of the object. Thus, the transformational invariant specifies how far away the viewed object is. Second, it can be shown that transformational invariants distinguish among *all* monocularly equivalent shapes. So, at the very least, the binocular transformation renders unambiguous any shape that is monocularly ambiguous. Finally, the specificity of the information also applies to shapes and sizes of objects.

With respect to the "problems" of singleness and three-dimensionality, the former can be easily explained. The binocular organ does not deal with two things, only one: a transformational invariant. Similarly, three-dimensionality is no longer a problem, because the information specifies the three-dimensional character of the world.

We have concerned ourselves here with the essentials of a theory of direct binocular perception. At the core of the reformulation is the assertion that binocular information does not consist, as traditional theory would have it, of two things which must be compared and conjoined, but of single entities—transformations—which must be detected. That such detection requires two properly configured eyeballs does not require that the information be in two separate parts that must be combined. Rather, there is a spatial transformation (binocular rotation) specifying the properties, including singularity, of an object. Singleness and three-dimensionality are environmental properties that are specified in the light and detected by a properly attuned visual system.

PERCEIVING THE AGE OF A FACE

For centuries the human face has fascinated everyone from artists to advertisers, poets to perceptionists. And, like everyone else, proponents of ecological psychology are not immune to this allure. In recent years, various issues in face perception have been addressed from the ecological viewpoint.

Of these, the issue that has commanded the most attention concerns the properties of faces and heads that are relevant to perceivers' estimations of another's age. This research program, carried out by Shaw and his associates asks, quite simply, what kind of information allows one to perceive growth and aging? The program has investigated the biology of growth, seeking correlates in the information that people detect when they perceive age. It investigates the nature of that information and compares it with the perception of the growth of other living things. Before proceeding to some of the details of this approach, it is of interest to compare the more traditional approach to face perception with the ecological perspective.

The Face as a Set of Features

For the most part, experimental investigations of object perception are concerned with how an object might be recognized—what processes underlie the determination that an object is a chair, for example, and not something else. Regarding the case of faces, this question includes not only how an individual might be recognized but also, perhaps, how a particular facial expression might be identified. A fairly common explanation of recognition supposes that there is a mechanism that analyzes features of the visual input. Feature detectors in the visual system are thought to respond in some selective fashion to the appropriate features of the retinal image (cf. Neisser, 1976). This feature "information" is integrated with some kind of preexisting knowledge structures (e.g., feature lists, structural descriptions, schemata, frames) which guide the construction of perceptual experience.

For example, the pattern of excitation of detectors indicating lines of various lengths and orientations can presumably be fitted to (cognitive) structures which determine that a particular object is present. The features into which the object is decomposed by the visual system must be recombined in higher stages of the brain in order to allow recognition of the object. Recognition (object identity) occurs if features of the object in the world have the same "shape" as and are numerically equivalent to those represented in the memory of the object. If an object is similar to but not identical with a representation, that, too, is thought to be determined by how many features have the same shape or, alternatively, how closely individual features approximate each other.[2]

For the particular case of faces, the target-face is presumed to be compared to a prototype, although the generality of this prototype is not clear. (Is there, for example, one representation for the "universal" face or separate racial and species prototypes?) After this initial comparison, individualizing features are noted (Hochberg, 1978) so that the face may be recognized as someone in particular, as looking like someone (family resemblance), or as presenting a particular expression (smile, frown) or emotion (happiness, sadness).

Problems with a General Feature-Comparison Model

Despite the ease with which the face seems to lend itself to feature breakdown (eyes, nose, mouth, and ears are able to stand more or less on their own, isolable from each other and the face as a whole), generalizing theories of object perception to face recognition is not altogether straightforward. Face stimuli yield data different from those of other objects in

---

[2] Actually, it is not proper to talk about the "shape" of features, but, more accurately, the way features are represented. While shape is often described as the two-dimensional projection of a three-dimensional form (Hochberg, 1978), it must somehow be coded from the retinal projection for storage and retrieval. Our discussion of feature-comparison models presupposes, for purposes of simplicity, that such processes can be carried out successfully.

recognition paradigms. For example, standard pattern-storage and pattern-recognition accounts do not hold for inverted faces, even though inversion leaves the pattern—and features—unchanged (Hochberg & Galper, 1967). A number of such manipulations show that faces are treated differently from other objects (e.g., photographs presented in the negative [Galper, 1970; Galper & Hochberg, 1971]).

Attempts to account for the differences between faces and most other objects have turned up nothing more substantive than the conjecture that face recognition involves not only perception of distinguishing features but also a special factor such as "general personal impression" (Yin, 1969). It is the personal impression that cannot be used when faces are altered in particular ways. The precise nature of this special factor, however, has not been addressed directly. While most theories of face perception assert that faces are special in some way, the nature of this specialness is not pursued seriously. Investigators concentrate on questions of how specific tokens are recognized and ignore the fundamental question of what a face is.

Questions of the former type provide no insight, for example, into how the quality of faceness is perceived across wide varieties of facial features. Among humans, facial features show great diversity as a function of sex, race, and stage of development. When the class of animal faces is admitted—from the more or less humanoid mammals to the somewhat less than person-like visages of birds, fish and insects—the variability in what constitutes a face is astounding. If we also consider those inanimate objects which can be said to look as if they have a face (e.g., the front view of an automobile), the notion of Euclidean equivalence of features seems wholly inappropriate. Before asserting that faces are special, therefore, it is necessary to consider what that could mean for all the entities that constitute the class *face*.

There is also evidence that seems to suggest that at least some information for faces is so abstract as not to depend on common features at all. For example, subjects can properly rank-order according to age a set of facial photographs, none of which appear twice and none familiar to the subjects. This suggests that when subjects make such judgments, the difference relations they pick up on cannot depend on different topographical states of the same face (Pittenger & Shaw, 1975b). The specific facial features are of little consequence here. Rather, "perceptual information for age level is both abstract and global, inhering in the effects that the [growth] transformation has on any object to which it can be applied" (Shaw & Pittenger, 1977, p. 129, all italicized in original). It is suspected that information for properties other than aging will be just as global and just as abstract.

Faces as Nonrigid Objects: An Event Approach

Evidence of the kind cited above suggests that some problems may arise with trying to fit faces into feature models because such models were developed to deal with rigid objects; they must be generalized and accommodated in order to deal with nonrigid objects such as faces. It may be the case, however, that treating rigid objects as the standard is misguided. Flexible, malleable, and growing objects, after all, are legion. Within individual faces, for example, the malleability of features is considerable. Changes in both the short-term (expressions, chewing, speaking) and the long-term (aging) alter individual features in significant ways so as to make strict feature comparisons extremely difficult. Feature-comparison models of the recognition of rigid objects are difficult enough; nonrigid objects make matters even worse. Just to recognize a static, nontransforming object, the mechanism must somehow discern which descriptors characterize the input *and* are commensurate with those descriptors in memory. Then the proper memory representation must be found that matches the structural description so derived. Solving these problems becomes exponentially more difficult as the number of possible comparisons increases (Gel'fand & Tsetlin, 1962). Obviously, choosing and matching descriptors becomes very arduous indeed if the object is also undergoing elastic transformations while the recognition process is occurring.

In order to avoid the kinds of problems feature models create, the approach to face perception that has developed within the realist framework exploits more fully the nonrigid nature of faces. In part, this approach holds that the transformations an object supports are integral to its nature. The kinds of things an object can do are reflected in its structure— round objects roll, living things grow—and should be included in the object's description. That is why the ecological research program deals with the perception of faces undergoing various transformations that simulate growth and aging (e.g., Pittenger & Shaw, 1975a, 1975b; Shaw & Pittenger, 1977; Todd, Mark, Shaw, & Pittenger, 1980). These particular transformations would be inappropriate to consider for most objects, but they are intrinsic to the study of faces. The differences between a featural approach and the transformational or event approach used in Shaw's research program are fundamental. In a feature model, explanations of perception need not take into account the nature of the particular object being perceived; all objects are thought to be reducible to the same kind of static descriptors that are analyzed and then constructed into the final object.

In contrast, the approach taken by Shaw and his colleagues considers faces in light of the transformations they support. The structure of the face is such that its identity (not only who the person is but also that it is, indeed, a face) is preserved under only certain kinds of changes—it is compatible with a limited class of transformations. Faces support transformations of aging, weight gain, tanning, and yawning, but they do not support transformations of folding or melting. While some of the transformations they do support may be shared with other objects (perspective changes, growth), others are uniquely facial (talking, smiling). All transformations considered in this research are examined with regard to how they affect the perception of faces as distinct from other objects.

The transformational approach requires, of course, that the face be treated as a dynamic event over time rather than as static fodder for a feature-comparison model. The face is not often seen in complete repose; rather, faces continually talk, eat, yawn, emote, and twitch. The face-event is composed of these kinds of changes wrought over its structure. Thus, it is claimed that a perceptually valid characterization of faces must allow for those transformations that are peculiar to faces, and static featural models do not easily accommodate them. To follow this analysis, we shall now examine how this theoretical backdrop translates into actual research.

The Perception of Human Growth

To reiterate, the research program has thus far devoted the most attention to transformational information relevant to perception of the aging event. Fundamental to this investigation is the need for a rigorous description of the changes that take place during growth and aging. Shaw and his colleagues have investigated the possibility that a single geometric transformation might successfully capture these systematic changes. That is, if an object were considered as a set of points (for present purposes, in two dimensions), each of whose coordinates (X and Y) are altered by growth, then could a transformation be found that maps them onto the two new variables (X' and Y') describing the grown or aged object?

While many transformations have been studied in an effort to simulate growth, research has found the *cardioidal strain* to be the most promising option. Cardioid is the geometrical name for a heart-shaped figure with a rounded tip (see Figure 6-3a). Interestingly, this shape not only describes the shape of the cranium in profile, but cardioidal strain also accurately describes the growth pattern followed by the human head in profile: essentially symmetrical growth around a nodal point. Strain is basically a nonlinear stretch in more than one direction at a time. Figure 6-4 shows a grid before and after such a strain. For example, a circle could be transformed into a cardioid by drawing it on the grid and stretching the grid.

a

b

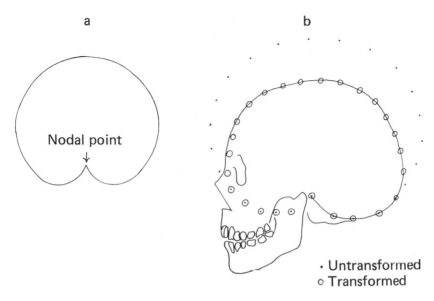

Nodal point
↓

· Untransformed
o Transformed

Figure 6-3. *A:* a cardioid. *B:* a cardioid fitted to a skull. (After Shaw, McIntyre, & Mace, 1974; with permission)

The strain transformation was suggested originally by the naturalist D'Arcy Thompson (1917) as one of a number of candidates to model changes in shape due to growth. During growth biological and physical forces on the different types of tissue interact to produce strain on the bony tissue. The direction of growth along which skull shape is strained

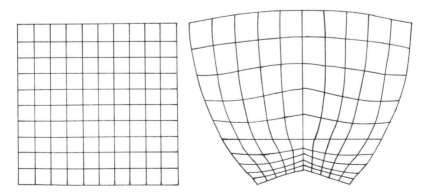

Figure 6-4. A grid before and after a cardioidal strain. (After Shaw & Pittenger, 1977; with permission)

follows lines of least resistance against such factors as muscle, cartilage, fluid pressure, gravitational attraction, atmospheric pressure, and growth of the brain. Such natural forces are illustrated in an idealized model from Todd, Mark, Shaw, & Pittenger (1980). If the craniofacial complex is considered as a spherical tank filled with fluid, "the pressure at any point on the surface of the tank is directly determined by the amount of fluid above it." The gradient of pressure so obtained would remodel the head in accordance with a transformation not unlike the cardioidal strain transformation suggested by Shaw and Pittenger (1975a).[3]

Thus, the cardioidal strain transformation seems to be a reasonable candidate for the growth transformation—it follows the proper direction determined by the interaction of physical and biological forces and results in a shape that is appropriate for a great proportion of the skull. Perhaps most persuasive in the choice of cardioidal strain as a model for growth is that it has been demonstrated to fit actual growth data. Given two outline tracings of an individual's skull, based on x-ray pictures of the same person at two different ages, the first can be transformed by the cardioidal strain so that the result is almost identical to the older skull outline (see Figure 6-5). In other words, the direction of changes due to growth is accurately predicted by cardioidal strain (Todd et al., 1980).

It is clear that cardioidal strain is a valid physical correlate of growth. But what of its perceptual relevance? Are perceivers at all sensitive to cardioidal strain in their appraisals of age? The answer appears to be a resounding yes. A number of experiments have been done which demonstrate such information is useful in subjects' age estimations. Subjects presented with a randomly ordered series of transformations of a standard profile consistently estimated relative age as if cardioidal strain produced monotonic perceived-age changes. That is, the greater the coefficient of change applied to the standard profile, the older the transformed profile was seen to be (Pittenger & Shaw, 1975a). Moreover, such results are obtained without benefit of internal features. (To verify this result, the reader is invited to order the randomly arranged profiles drawn in Figure 6-6.)

The earlier contention that growth is an abstract form of change not dependent on any particular set of object properties was supported by a series of experiments illustrated in Figure 6-7 (Pittenger, Shaw, & Mark, 1979). The same kind of relative age judgment can be performed consistently on nonhuman stimuli such as facial profiles of monkeys, birds, and dogs and even on front and side views of Volkswagen "beetles." The information for growth is in the effects the transformation has on the object and not the object's particular features.

Because information for individual identity is preserved in real

[3]This "revised cardioidal strain," unlike the earlier version, also accounts for size changes that accompany growth.

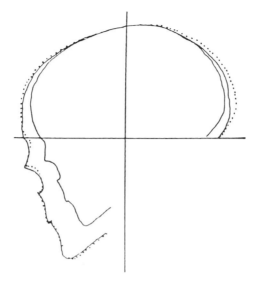

Figure 6-5. The cardioidal strain transformation fit to actual growth data. The solid lines were traced from x-ray pictures of a male at ages 5 and 17. The dashed line is the transformed version of the younger profile.

growth (i.e., people retain a characteristic "look" despite the substantial changes their faces undergo over the years) it is crucial that the cardioidal strain transformation also preserve this information. In a preliminary effort to determine whether it does, subjects were asked to judge which of two skull profiles was the same person as a target profile. One of the alternatives was some level of strain on the target while the second was the same level of strain but of a different skull (see Figure 6-8). The fairly low error rate suggests that sufficient information is left invariant to specify individual identity. This identity, too, can be established without benefit of facial features as these stimuli were just skull outlines.

Figure 6-6. Five profiles representing different degrees of strain. The order is, youngest to oldest: 4, 2, 3, 5, 1. (After Pittenger & Shaw, 1975a; with permission)

129

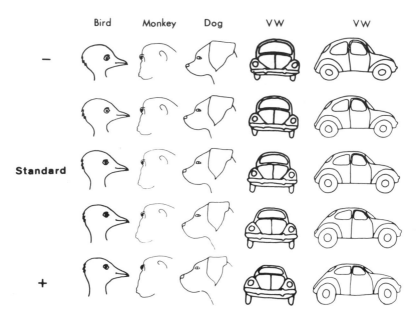

Figure 6-7. Examples of the cartoons produced by applying cardioidal strain to standard profiles. (After Pittenger, Shaw, & Mark, 1979; with permission)

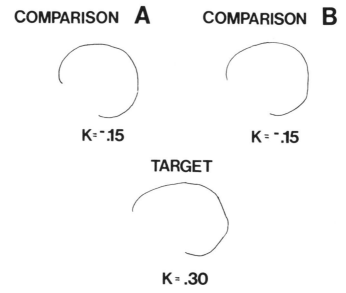

COMPARISON **A**   COMPARISON **B**

K = ⁻.15   K = ⁻.15

TARGET

K = .30

Figure 6-8. The upper figures show a strain of —.15 applied to two skulls. Which is the transform of the target skull? *B.* (After Pittenger & Shaw, 1977; with permission)

Finally, it should also be noted that the two strain transformations (early cardioidal and revised) have been compared with a number of other growth-simulating transformations—affine shear, reflected shear, rotation and a control (no change)[4]—in order to determine if (1) strain is perceptually equivalent to growth, and (2) any other transformation might be just as effective. Subjects were presented with a number of different sequences of facial profiles, arranged from left to right, with increasing values of one of the aforementioned transformations for actual growth. Some observers merely had to describe the pattern of change within a sequence, while others rated each sequence for its resemblance to growth. It was hypothesized that if the pattern of subjects' responses corresponded to actual growth sequences, it could be taken as evidence that that transformation closely approximates important effects of growth. Indeed, subjects are quite selective and consistent in those transformations to which they will give growth responses: Only actual growth and the strain transformations elicited growth responses significantly greater than the control (Todd, et. al., 1980).

To summarize this research together with its theoretical backdrop, the human face has been characterized as a dynamic event—an object that undergoes transformations that are as fast as the wink of an eye and as slow as aging. In keeping with the characterization of face as event, the research described here has attempted to provide an account of perceivers' ability to perceive age. The process of aging itself was examined and the growth pattern of the human skull was found to be that of a cardioid undergoing strain. But finding an invariant, as noted in Chapters 2 and 3, is not the same as finding information. For the former to constitute the latter, it must be shown that perceivers can detect it. Several types of experiments have indeed revealed that degree of cardioidal strain is information about age.

Perceiving Growth: The Traditional Approach

But do these facts in themselves support the viability of the theory of direct perception? Certainly we would have to accept the claim that the event approach encourages some new and interesting questions. Psychology, however, has never had trouble generating questions. The real value of a theory is whether it can account for phenomena that other theories cannot account for. In our view, the interpretations established by traditional psychology cannot answer the question of how age might be perceived.

Can age estimations be accounted for by feature-comparison? Is seeing age merely a matter of seeing, for example, that a profile's nose is

---

[4] These transformations are considered growth-simulating because they all—with the exception of no change—effect a change in facial angle that occurs in craniofacial growth.

bigger, longer, or flatter, and, therefore, that it is the older profile? If Shaw is right in claiming that the perception of age-level is the pick-up of invariant growth relations, then individual features should matter little. Recall that individuals asked to rank-order photographs of unfamiliar people of different ages, none of whom appears more than once, can do so without difficulty (Pittenger & Shaw, 1975b). Obviously, they cannot be comparing the featural layout of an older face with its younger self.

But a more fundamental problem emerges if we press a traditional interpretation to explain the dual recognition of a face and how much it has aged. As an example, recognizing a grade-school acquaintance is perceiving an older version of a young face. Can the traditional story of perception account for this dual recognition of identity and aging? We think not. It can account for either but not both, because in order to account for one it must presuppose the other. The details of this dilemma are as follows.

In order to perceive (deduce) the change called aging, one would first have to identify the face with its younger representation in memory. But obviously those two faces are not an exact match. In order to even find the representation, the input would have to be adjusted. The changes that had produced the older face would have to be reversed at least to some degree so that the comparator could determine that this was indeed the same face rather than a novel old person or a look-alike. Once the match had been achieved, differences between the two faces could be assessed and the aging could be deduced. But careful scrutiny of this process reveals a requirement that to perceive aging, one must perceive aging. This act of deduction presupposes the very process it seeks to explain.

This point is worth belaboring because it contains an indictment not only of a feature-comparison scheme of face perception, but a feature-comparison scheme of event perception in general. Events are changes wrought over objects. For feature-comparison to yield the nature of the change, the inputs must be matched, but to match them the nature of the change must be known. Therefore, change cannot be deduced. For a comparison to yield the identity of two inputs (e.g., recognition of a face), the change that relates them must be known, but the deduction of the change requires that the faces are recognized as the same. Thus, the identity of the object cannot be deduced either.

The event approach to faces does not fall prey to these paradoxes. The identity of the head is preserved in certain invariants, and the age of the head is described by certain other invariants. And, this structural and transformational information taken together provides the minimal description of the information that permits face perception. A theory that ignores either one can explain face perception only by sleight of hand.

Criticism of feature theories should not be taken as a denial of features as components of a face (see, for example, Mitchell, 1976). On the contrary, it should be taken as the impetus for a more rigorous approach to what a feature is or can be in the context of a face. There are any number of elements that might be offered as candidates, but in general, experiments on which theories of face perception are based have treated the notion of feature too cavalierly. They assert that features are important but pay little heed to what they might be. At one level of abstraction, features can be said to be those countable elements that comprise an object. That assumes, however, that faces and other objects ought to be commensurate at that level. But if what we choose to call a feature is well defined (e.g., a thoroughly articulated eye), the other features are dictated by that choice—that is, nothing but a face has such an eye and its other elements must align in a particular way with reference to that eye. If, on the other hand, what we call a feature is not sufficiently constrained (e.g., each of the accents and highlights that comprise that eye), the other features can take on any values and specify an infinite set of objects.

Such constraints speak to a second issue, that of the configurations in which the features relate. The suggestion that the relations among features are important belies the common claim that features are isolated and context-independent. It is important to note that such a possibility has not been entertained in the literature on the specialness of faces, for example. Although faces are composed of features that are highly constrained—an eye in one place necessarily entails an eye in some other particular place—other objects of supposedly equal complexity with which they have been compared are not so restricted. For example, houses have certain featural requirements (doors, windows, roof) with few absolute constraints (roof must be on top) and a good deal of free variation (number and location of windows). In other words, placing one feature does not dictate as strictly what, where, or how many other features there are.

In sum, the event approach asserts that configurational and transformational *constraints on features* are integral to describing the entities that constitute the class face. It is thought that an approach that exploits the endogenous properties of faces will provide an answer to the question "what is a face?" that will stand as an example of, rather than as an exception to, "what is an object?"

ACTION

We have placed particular emphasis on a consideration of activity. Because animals' activities restrict the kind of information that they find useful, a theory of perception cannot be developed independently of a theory of action. In addition to these rather broad logical arguments, Chapter 3 provided a sketch of such an action theory. In particular, it was suggested that the motor machinery is organized so as to take advantage of certain kinds of information. We shall now elaborate the details of such organization and, perhaps more importantly, illustrate the style of inquiry into complex systems *as coalitions,* which has emerged out of an attempt to explain coordination.

This more detailed discussion of the perception-action relationship begins with a description of the form of conventional theories of coordinated movement, which is colored by the traditional dichotomy between perception and action. We criticize this perspective, focusing on two major problems which derive from it. The ecological alternative, which we summarize from the work of Turvey and his associates (Turvey, 1977b; Fitch & Turvey, 1978; Turvey, Shaw & Mace, 1978; Kugler, Kelso, & Turvey, 1980) treats perceiving and acting not as independent, interacting systems, but calls upon a different type of organization—the coalition—to characterize their interrelationship. The coalitional approach which seeks the basis of the apparent "control" of activity in the mutual constraint of perception and action, avoids the pitfalls of more traditional approaches and, in addition, illustrates a style of scientific inquiry whose domain may extend far beyond investigations of coordinated activity (see Shaw & Turvey, in press).

The Domains of Perception and Action as Nonoverlapping

Many psychologists have presumed that the problems of coordinated movement are logically independent of the problems of information pickup. For example, theories of how one does the broad-jump bear little or no relation to theories of how one perceives the location of the take-off board. The problems with which perception and action are thought to deal are nonoverlapping: Perception registers sensory events and constructs meaning for them, while action writes and executes motor commands. Of course, no one argues that the two processes are totally unrelated, because actions must be made with reference to an environment that is revealed through perception. There must be some point at which perceptual information is allowed to influence the organization of acts. Typically, however, this influence is assumed to be simple—the motor system is controlled (somehow) by the products yielded by the act of perception; the *results* of the perceptual process are used in the design of the act. The nature of perceiving, however, is not thought to logically condition the nature of acting. Put another way, there is the implicit suggestion that *how* a perceptual system determines and delivers its products—perceptions—neither influences nor is influenced by how the motor system receives and uses these products.

This dichotomy of perception and action accords an inferior status to action. The action system depends on information from perception *before* an act can be formulated. The underlying theme is essentially unchanged from Descartes' Response Doctrine—the motor machinery must wait for perception before it can be put into operation. Perception, it is supposed, is not so indebted to the action system. Given this general perspective, we shall examine the particulars of a theory that this tradition suggests.

Briefly, the classical view claims that the products of perception permit a motor executive to write a plan that controls contractions of muscles. Consider a characteristic, though simplistic, account of walking that this approach fosters. First, the environment to be negotiated must be appraised. The process of perception is called upon to assess the terrain. Are the surfaces slippery? Are there any obstacles? Is there an incline? The products of this process can then be used in writing an action plan geared to these local conditions. Such a plan would include, presumably, not only the general path to follow but also the particulars of which muscles to contract, how fast, how much, and in what order. This plan would then be used as a script for some kind of executive who ultimately gives the proper command to the proper motor units so that the act is carried out (Figure 6-9).

Theories differ, of course, on the individual details of this process (e.g., Is the unit of movement control an alpha- or gamma-motoneuron, muscle, or muscle sequence? What form does the executive take? What is the role of feedback?). Regardless of the particulars, however, these theories all take the same approach: A plan must exist in order that an act can be executed. This is explicit, for example, in Schmidt's description of his schema theory:

> It is also assumed that there are "generalized" motor programs formed in the central nervous system that contain stored muscle commands with all of the details necessary to carry out a movement. The program requires response specifications that determine how the program is to be carried out (e.g., rapidly, slowly, etc.). Given the response specifications, the program can be run off, with all of the details of the movement determined in advance. (Schmidt, 1976, p. 46)

In other words, the prescription for the movement is stored before the movement is attempted. In this general approach, schematized in

Figure 6-9. Cartoon of "Motor Executive" using scripts based on local terrain in order to control movement.

Figure 6-10, the plan or representation of the movement with which action begins is based on the product or representation with which perception ends. In such a view, action deals not with the environment, but with a representation of that environment as yielded by perception. Of course, this general model encourages the perception theorist to consider perceiving and acting as distinct theoretical districts.

At first glance, the logic of this traditional scheme may seem adequate: One recognizes a rock, for example, and then commands the muscles to step over it. But when pressed, such theories create unnecessary and persistent problems. In what follows, we look at some of the most bothersome and show how a solution cannot be found within the framework of animal-environment dualism.

The first problem encountered by this kind of theory is the vast

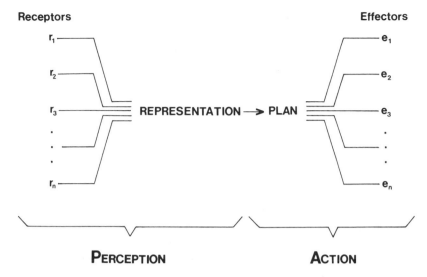

Figure 6-10. A schematization of the relationship between perceiving and acting in traditional psychology.

number of free variables (e.g., muscles, joints) which would have to be regulated by the executive. To write a plan of the kind described would require, first, a selection of which variables are to be manipulated and, second, a specification of the degree and timing of manipulation. As an illustration of this, imagine that separate levers controlled the five mechanisms that are manipulated in flying planes (left and right ailerons, elevator, rudder, and throttle). To control the plane, the pilot would have to assess the current state of all these variables and decide which variables need to be changed and how much. If planes were controlled this way, flying would be a difficult, though not impossible, task. But, if instead of five variables, the pilot were put in charge of a hundred or more (as in the number of muscles in the hands and arms) the task of control does become impossible. Choosing the proper combination from all the possible combinations exceeds the processing capacity of any known algorithm (Gel'fand & Tsetlin, 1962; cited in Turvey, Shaw, & Mace, 1978). This "degrees-of-freedom problem" (Bernstein, 1967) arises because the number of things in need of regulation exceeds the number of things that can regulate. That is, the executive has fewer degrees of freedom than the mechanical degrees of freedom it must control.

The degrees-of-freedom problem is an important concept and deserves another illustration. Imagine that the device that we want to control is a player piano. The degrees of freedom requiring regulation are the keys to be played, how long, and in what order. The roll specifies each of these variables—there is information in the roll that specifies order, key, and duration. The degrees of freedom on the thing being controlled (the piano) are equal to the degrees of freedom of the thing doing the controlling (the roll). But what if the roll had 10 commands of the type that only conveyed to the piano "play a happy tune" or "play a C-major chord"? The piano needs to know which keys to depress, for how long, and in what order. Obviously, the number of things controlling is far less than the number of things requiring control, and a degrees-of-freedom problem emerges. Coordinated activity is like making music; the roll corresponds to the action plan and the keys are the units of movement.

One reasonable solution to the degrees-of-freedom problem assumes that the variables (aileron, key, or muscle) are not regulated individually. Rather, groups of those variables may be partitioned into standard units or subprograms. If commands could be issued to these units which, in turn, would take care of the finer details of the act in some stereotyped fashion (e.g., if the command for a happy song engaged some subprogram within the piano to play "Happy Talk," and the subprogram specified the details), the degrees of freedom that would have to be regulated would be reduced. Indeed, this can be the solution to the degrees-of-freedom problem in the case of the airplane. Two ailerons and the rudder are (sometimes) mechanically linked into a "collective" so that one command from the pilot affects all three mechanisms. The particulars of what the individual members of the collective do are standardized to the kinds of commands they receive (e.g., one possible command could move the left aileron up, right aileron down, and turn the rudder to the left).

While the notion of a fixed collective or standardized program commanded by an executive (pilot, roll) suits the explanation of the co-ordination of parts of an airplane and our player piano, it is not an adequate solution to the problems in coordinated animal activity. This is so because the style of organization that underlies this command formulation is that of an hierarchy. The language of commands implies that someone or something has a movement plan or rule which it applies to the motor machinery. In other words, total responsibility for control is entrusted to an executive. In a pure hierarchy,[5] this centralization of control means that the executive always dominates the variables or nodes below it, which, in turn, dominate variables below them. So in Figure 6-11, for example, the executive might prescribe which collective to excite so that its alpha-motoneuron (A or B) activates certain extrafusal muscle fibers ($a1$ and $a2$,

[5] Turvey, Shaw, & Mace (1978) distinguish a number of pure control systems from which "mixed-types" may be derived. To make the characteristics as clear as possible, we follow our colleagues' lead in focusing on the pure case.

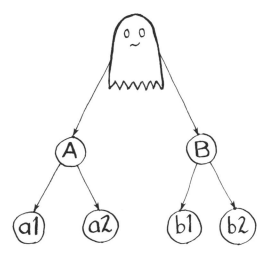

Figure 6-11. Diagram of an hierarchy. The executive can excite collective *A* or collective *B.*

or *b*1 and *b*2), causing the proper muscle to contract. The state of the muscle fibers or the muscle itself should have no influence or control over the plan for the movement which is above them in the hierarchy.

It is also interesting to note that an hierarchically organized control system requires that each variable has only one job that it can do, and it executes this function only when it receives a command to do so. To see why this is so, consider the following. Because the actual execution of the act is accomplished by muscles and joints, the plan must ultimately be written over these variables. A plan for "step over," for example, might include something like "contract the thigh muscles and then extend the knee." A plan written with these ends in mind must assume that each time the muscles are activated, they yield a particular movement. In order that a given command always yields the same consequence, the entire complex of commands on the way to "contract the thigh muscles" must be standard. The linear transitivity of control that characterizes hierarchies—i.e., variables above always dominate variables below—makes this standardization necessary. All variables are, in a sense, ignorant of what the others are doing. For control to be possible, therefore, all variables must be reliable in what they do.

While hierarchical organization seems to allow a certain amount of savings in the control burden borne by the executive—each collective, a subsystem containing several variables, can be treated as one degree of freedom—it extracts its cost in other areas. First, this version of a collection of variables poses difficulty in accounting for how such variables come to be joined. If the collective or subprogram is thought to exist prior to the execution of the act, how did it arise? Alternatively, if the collective or subprogram arises at the time of the act, the action plan would still have to prescribe which muscles join together. Of course, this latter alternative revives the degrees-of-freedom problem.

Second, the assumption that a given command to a muscle will have a standard consequence is simply not justified. When one plays a key on a piano, some particular note will come out; when a muscle is commanded, however, the outcome of a command depends on a number of other factors. The influence of these factors is especially troublesome to hierarchical organizations because they often occur "below" the command node or are of a type not usually considered relevant to the design of an act. We take three such factors (from Bernstein, 1967; and Turvey, Shaw, & Mace, 1978) that illustrate various sources of "indeterminacy" between command and consequence: anatomical, mechanical, and physiological.

One factor concerns how the anatomical relationship between a muscle and joint affects the outcome of a given command. As an example, a command to contract pectoralis major, one of the muscles that connect the upper arm to the chest, will produce two different movements depending on the arm's position relative to the horizontal plane of the shoulder. In particular, if the arm is to the side of the body and even with or below the shoulder, contracting pectoralis major will pull the arm forward in front of the body. On the other hand, if the arm is above the plane of the shoulder, contracting that same muscle will bring the arm upward toward the head (Figure 6-12).

Besides such anatomical relationships, a muscle's dynamic state also has mechanical influence on the kind of movement it will produce. A given command (defined as some particular innervational state) to a muscle of a moving arm, for example, may slow the movement, arrest it, or reverse its direction, all of which differ from what that command does to a static arm. The influence of a muscle's dynamic state can also be found in evidence that one link (e.g., the thigh) in a kinematic chain (e.g., the whole leg) will generate forces in related or attached links thereby generating kinetic energy which, in turn, reacts back on the first link, further complicating its control.

A third case in which variability arises from the context of the motor machinery involves physiological factors. Briefly, it has been shown that the *state* of the spinal machinery is as important as the commands themselves. For instance, stimulation of the underside of a dog's paw elicits an extension reflex in one posture and a flexion reflex under a different posture.

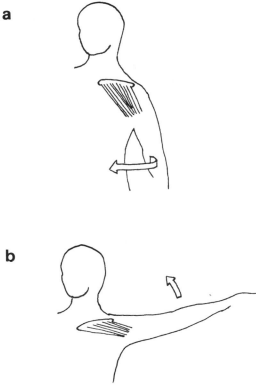

Figure 6-12. The consequence of contracting
pectoralis major when the arm is (*a*) lower than
the plane of the shoulder and (*b*) above the
plane of the shoulder.

Turvey, Shaw, & Mace (1978) mention a number of other examples
of these three sources of variability in the command-consequent relation
that would undermine an hierarchically organized control system. Given
that natural systems exhibit coordination in the face of such context-
conditioned variability, it would appear that pure hierarchies simply cannot
account for the plasticity that coordination evidences.[6] In sum, an hierarchically organized action system in which commands come from the top

---

[6]This shortcoming is even more obvious when one considers that an hierarchy
would be seriously damaged by any kind of insult to a high-level variable (e.g.,
destruction of neural tissue): Any variables under its domination would be left
uncontrolled. But in acting animals, this does not usually happen; they often continue
to function properly in spite of such insults.

and in which details emerge in a standardized way through successive nodes does not work. Coordination cannot be indifferent to the ever-changing state of the body.

A style of organization that could deal more successfully with these difficulties would be one that allows *feedback*—information passed "upward." As illustrated in Figure 6-13, if for some reason node *c* cannot pass its command along a standard route, this information is passed back to call upon an alternative subsystem. Unlike a strict hierarchy, the whole system need not be infirmed. No one variable is solely responsible for a particular function; a number of subsystems could be functionally equivalent.

An organization with feedback also seems to have the advantage of being fairly adaptable to context-conditioned variability and, perhaps, even to the changing aspects of the environment. Because it conveys information about what the variables have done and, therefore, whether the act is being carried out, feedback can presumably be used to adjust the action plan to factors unforeseen when the plan was written (e.g., as when a hidden rock causes one to stumble). Unfortunately, theories of coordinated movement usually restrict the use of feedback to information about the consequences (success or failure) of some act as depicted by the current state of the

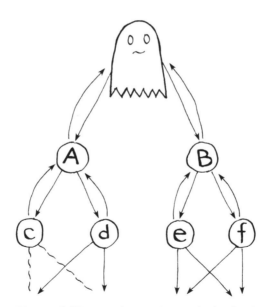

Figure 6-13. An hierarchy with feedback. Information about the infirmity of node *c* can be passed back to node *A* so that it can call upon an alternative subsystem.

machinery. In such a formulation, the act, or some part of it, serves as a reference value against which error signals are determined.

Thus, an animal that attempts to walk forward receives confirming or disconfirming feedback from a variety of sources such as muscles, joints, and orienting system. If feedback indicates an error, the plan is modified. But feedback in this strict sense is essentially reactive; the act is carried out and *then* checked. Such feedback could inform the organism only of conditions that no longer exist. That is, if one trips on a rock, feedback could tell only that an error had occurred. But the organism does not need to know that it has tripped; that is unalterable and no longer relevant. The real need is for information about how to recover without falling—feed-*forward*, so to speak (Greene, 1972; Turvey, 1977b). Registering error or even direction of error is not enough. It simply says that some or perhaps all of the elements are wrong. It does not carry information about which elements to fix or how much to fix them. Indeed, the same error signal could be caused by any number of combinations of elements all doing the wrong thing to varying degrees.

Thus, feedback, the very mechanism that allowed for the plasticity or adaptability necessary to deal with context-conditioned variability, has reintroduced the degrees-of-freedom problem. Feedback increases the supposed processing load on an action system beyond the normal burden of planning and control. Moreover, there is no source of constraint on the kinds of surprises that the environment might offer. Unless such surprises are somehow anticipated in the design of the act, feedback cannot control for them. Clearly, the concept of feedback as usually formulated is not sufficient to permit an animal to accommodate to that environment.

To summarize, the problems of degrees of freedom and context-conditioned variability make the writing of commands an impossibly complex task. There cannot be a pat command for "step over"; the plan must take into account current states in the motor machinery and precise conditions of the environment, and allow for accommodation to environmental surprises. To make matters worse, all of these tasks fall upon a control system whose plan must be written from a representation created by a perceptual system that, according to typical theory, can be studied without a whit of attention to action.

Coordination in the Coalitional Organization of Animal-Environment Systems

Obviously, organisms do exhibit coordination in the face of many kinds of perturbations and seeming uncertainties. The cheetah that chases and catches the impala or the basketball player who dribbles through the defense into the key are elegant testimonies to the adaptability of actions to the details of a changing environment. If one were to itemize the contractions of all the muscles involved in the cheetah's chase or the player's shot, the length and detail of the list would be overwhelming. But ascribing the complex structure of an act to a plan or design is like ascribing the complex structure of an animal to the *plan* of evolution. Just as the structure of an animal must be understood with reference to the larger system in which it arose, the structure of an act must be understood with reference to the system in which *it* arose. Thus, the realist perspective asserts that the style of organization of coordinated movement must be consistent with the tenets of animal-environment synergy. This means that coordination cannot be accomplished by means of a controlling executive, but must fall out of the natural compatibility between an animal and its ecological niche. Adaptability to environmental contingencies must be naturally constrained by the organization of the musculature with respect to the environment. An act is not programmed internally, but is entailed by environmental information of use to the animal.

Structures and processes that are complex are usually taken to be controlled or planned; complexity is, indeed, often taken as evidence of control. At issue here is how one kind of complexity—that of coordinated activity—might arise in the absence of mechanisms that design or control. Thus, the origins of the organization of an act are sought in the organization of the larger system (animal-environment) in which it arose. By treating structure as arising not from control mechanisms in the actor, but as a description over an animal and its environment, this approach seeks its explanation in that system. It seeks a solution to the problems of degrees of freedom and context-conditioned variability in the natural constraints of that system. Specifically, a solution is to be found in the style of organization termed *coalitional* (Turvey, Shaw, & Mace, 1978).

Coalitions are distinguished from other styles of organization in that there is not just one component—the animal—that has to be "controlled." Rather, coordination must be defined over three components: an action system, a perception system, and an environmental niche (Figure 6-14). Arguments for the mutual fit in all combinations of these components have been made in this book and elsewhere (cf. Chapters 3 and 5; Turvey, Shaw, & Mace, 1978; Turvey & Shaw, 1979; Shaw & Turvey, in press). Action and perception are mutually constraining, and together they constitute the animal; the animal and the environment, in turn, are mutually constraining, and they constitute an ecosystem. Therefore, it is at the level of the ecosystem that "control" must be defined.

The realist attitude asserts that an ecosystem is not just a casual pairing of an animal with environmental factors that might affect it; rather, they have coevolved. This is especially important to the requirements of

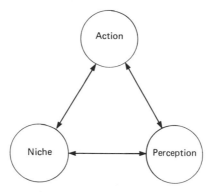

Figure 6-14. Schematic of the coimplicative relations among actions, perceptions, and the environmental niche.

control because a casual pairing would not solve the degrees-of-freedom problem. Without the mutual constraints guaranteed by evolution, the environment would merely provide additional degrees of freedom in need of control, additional sources of variability. If the organization of the animal were indifferent to the organization of the environment, the problem of control would be immensely complicated. Rather, the relationship must be of a special kind so that each component constrains or tailors the other. This *dual complementation* (Turvey, Shaw, & Mace, 1978) is the source of the complex coordinations exhibited by individual components of ecosystems.

> An organization which can be characterized as having this style of control is what we call a coalition; and we take a coalition to be the minimum sufficient organization to capture the intuitive notion of an ecosystem. A coalition is not a system-plus-context. It is the minimal system that carries its own context. (Turvey, Shaw, & Mace, 1978, p. 592)

Obviously, the coalitional style of inquiry has been implicit in much of what has been presented already in this book. We now examine how the notion of mutual compatibility or dual complementation might help us to understand coordinated activity.

First, given that there are a large number of elements (e.g., muscles) that take part in an act, how might they be collected into units without giving rise to the degrees-of-freedom problem? The choice of the unit (e.g., motoneuron, muscle, joint) quite obviously determines the number of degrees of freedom and, hence, the degrees of constraint required. Given

145

that an indefinitely large number of constraints is not available, regulation could not happen even at as coarse a level as joint angle. The vocabulary of control must be at an even coarser grain; it must account for a larger part of the body. But, once more, this larger collection of the fine-grained variables cannot be arbitrary because certain collections of variables would be useless for activity. Moreover, the collectives must be naturally constrained, requiring no extrinsic device to link them. Recall from our earlier discussion that merely collecting the variables into standard units is not enough because the very process of collection involves degrees of freedom that must be controlled.

Such a unit or, more properly, autonomous collective, has been termed the coordinative structure (Easton, 1972; Turvey, 1977; Turvey, Shaw, & Mace, 1978) or coordinative cycle (Kugler, Kelso, & Turvey, 1980). A coordinative structure is defined as a group of muscles, often spanning several joints, constrained to act as a functional unit.

> Through biasings or tunings of the spinal cord that arise [in the spine or brain], the individual members of an aggregate of skeletomuscular variables are linked or constrained to act as a functional unit or collective. These are not commands but constraining patterns of facilitation and inhibition on spinal brainstem interneurons. (Kugler & Turvey, 1978)

Some examples of coordinative structures were presented in Chapter 3. Recall that the wrist and shoulder are linked in the act of aiming a gun (Arutyunyan et al., 1969). The wrists of the two arms, although not connected mechanically, are functionally linked in the act of drumming (von Holst, 1973). These kinds of coordinative structures are conveniently illustrated in the simple model for regulating an airplane. The mechanical link on the rudder and ailerons harnesses those free variables so as to bring about a simple change in a coarse-grain variable (bank). The form of the linkage is such that it supports the activity—flying—where another combination might be useless—for example, if the ailerons were linked to move in the same direction. The airplane model is not ideal for our purposes, however, because it requires a pilot to exert control. In coordinative structures, the constraint arises in perception, and to illustrate this, we return to the clock metaphor.

Recall that the pendulum clock is a self-sustaining device whose organization is such that it taps a continuously available energy source at those times appropriate for its function, i.e., periodic regular oscillation. Regulation is a consequence, not of a separate monitoring device, but of the organization of the system. This self-maintaining periodicity is also characteristic of coordinated movement. This is best illustrated by the act of locomotion. During each step, a single limb goes through a characteristic pattern of positions, some of which are diagrammed in Figure 6-15. If the flexed position of the limb is labeled (1), the rest of the cycle is as follows: (2) the limb is extended in front of the body, (3) the limb is under the body so that the body weight is directly over the foot, and (4) the limb extends back, thereby shifting weight forward. So the step-cycle of a single limb consists of a leg flexed in mid-air, which extends to land on the ground, where the body weight is transferred over it until the leg again leaves the ground as it flexes and starts the cycle once more.

Coordination of the step-cycle is evident in four phases which these positions distinguish. There are three extension phases: E1 occurs in the movement from position (1) to position (2), E2 is the shift from position (2) to (3), and during E3, the limb goes from position (3) to (4). The flexion phase (F) occurs in going from (4) to (1). When the limb is so organized for locomotion and the muscle activity is recorded, an interesting systematicity is revealed. If we look at those muscles responsible for extending the leg, the ratio of their electrical activity does not change, regardless of the speed of locomotion (Grillner, 1975). While the absolute amount of activity will change as speed increases, *the relationship among the muscles is constant.* They are organized for the act of locomotion and that organization remains fixed.

The amount of time that the limb spends in each phase reveals another aspect of this organization. While the E3 phase shortens dramatically with an increase in speed, the durations of the other phases remain relatively constant. This is not unexpected because the speed increase is accomplished by applying more force during E3, thereby shortening its

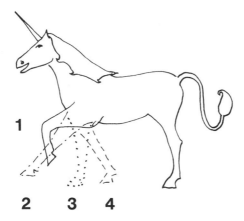

Figure 6-15. The step-cycle of a single limb.

duration (Shik & Orlovskii, 1976). But notice what is happening: The power is being tapped at just the phase in the organization of the structure where it will have the appropriate effect for the act.

The coordinative structure for a step-cycle in locomotion selectively percolates continuously available force, just as the pendulum clock selectively percolates continuously available energy, in embodying its function as a self-maintaining periodic oscillator. This unique interpretation of the step-cycle from Kugler, Kelso, & Turvey (1980) is an example of the complex structure exhibited by individual muscles joined together during coordinated movement. These investigators seek the origin of complex organizations such as coordinative structures in the constraints that arise in accordance with physical principles that apply to natural systems at all scales. This approach finds support, for example, in the efforts of many contemporary physical biologists (e.g., Morowitz, 1968; Iberall, 1969; Nicolis & Prigogine, 1978; Yates, in press) who characterize the organization of living systems (as members of the class of *dissipative structures*)[7] in the same way.

The notion that order can arise according to physical principles is in marked contrast to a theory that seeks the origin of order in plans, instructions, or controls. Complex control in the absence of (internal) control programs has already been demonstrated in artifacts such as the pendulum clock. We now turn to an example of such organization in a living system.

The nest building of termites displays the orderliness and systematicity that might be given a superficial explanation in terms of a preexisting plan. Termites repeatedly deposit building material on certain sites, some of which join to form the arches characteristic of their nests. But instead of having a collective plan by which the colony of termites builds its nest, the order can be explained by the dynamics of the termite-nest system (Prigogine, 1976). Material initially is deposited randomly. Because the material is infused with a pheromone or chemical attractant, however, subsequent deposits will tend to be made on those same sites. In this way, "pillars" are formed. If two such pillars occur close together, the highest density of pheromone chemicals will actually be between the tops of the two pillars (Figure 6-16) and that will attract the deposits which will complete the arch.

---

[7]Structures that arise as a function of the dynamic interplay of forces in nonequilibrium systems (systems through which there is a flow of energy) are known as dissipative structures (Prigogine & Nicolis, 1971). From the viewpoint of thermodynamics, such "open systems" can, at the expense of energy dissipation, maintain complex structures. Plans, instructions, and the like are simply not involved.

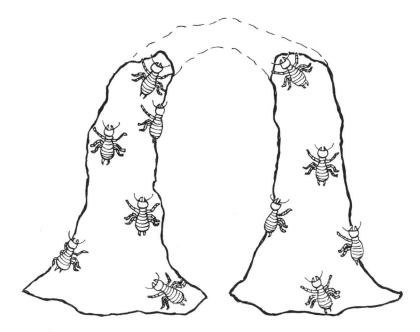

Figure 6-16. Pillars and arches formed during the nest building of termites.

> The form of the nest arises as an *a posteriori* fact of the termite ecosystem. It is not owing to a plan or program invested *a priori* in the individual termite or in the "collective" termite. (Kugler et al., in press)

Such structures are useful to understanding activity because the structure of an act is, by the ecological view, not represented in the system; rather, it is entailed by the organization. Both nest building and time keeping exhibit the kind of control or stability which, when it appears in rational systems, is usually ascribed to internalized (mental) plans.

Coordinative structures were identified as dissipative structures by Kugler, Kelso, & Turvey (1980) to buttress the argument that spatiotemporal order and its regulation need not be determined by an extrinsic monitoring (control) device. Insofar as living systems characteristically exhibit such regularity which can be accounted for on the basis of physical principles and not mental entities, a case is made for the reasonableness of the concept of coordinative structure as the device in which the free variables of movement are harnessed and regulated without recourse to mental representations or motor programs.

The coordinative structure concept allows us to avoid one problem that has perennially plagued theories of action: the degrees-of-freedom problem. But recall that if such devices are formed, they must be flexible enough to adjust to environmental fluctuations. If they are too stereotyped, they will, of course, succumb to context-conditioned variability. Let us now look at how coordinative structures stand up to this challenge.

Notice that in the examples of coordinative structures we have examined, the organization was manifested in the relationship among the variables and not their absolute values. Herein lies their flexibility. While the *organization* of the variables allows the particular act, adaptability to changing contextual circumstances comes about through the *tuning* of those variables (Greene, 1972; Turvey, 1977b; Turvey, Shaw, & Mace, 1978). Tuning is the means by which a coordinative structure that has already been organized for an act is modulated. Tuning describes that aspect of the coordinative cycle wherein information is accepted during certain phases of an act, thereby allowing its regulation.

The labyrinthine reflex provides one example of tuning. If a decerebrate cat with its neck immobilized is suspended in mid-air, upright and facing straight ahead, its limbs go into total flexion. If it is suspended on its back, however, and looking upward, the limbs go into extension (Fukuda, 1961; Figure 6-17). Aligning the head in certain positions relative to gravity

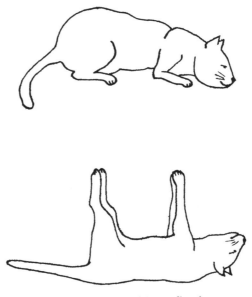

Figure 6-17. A labyrinthine reflex in a cat.

predisposes the body to certain postures. While adult humans do not exhibit this reflex overtly, tuning induced by such movements of the head can facilitate certain acts.[8] A long-jumper, for example, could keep her or his head up to inhibit flexion (which would result in a too-rapid landing). Rather, flexion would occur at just that point in the act where it would be most effective.

Perhaps this selective aspect of information is more obvious in the step-cycle where tuning occurs in the third extension phase, the only phase during which more force may be applied so as to effect an increase in running speed. In the baseball-batting example as well (see Chapter 3), information selectively modulates one aspect of the act: The influence of time-to-contact information is seen in the speed of opening of the stance. Other aspects of the organization for batting remain constant (e.g., duration of the swing).

Therefore, tuning is the way in which coordinative structures are able to *take advantage of* contextual information—not only about the body but about the environment and the relation of the body to the environment as well[9] —and thereby dissolve the problem of context-conditioned variability.

What we have presented in this section may be characterized as principles of coordination and control from the ecological perspective rather than a theory of action. Such a theory is being pursued by others. Our aims have been merely to focus attention on the importance of a theory of action to a theory of perception (and vice versa), to point out the immensity of the problems that emerge out of approaches that assume their logical independence, and, finally, to characterize the relationship between action and perception (and environment) as coalitional: Each constrains—rather than controls or instructs—the others.

The first part of this section examined the perceiving-acting relationship from a perspective that assumes animal-environment dualism. This attitude conceives of the organization of acts as a process within the animal. From the deliverances of the senses, the perceiver creates some sort of representation upon which is based the plan for muscle contraction. As it turns out, the computations required for the plan are impossibly complex. To assume that an act is accomplished by a plan for the execution of commands is to assume, first of all, that there is "someone" to write and issue those commands and, second, that that commander or executive possesses the set of rules for issuing those commands. This fosters a notion of very strict control of the act by an executive (or executive program) and,

---

[8]The same effect that is had with the cat can be obtained with intact children.

[9]In keeping with the conventional use of *proprioceptive* and *exteroceptive* for the first two kinds of information, respectively, Lee (1978) uses the term *exproprioceptive* for the third kind.

hence, creates the two problems on which we have focused: degrees of freedom and context-conditioned variability. Lost in the shuffle of commands, errors, and feedback are the logically prior problems of origin—what is the executive, how did it arise, and from where did it get the rules needed to issue commands?

We have outlined here what are offered as more reasonable solutions to the problems of coordinated activity. Guided by the coalitional style of inquiry, the origins of the apparent complexities of this coordination were sought in the natural constraints of an animal-environment system. Specifically, coordination was defined over an action term, a perception term, and an environment term. Control at this level—the ecosystem—is thought to be the natural consequence of the mutually compatible fit of (an) animal (perception + action) and (its) environment. The notion of a coordinative structure as a member of the class of dissipative structures was offered in support of the contention that organized, complex behavior is due to the nature of physical systems and does not require an "intelligent" regulator. The essence of dual complementation as a control principle is that it binds the animal to its environment:

> To say that an organism is the dual complement of its environment is also to assert that an environment is a dual complement of the organism, i.e., that the environment is just as thoroughly organized as its organism *and is specific to it* (cf. Gibson, 1977). The relation of dual complementation also carries with it the idea that it is the overarching whole formed by the duals which is the proper unit. Neither member of a dual pair is properly constrained without the other, or without the whole being defined by their closure. (Turvey, Shaw, & Mace, 1978, p. 592)

In summary, the ecological view asserts that perceiving and acting are complementary descriptions of the same event. The animal and environment are in a relationship of mutual constraint. For example, the precise motor activities by which a perceiver-actor adjusts her or his footfall to the vicissitudes of a path are complementary to optical information that tunes that adjustment. At the heart of this is the view that understanding perception is understanding how actions are organized and tailored, both macroscopically (as in affordances) and microscopically (as in tuning) by perceptual systems.

SUMMARY

In the first five chapters, the general ecological approach to perception was presented. The aim of this chapter has been to illustrate the variety of directions that the ecological reorientation invites for specific theoretical a plan must be written in order to effect the control of muscles. The ecological reformulation, in contrast, seeks an explanation of "control" in the organization of biokinematic variables into coordinative structures (and their tuning) by perceptual information. The coalitional nature of perception and action requires also that the organization and tuning of these collectives constrains perception.

issues. In particular, we described three avenues of inquiry tha
either in content or in emphasis from their traditional counterpart
    Binocular vision was presented as a demonstration that an e
approach can change the questions that theories in a given line of
try to answer. Two fundamental problems that are usually addr
theories of binocular vision are singleness and three-dimensionalit
problems are spawned by the apparent discrepancy between th
three-dimensional character of experience and the double, two-din
character of the input. This approach assumes that the metrical p
of the two images must be determined and compared and that
images must somehow be unified. In consequence, theories of t
vision propose mechanisms that determine metrical properties o
compare two sets of such properties, and unify them.
    The ecological perspective on binocular vision focuses on c
ing how the light to two eyes (i.e., the binocular array) might sp
properties of the world that perceivers know. It was argued tha
binocular viewing transforms the optic array in a way most easily c
of as a rotation. The distances, sizes, shapes, and relative pos
surfaces can be shown to be specified by transformational inva
that binocular array. For those interested in mechanism, then, the
becomes one of how the single, spatial transformation that in
singleness and three-dimensionality might be detected.
    The topic of face perception was introduced to highlight twc
cal concerns that are not usually brought to bear in more tradit
proaches. The first concerns identifying the very nature of th
under investigation. It was argued that an object is what it is be
what it can do or what it can have done to it, and that those
mations should be exploited by attempts to understand perceptic
are not considered static objects, but structures continually ur
transformations.
    The second and related point concerned temporal aspec
event orientation and, more specifically, illustrated the extended
of perceptually salient events. The unit of analysis for ecological r
gy is an event, whether that occurs in a moment (smiling) c
lifetime (aging).
    In the third section, we turned our attention to coordinat
ment and, again, two aspects of that discussion deserve recap
First, the very presence of a section on action highlights the e
claim that understanding activity is central to understanding pe
Second, in light of the suggested importance of understanding act
presented the kinds of problems that theories of coordination ad
it turns out, the motivation for many traditional problems derives
assumed independence of action from perception. On such an ass

7

Summary and Conclusions

In the last several decades of mainstream psychology, there have been two traditional approaches to understanding perception. One of these has been to describe the physiological mechanisms of perceiving and the other has been to model the act of perceiving by describing it according to the rules of a device such as a switchboard or computer.

The physiological approach asks how light, sound pressure, airborne chemicals, etc. are transduced. Of course, most questions are asked more particularly: How do different wavelengths of light lead to different patterns of firing in the optic nerve? How do certain combinations of wavelengths lead to the same pattern? How do different amplitudes of sound waves lead to different patterns of auditory neural activity? While these questions still enjoy wide attention, recent years have seen a new variety of questions emerge: How are edges detected? How are contours enhanced? How are angles, curves, velocities, orientations, and directions computed by neural circuitry?

The modeling approach, on the other hand, is for the most part unconcerned with receptors, neurons, and their properties. Rather, it seeks to describe, in a metaphoric way, the processing of stimulus input. The common metaphor is the digital computer, but there is a large measure of variability in how seriously theorists exploit the metaphor. Some theorists attempt a fairly precise transfer of computer concepts (e.g., bits) to perception, while others are satisfied to borrow for psychology only the global characteristics of computing machines (e.g., stages of processing, processing capacity). In spite of their differences, the questions asked by these information processing approaches are fairly similar. How is information stored and retrieved? How are images recognized? How might a pattern be constructed from features? And, more generally, how might one describe the sequence of processing stages that convert the proximal stimulus into meaningful experience and appropriate action?

The physiological and information processing approaches ask, each in its own way, how what is perceived is perceived. All of the above questions ask how the input is processed. Quite plainly, a theory of how perception is accomplished must contain in it a theory of what it is accomplished *on;* therefore, these questions presuppose a theory of what is processed. That is, they necessarily embody a statement of what constitutes perceptual information. For the sensory psychologist, perceptual information appears to include such variables as wavelength, amplitude, convex edges moving across the retina, image angles, image velocities, and image orientations. For the information processors, it includes amounts of energy, images, and a similar roster of features. For these theories of indirect perception, be they rooted in models or mechanisms, the "stimuli" have been properties of the light to an eye or the sound to an ear that are inadequate bases for perception. All of the "whats" described above—features, images, wavelengths—are not specific to the facts of the environment. To assume that the input is nonspecific, ambiguous, or piecemeal makes a theory of *how* into a theory of correction, elaboration, calculation, and inference. These are exactly the concepts of which traditional theories partake.

The notion that these ambiguous data are relevant to perception, however, seems to contradict evolution. Given that visual systems evolved in a sea of patterned energy—some of which was specific to the facts of the world and some of which was not—can we suppose that animals evolved sensitivity to the latter? We have argued, after Gibson, that it makes better sense to suppose that a visual system that can detect the informative energy patterns is a more likely consequence of evolution.

THE ECOLOGICAL APPROACH: A SUMMARY

The conceptual starting point for the ecological approach to perception is summed up in the following: The useful dimensions of an animal's sensitivity are to the structured energy that invariantly specifies properties of the environment of significance to that animal. The entire ecological approach revolves around this simple and eminently sensible premise. Every assumption that is made, every hypothesis that is forwarded, every criticism levied against traditional psychology, and every experiment that is run has its roots in this principle.

To elucidate the ecological approach, we began with an emphasis on information and the ecological requirement that it be unique and specific to its source. After establishing that information can convey fairly high-order properties of environments, the significance of those properties for the activities of animals was elaborated. Eventually, we arrived at the claim that, at some level, information had to be in the dimensions of the particular perceiver—body-scaled. It is this more complete description of the animal-environment relation that allows the position of direct, or ecological, realism. A chapter-by-chapter review of its major ramifications in the psychology of perceiving is now presented.

Chapter 1. The ecological approach is set apart from all other mainstream perceptual theory by the assumption that animals detect structured energy that specifies properties of the environment. This chapter outlined the contrasts between the ecological orientation and conventional theories that suppose (at least tacitly) that nervous systems register impoverished, ambiguous, or otherwise inadequate variables of stimulation. The main distinction rests on the question of whether perception must be mediated. The ecological position is that perception is a matter of detecting information that is unique and specific to its source, while the alternative approach contends that inadequate "information" is detected and must be converted, through some process of mediation, into meaning.

The idea that the senses register inadequate input may not be an *explicit* assumption of traditional approaches, but, where it isn't, it can be inferred from certain other assumptions. In vision, for example, it is supposed that the stimulus is the retinal image and, as we noted, images are, of necessity, ambiguous with respect to the third dimension. A more general assumption that results in uninformative inputs is that events are broken into space and time components and the time over which an input is defined is an instantaneous "now." It is obvious that if the perceiver is to know the three dimensions of the world as it changes over time (the fourth dimension), and the input from such an event is presumed to be a *static,* two-dimensional image, a theorist *must* impart to the brain the tasks of inferring or constructing both the third and fourth dimensions.

Therefore, the ecological and traditional approaches part ways at the outset. Following Gibson's lead, an explanation of the richness with which animals (human and otherwise) know their environments begins with the information to perceptual systems. Information processors (and constructivists, in general) seek the origins of such richness in the calculations of, supplements to, deductions from, and inferences about the scant data provided by the senses. Because the two camps differ so dramatically in their approaches to perceiving, it is not surprising that they characterize and attempt to study the perceiver in very different ways.

In the ecological view, the perceiver is an active explorer of the environment—one who will make an effort to obtain sufficient information. The more traditional view portrays the senses as passive conduits of sensation and the perceiver is active only insofar as he or she constructs or deduces the facts of the visual world. These disparate views of the perceiver, together with disparate views of perception as an ongoing activity vs. perception as a succession of processing stages, lead, in turn, to very different experimental strategies. The emphasis of direct perception is on approximating natural viewing conditions so that the perceiver as explorer can be investigated. Information processing experiments usually employ impoverished stimulus conditions so that the perceiver as constructor or deducer might be investigated. As sensible as this latter endeavor may sound insofar as it allows close control on those variables to be investigated, theorists of this persuasion do not seem compelled to demonstrate logically or experimentally how their findings (e.g., from tachistoscopic recognition) relate to ordinary perception.

Finally, we claimed that many of the disputes between theories of direct and indirect perception are due to what each considers to be the appropriate unit of analysis for studying perception. For traditional approaches, the subject matter of perception is bounded by the skin; for ecological psychologists, it is the animal-environment system.

Chapter 2. Information was described as those patterns of energy that specify for the animal the objects, places, and events of the animal's environment. We showed, in an approximate way, how these event-specific energy patterns are structured and how they might be described.

As we shift from an analysis of energy as a classical physicist views it to energy as a psychologist (*qua* ecological physicist) views it, we abandon the so-called lower-level measurements of light (amplitude, momentary retinal form, wavelength, etc.) in favor of descriptions of the *structure* of energy patterns. The lower-level descriptions are variant: They change with angle of regard, distance, and viewing conditions. Such descriptions offer little leverage in understanding why or how animals perceive objects of constant properties. Thus, instead of studying these metrics of energy, ecological psychologists seek to identify the structures in the light to an eye or the sound to an ear that relate invariantly to the events that gave rise to them. It is to these invariants that the basis of perceptual constancy is attributed.

Although it is easy to understand how the environment imparts structure to energy, the description of that structure sometimes requires significant mathematical sophistication. The pattern of light to an eye, for example, is due to the scatter-reflection of incident light by the surfaces in the surrounds and to the transformations upon the optic array that are induced by motions of the surfaces or of the perceiver. Some energy patterns are invariant with respect to some group of transformations; these were termed structural invariants. Similarly, groups of transformations that preserve some structural property are termed transformational invariants.

To provide a rigorous analysis of these patterns, we turned our attention to mathematics as a source of appropriate descriptive tools. Geometry provided a solid foundation for properties of information that would otherwise remain only intuitive. One of the first aims, then, in describing perceptual information is the identification of a geometry appropriate for that description—an endeavor later exemplified in the Chapter 6 treatments of face perception and binocular vision.

The search for information begins with the search for invariants. Whether the identified invariants constitute information and how they might be detected are separate questions. Chapters 3 and 4, respectively, addressed those questions.

Chapter 3. The relation between structured energy and the animal was discussed in this chapter. The reasons for including the animal in a consideration of information are (1) that not all invariant energy patterns have ecological significance and (2) the animal's own activities make additional information available (e.g., motion perspective). We asserted that energy structures only qualify as information if they have ecological significance. Of course, this requires that we be explicit in defining that significance. Energy patterns are said to be ecologically significant if they permit or guide adaptive behaviors. With that claim, the concepts of perception and action flow together into the notion of affordances.

The theory of affordances is a theory of what information informs about. In brief, affordances are descriptions of the environment with reference to an animal; affordances are what the environment *means* to an animal. The affordances of an object, place, or event are the behaviors it invites or permits by virtue of its structure, composition, position, and so on—and by virtue of the animal's effectivities.

Perhaps one of the most important consequences of this confluence of perceiving and acting is the notion that a theory of perception should not be divorced from a theory of action. That is, if a theorist embraces the concept of affordances, it is incumbent on that theorist to understand what an act is and how that act is modified to suit local conditions. It is only within the context of such an understanding of action that a theory of perception can be written. Noting that "while theories of perception abound, theories of action are conspicuous by their absence," Turvey (1977b) and others have attempted to bring action concepts to center stage in cognitive psychology.

The major issue in a theory of action (with reference to vision) concerns what constitutes an act, how that act might be organized, and how that organization might be entailed and constrained by perception.

Once again the ecological approach is compelled to reject traditional answers. Instead of proposing that the products of perceiving are used by an executive to write an action plan, it was claimed that the organization of musculature and the information are mutually constraining. Because neither the information nor the organization of musculature has the upper hand, the notion of control was abandoned. Rather, the organization of the musculature into collectives for a particular act invites regulation by certain information, *and* information constrains muscles and joints into collectives for the act. Such mutual constraint reflects the natural compatibility of the coevolved processes that action and perception must be. This coevolution of perception and action is the heart of the theory of affordances.

Experimental support for the theory that animals perceive affordances was then presented, citing research on "biological constraints on learning." It was claimed that what passes for an *inability to learn* a particular act in the presence of certain "detectable" information might be the failure of the information to *afford* the act that the experimenter deems correct.

Chapter 4. This chapter dealt primarily with two issues: the detection of information and of learning. The way these topics were treated derived from two premises developed in earlier chapters. The first was that perception is the *ongoing* activity of maintaining epistemic contact with the environment. This view is contrasted with an approach that considers perception to be a single act that yields perceptual products. The second premise was that perception is the detection of the higher-order variables of stimulation that specify to the animal the affordances of the environment. The tasks for Chapter 4, then, were to come to terms with *how* information might be detected and how experience affects that detection. Because this part of ecological theory is not, at this stage of development, well-articulated, our description of how perception is done was metaphoric. We summarize Chapter 4 by reviewing the three important metaphors and by distilling the lessons that might be drawn from each.

Perceptual systems are devices that register higher-order variables of stimulation; they do not calculate or compute these variables from the values of more elementary variables. One commonplace device that instantiates this notion is the polar planimeter. The planimeter is a simple machine that registers the area of a planar figure without measuring any of the more rudimentary variables that one might ordinarily suppose area must be computed from. The value of the planimeter as a metaphor for perceptual systems is that it permits the conceptual dissociation of detection and computation. Specifically, it demonstrates that a process can take time and yet not involve an explicit algorithm to mediate between antecedent states and the consequent state (area). Thus, by extension, the claim that higher-order invariants are embodied in neural activity does not require that those invariants shall have been derived from more elementary variables through a chain of calculations.

The radio was taken as another limited metaphor for the activity of perceptual systems. Here, the environment was said to "broadcast" information and the job of the perceptual system is to resonate to that information. Much information is broadcast and the perceptual system, like the radio, must attend to or tune in whatever is currently salient. Perception is thereby characterized as the controlled detection of information.

The control of detection, our new phrase for attention, is, in part, a manifestation of the algoristic basis of perception. That is, what information is detected is constrained by the needs and intentions of the perceiver. However, this role for the algorist is the role of selector of information, *not* creator or contributor.

Being able to tune in information is the consequence of two types of history: phylogeny and ontogeny. Evolving a sensitivity to informative invariants results in the genetic attunement to information. In addition, some animals can learn, in their lifetimes, to detect the meaning of other structured energies. It is for understanding the ecological interpretation of "learning to detect meaning" that we called upon a third metaphor. Evolution was asked to do double duty, first as the route for genetic preattunement, and second, as a model for learning without memory storage. In brief, it was claimed that the consequences of learning should be conceptualized the same way we conceptualize the consequences of evolution. Just as we need not call upon notions of storage and retrieval to account for evolutionary success, we need not call upon notions of storage and retrieval to account for the effects of past experiences on current behavior. Certainly the animal may change as a consequence of experience, but we view that change not as accumulation of knowledge, but as a keener ability to detect the affordances of the environment.

Chapter 5. The mutual compatibility between animal and environment is the hallmark of the ecological approach. In Chapter 5 we explored some of the philosophical implications of animal-environment mutuality and synergy. This mutuality provides necessary support for the realist's claim that animals know the real world. It undercuts arguments against veridicality because it demands a description of information that is specific to the environment as it relates to the animal rather than a description in the animal-neutral variables of regular physics. Moreover, it makes the question of error in perception a nonissue: Perception is deemed "successful" insofar as it guides activity because acting on an environment is knowing that environment. Judgments that an error has occurred come from biases, human or theoretical, about what is happening or can happen in perception.

The synergy of animal and environment is also used to buttress the argument that describing the environment is within the legitimate domain of psychology *for those questions within the grain of psychology.* Physics and biology are, in turn, appropriate for describing physical and biological phenomena, respectively. Because psychology is concerned with perceiving and acting, reality—the environment—should be described at that grain, and such a description is necessarily animal-referential. A model was presented in which only horizontal (within-grain) and vertical (within-subsystem [animal or environment]) questions are deemed legitimate. Diagonal questions, which cross grain and subsystem, constitute category errors, and are, therefore, not legitimate scientific questions.

A new scientific attitude called evolutionism was offered as the rationale for the animal-environment fit. Put more strongly, it is the guarantee that perceiving-acting-knowing and reality are compatible. For an animal and environment to coexist it could not be otherwise. It takes the stance that perceiving-acting-knowing is not a matter of making propositions about the environment. It is simply a state of affairs, and, as such, can be neither true nor false: Just as an animal's physical characteristics stand in some kind of adaptive relation to the environment so, too, do its psychological characteristics or knowings. One is not a proposition about the other.

Chapter 6. In this chapter, we examined several applications in order to outline the ways in which the ecological approach affects perceptual theory and research. In general, before psychological theory comes to the point of experimentation, three issues must be settled. First, we must inquire as to what phenomena are to be investigated. Next, we must determine what questions need be asked of these phenomena. Finally, we must decide where to look for the answers. Much of the emphasis in the ecological approach deals with how these protoquestions are handled.

With respect to what constitutes a phenomenon worthy of investigation, the realist's emphasis is on ecological significance. We ask whether the phenomenon *clearly* bears on how an animal perceives and acts adaptively in its environment. Therefore, direct perception theorists are not likely to engage in the manufacture of phenomena. There is sufficient grist for the mill without contriving additional phenomena (e.g., tachistoscopic recognition).

However, even if ecological and traditional psychologists settle on the same phenomena as interesting, the questions they ask and the area in which they seek answers are different. For traditional psychologists, the system about which the questions are framed and within which the answers are sought is the animal, or, more precisely, in the computations and deductions that intervene between receptors and effectors. For ecological psychology, the questions and source of answers are in the animal-environment system. The theoretical *modus operandi* is to *identify the information* that supports the ability, and, ultimately, to determine how that information is detected.

Assuming that traditional psychology and ecological psychology can both, in time, answer the questions they pose, the psychologist's choice of metatheory—traditional or ecological—will be based on the integrity of the questions. In Chapter 6, we illustrated the kinds of theoretical questions that emerge from the ecological approach.

This general orientation toward theory and research was illustrated by three examples from the ecological movement. First, our concern with the phenomena of binocular vision is motivated by its relevance to the kind of information needed by animals with frontal binocularity. For example, predators can detect the position of prey without using head or body movements that might frighten prey. The information that supports this ability was sought, not in the comparison of two anatomically separate images, but in the (spatial) transformations of the binocular array that specify properties—for example, three-dimensionality—of objects.

Our second example focused on phenomena of face perception insofar as they might answer the question "what is a face?" It was suggested that the answer to this question was to be found within the constraints of the biological forces to which living, growing objects are subject. In contrast to conventional endeavors that limit the investigation of face perception to static features, the ecological emphasis is on the *transformations* or changes that are intrinsic to the nature of faces.

Finally, the inclusion of an account of coordinated activity is a departure from what is traditionally held to be a matter of interest to perception theories. The question of how activity is regulated was shown to lie in the realm of how perception constrains action. Indeed, all of the themes of ecological realism seem to converge in a theory of action. Information that is unique and specific to its environmental source and that is at a grain meaningful for an animal was shown to constrain the form and timing of activity without recourse to mediating plans or programs. Such apparent "control" was viewed as the natural consequence of the dynamics of complex systems.

DIRECT AND INDIRECT: A RECONCILIATION?

Many of those who write on the topic of perception gratefully acknowledge *research* by Gibson. Moreover, much ecological research can be translated rather handily into traditional language; for example:

> One can grant this point readily enough; it is evident that complex stimulus attributes such as texture, perspective, movement, and disparity gradients exist, and that they are effective as purely visual *cues* . . . . (Dodwell, 1970, p. 206, italics added)

(Here information is demoted to the status of a hint or signal; the term "cue" has no home at all in ecological theory.) Whether ecological *theory* can stand alongside and peacefully coexist with traditional theory is quite another matter. In our view, such a marriage—or even détente—would not work for several reasons.

First, the two positions take as their theoretical objectives two very different goals. For the traditional school, the object of study is a process inside the animal, beginning with receptors and ending with effectors. In the ecological approach, the object of study is in the relationship between the perceiver and what is perceived: the ecosystem.

Second, the two positions may not even agree on what the subject matter of psychology should be. Recall from Chapter 5 that traditionalists reserve psychological terms for certain processes going on, again, inside the animal. The ecological approach, especially as described by Shaw and Turvey, supposes that psychology is a particular scale of analysis of phenomena.

The importance of these distinctions to the reconciliation of the approaches bears on the role of environment in the theory of perception. For traditionalists, there is the implicit doctrine that the environment is the business of physicists, and is of little concern to one who wants to describe the processing rules relating receptor input to effector output. For ecological psychologists, the environment is an integral part of the system in which perception resides.

On this view, we must reject any suggestion that direct perception might account for certain lower-order perceptual abilities while a mediational theory is required to explain fancy perceptual abilities such as those entailed in speech perception or reading. Nor can we accept the view that ecological psychology is a theory of what is processed while "information processing" is a theory of how it is processed. Implicit in this latter view is the idea that the two endeavors—identifying information and determining how it is detected—can proceed independently. As we have emphasized throughout, a theory of *how* presupposes a theory of *what*. Moreover, neither theory can be developed with indifference as to *who* is doing the perceiving.

This last point bears repeating as it is often overlooked in criticisms of the ecological approach. The long-overdue attention that Gibson and his followers have paid to the role of the environment has been misconstrued by some critics to indicate that the animal plays no role in the theory. Some have even gone so far as to say that Gibson's is no more than a "black box" account of perceiving (Krueger, 1980)! Such an interpretation is puzzling in light of the emphasis which ecological psychologists place on the mutuality, compatibility, and reciprocity that characterize the animal-environment system. Indeed, this approach is unique in that it is mindful that the *particular animal* cannot be ignored by general theories that purport to apply to all possible circumstances.

The heart of the matter is whether two frameworks—one that approaches perception as a phenomenon in an animal and one that approaches perception as a phenomenon in an animal-environment system—are reconcilable. We believe they are not. Indeed, the gulf between the two camps is so large that often one feels that the other is, at best, oblivious to what the *real* problems of perception are. Unfortunately, the schism in metaphysics often manifests itself as sanctimonious disdain—in both directions.

THE FUTURE OF THE ECOLOGICAL APPROACH

While the ecological approach may in time leave its mark on all of psychology, we have limited our presentation to its origins in perception. Even at that, we have discussed some perceptual phenomena only briefly, and others we have omitted entirely. This coverage reflects the order of business as it has been carried out by ecological psychologists and is not meant to imply that the potential scope of the approach has been exhausted. New areas have recently been attacked within the ecological framework, and others await concentrated investigation. The following discussion of the outstanding issues is divided into three parts, reflecting the informational, the algorithmic, and the algoristic bases of perceiving-acting-knowing.

The Informational Basis. This part of the ecological program identifies the invariants that support perception. Ecological psychologists who have sought to identify information, most notably Gibson himself, have concentrated attention on visual information. While strides have been made on this problem, a great deal of work remains to be done. It is not the case, however, that understanding the informational support for vision will or should be the central focus of the ecological program. The emphasis is always on animals as knowing beings, not just seeing beings. Indeed, Gibson's second book includes chapters on the basic orienting system, the auditory system, the haptic-somatic system, taste and smell as well as vision. The information detected by all perceptual systems is to be understood within the framework of ecological psychology.

For example, attention is now being turned to an investigation of the nature of information that specifies events with acoustic consequences. As with vision, it is expected that useful information is not to be found in elementary physical variables such as frequency, intensity, and timbre, but in the higher-order structure of complex acoustic patterns. Again, information is being sought which is unique and specific to its source—both to the object participating in the event and to the nature of the event itself.

The acoustic array, just like the optic array, arises from the ways in which surfaces structure the medium. During an event, an object set into vibration resonates at a range of frequencies characteristic of its size, shape, thickness, and density. The series of air pressure waves so produced is the acoustic array. As suggested in the analysis of melody presented in Chapter 2, complex temporal relationships among acoustic components may constitute information for the identity of an event. This kind of information has been demonstrated to be of value in identifying musical instruments by their sounds, for example (Saldanha & Corso, 1964). Higher-order relations defined over time (e.g., complex changes in frequency and amplitude) have also been investigated as information for distinguishing breaking from bouncing (Warren, 1980) and for the perception of the velocity and distance of objects passing by (Warlick, 1978). It is assumed that similar analyses will reveal the information relevant to events such as rolling, sliding, exploding, and so on.

Again, as with vision, care is taken to examine the acoustic array *as it relates to the activities of the hearer.* The compatibility of acoustic information and activity is not a one-way street. That is, it is not only to information that we look for a basis for activity; we also look to activity to provide a basis for information. This latter direction is illustrated by emerging attempts to identify the information for speech perception. A brief description of one such attempt should serve to convey the flavor of this general endeavor.

From the ecological perspective, an appreciation both of the coordinated activity that is speech and event perception, in general, is fundamental to an understanding of the perception of speech events. These two emphases provide the guidelines for the ecological approach to speech currently underway by Verbrugge, Rakerd, Fitch, Tuller, & Fowler (to be published).

In keeping with the principles of motor coordination as outlined in Chapter 6, the articulatory gestures for a particular phoneme are expected to reveal a common organization in the face of context-conditioned variability. For example, the phoneme /d/ is expected to have a common articulatory organization in spite of changes in tongue position that accompany different vowels. The first ecological attack on speech, then, is the determination of how phoneme identity is preserved in the organization of the act. In Verbrugge and associates' terms, this is identifying the nature of the source event. The next step in this attack is to ask how the medium—air— is structured in a way specific to that articulatory organization. It is expected that for a particular phoneme, any one of its acoustic invariants is a manifestation of a common, underlying constraint. For example, variations in frequency transitions are expected to be specific to the controlling constraint. The final stage of this proposed strategy for investigating speech is the perceptual: It asks which of the invariants specifying the organization of the speaker's articulations are detected by listeners. Of course, one might want to couple this with questions about how the auditory system is organized so as to detect these invariants.[1]

The ecological approach to speech perception does not begin with vibrations at the eardrum; it begins with an examination of speech production. What are the coordinative structures in speech? How are they tailored by context? How do the constraints on production engender acoustic patterns that are specific to those constraints? Do perceivers detect them? How?

As Verbrugge and his colleagues point out, there are obvious parallels between this strategy for speech and the Shaw and Pittenger strategy for faces (see Chapter 6): How do physical and biological forces remodel a

---

[1]Emphases on the articulatory basis of speech perception are, of course, not new. However, the usual attack is on phoneme constancy (hearing a particular phoneme despite variation in the acoustic array). For example, it has been noted that the portion of a speech signal that "is" /d/ (the second formant transition) varies with different vowel contexts (Liberman, Delattre, & Cooper, 1952). Phoneme constancy, then, becomes an achievement of the nervous system; according to the motor theory, perceivers use their knowledge of articulation to decode the signal (Liberman, Cooper, Shankweiler, & Studdert-Kennedy, 1967). The difference between this emphasis on articulation and the ecological is clear. For the motor theorist, articulatory mechanisms *inside the perceiver* are thought to be the basis of phoneme constancy. For the ecological theorist, the articulatory organization *inside the speaker*, together with its accompanying acoustic invariants, are thought to be the basis of phoneme constancy or, more simply, phoneme perception.

head over time? What structuring of the medium (light) specifies that re-modeling? Are those invariants perceptually salient?

The Algorithmic Basis of Perceiving. Ecological psychologists readi-ly admit that "explaining" perception by specifying invariants with no reference to how these invariants might be detected is not a full expla-nation. Indeed, our own descriptions of how information is detected are largely metaphoric. Inattention to these algorithmic concerns, however, is a problem of resources rather than a systematic bias against the importance of that particular class of scientific questions. Ecological psychologists recognize that the identification of the algorithms that are embodied in living tissue is a necessary part of a full theory of knowing. Unfortunately, the most the ecological approach can offer the neurophysiologist of today is a set of orientations toward what kinds of things to look for (e.g., single-step algorithms embodied in neural circuits) and what kinds of things not to look for (e.g., representations of the world embodied in tissue).

The kind of program of theory and research that the ecological ap-proach invites is one that considers not merely perception, but perception-action. Given the identification of some perceptual information and the activity that this information organizes, the theorist would attempt to de-termine the algorithms that could account for that organization. Simplisti-cally viewed, if X is information put into the machine and Y is the output act, what mathematical function relates Y to X? After determining this, one would ask how this algorithm might be embodied in the organization of receptors, neurons, muscle fibers, and bones that is an animal.

In short, this endeavor asks how a psychological description of an animal relates to a biological description. Put another way, how might a living system with a particular roster of qualities be organized so as to dis-play that which is called, at a coarser grain, perception-action?

The Algorist. While the algorithmic and informational bases of knowing require much theorizing and experimenting in the decades to come, the algoristic basis will require much more. A good measure of philo-sophical thinking will be needed just to generate the questions about the essential nature of a knowing agent that theory and experiment will ad-dress. It is not that the problem is a new one; it is not. Nevertheless, the problem has often been avoided, perhaps because of the apparent recalci-trance of the problems of purpose and intentionality for a science trying to deal with observables.

However, in the face of the seemingly obvious truths that knowing implies someone who knows, and that what is known and how it is known cannot be indifferent to who knows, the time has come to squarely face these issues. Psychologists who are hesitant to tread on this *terra incognita* or who feel that the ecological psychologists' "obvious truths" above are misty or spiritual exhortations should recognize that similar exhortations have been coming from the other side of science. Quantum mechanics has its own "algorist problems" in trying to understand what it means to *observe*. Shaw and McIntyre (1974) quote Wigner (1970):

> ... the basic concept in the epistemological structure of physics is the concept of observation and ... psychology is not yet ready for providing concepts and idealizations of such precision as are expected in mathematics or even physics. (p. 37)

Even though algoristic issues seem to be an indispensable part only of ecological psychology, they are rearing their heads in the writing of many outside of the ecological movement (e.g., Dennett, 1969; Fodor, 1979). The work of these thinkers will undoubtedly influence the ecological theorists as they build upon "The algoristic foundations to cognitive psychology," the seminal paper by Shaw and McIntyre (1974) summarized in Chapter 4.

The Harmony of Informational, Algorithmic, and Algoristic. Our division of this section into what, how, and who subsections does not mitigate the argument that the investigation of one area can be done with indifference to the other areas. For an invariant to qualify as information, it must be detectable by algorithms instantiated in living tissue and it must in some way guide the activities of the animal. For a particular algorithm to be instantiated in tissue, it must be tailored to the available information and it must satisfy the needs of the organism or, more generally, the requirements of life (e.g., a cost-effective utilization of energy). For an animal to be a goal-directed perceiver-actor, its needs and behaviors must be compatible with the affordances of the environment and they must be compatible with the algorithms realizable in tissue.

To summarize the ecological position, the phenomena of knowing are to be understood only by an holistic science that acknowledges that these phenomena exist in animal-environment systems and not merely in animals. In short, ecological psychology demands that both animal terms— who and how—and compatible environment terms—what—be included in any account of the phenomena exhibited by the system.

Appendix:
Discussion and Debate

In this appendix we attempt to answer questions and speak to criticisms that have been (1) raised by readers of drafts of this book, (2) raised by readers of earlier works on ecological psychology or, quite frankly, (3) raised by us to provide an occasion to fill in some missing links.

1. *Regarding the distinction between rich and impoverished stimulation that is used to contrast theories of direct and indirect perception, is it not the case that sometimes the input is rich and sometimes it is impoverished? Thus, does not the distinction bear more on two different conditions of perceiving than two different theories of perception?*

Two assumptions force the rich-impoverished distinction squarely on theoretical terrain, and to the extent that one embraces those assumptions, the distinction becomes far more than simply one of mere circumstance. The first is the assumption that impoverished inputs are typical of normal stimulation. The second is that perceptual systems operate the same way under the two conditions, or, put another way, that detecting impoverished data is representative of, or even a subset of, detecting more elaborate information. Let us summarize our objections to both of these assumptions.

For knowledge of the environment to be possible, information specifying that environment—"rich" information—must be *potentially* available. So the distinction between rich and impoverished stimulation is a matter of how much of the *potential* information becomes *actual* (or detected). The theorist who supposes that most or even some input is impoverished must specify the constraints that prevent potential information from becoming actual information. There is no doubt that constraints can be applied; experimenters often do so with brief exposures, Maxwellian peepholes, and blindfolds. But the question is whether the legitimacy of using such constraints can be defended. Are there naturally occurring circumstances in which an intact animal is prevented from engaging in activities that make potential information actual? The existence and frequency of such situations must be demonstrated to justify the use of constraints on information in the laboratory.

Even if such a justification of "legitimate constraint" were possible, would it necessarily follow that the perceptual activities revealed in the detection of impoverished inputs bears on the detection of more elaborate information? We think not. On our assumption that perceptual systems evolved to detect higher-order properties of stimulation, we must deny that detecting lower order, and perhaps, "impoverished" properties is constitutive of perceiving. A major thrust of the theory is that higher-order variables (e.g., optical expansion) are not calculated from or deduced from lower-order variables (e.g., momentary image size).

Our objections to the two assumptions—that of "legitimate constraint" and that registering lower-order variables is part of registering higher-order ones—might be made clearer by returning once again to Runeson's (1977) polar planimeter analogy (Chapter 4). We noted that the planimeter, an area-measuring device, *can* be constrained, by fixing the angle, to act as a length-measuring device. However, these latter measurements are not accurate. Now, what would one say to the physics student who, on the pretense of attempting to describe how the planimeter works, always constrains it and always uses it to measure length? Unfortunately, the constraint changes the nature of the machine and measuring length is *not* constitutive of measuring area. To be sure, the student is studying *something* and a variety of reliable results might emerge. But the something that is under study is a machine that cannot operate as it was meant to, measuring a variable it was not meant to measure.

In sum, then, we would answer that "impoverished input" is a theory of "stimulus" insofar as theorists take those circumstances to be justifiably constrained, and that the "cognitive operations" revealed by them are demonstrated to be part of the act of perceiving (see also Question 5).

In the absence of this justification and this demonstration, labeling impoverished stimuli as mere circumstances obscures theory.

2. *Isn't the account of the information processing approach presented in Chapter 1 oversimplified? Isn't it an easily criticized "straw-man" theory that any experimental psychologist would decry?*

There is no doubt that information processing psychologists would claim that their approach has been presented here in caricature, at best. At worst, we might be accused of wholly misrepresenting the approach. Indeed, many of the ideas attributed to them would be earnestly and honestly denied. For example, no one would explicitly claim that animals evolved to be sensitive to impoverished inputs. However, that doesn't mean that we have fabricated such a notion; it seems implicit both in theory and in research. To believe that species evolved and to believe that visual systems detect features of an image (which are necessarily nonspecific to the facts of the world) amounts to believing that animals evolved sensitivity to uninformative properties of stimulation.

One problem is that psychologists, like most scientists, rarely, if ever, make their metatheory explicit. To our knowledge, there is not a book or an article that puts forth the philosophical underpinnings of contemporary experimental psychology. The analysis presented in this book had to cull metaphysics from experiments and theory. But we do not believe that the metaphysics attributed to traditional psychology departs in any fundamental way from that which the dead hand of habit has carried into contemporary science.

To be sure, the puzzles presented by information processors are thrilling, and many of the solutions are ingenious and elegant. But the quality of an answer does not evidence the quality of a question.

Therefore, the charge to information processing theorists is to make explicit the origins of their questions, not allowing tradition or language to be the arbiter of the ontological status of hypothesized entities. Such an exposition is really the prior condition to arguing that ecological psychologists create "straw-men." We ask, simply, to be shown the real men.

3. *How can the information processing approach be called "traditional"?*

The information processing approach takes the high-speed digital computer as its model of the activity of the nervous system and is willing to talk of the organism's knowledge. In those ways, it stands apart from most historical traditions. Nevertheless, it partakes of traditional meta-theory in that its central question, handed down from Müller, is how animals might infer the world from the states of their nerves. We claim that the question can be described as traditional when contrasted with a meta-theory that denies that the brain draws inferences from the deliveries of the senses, and asserts that perceptual systems detect the affordances of the environment.

4. How does ecological theory, with its denial of "computation" and "intermediaries," explain the existence of feature detectors?

To accept the proposition that feature detectors exist is to subscribe to an entire theoretical position that we have up to now rejected. To re-phrase the question: How can it be that parts of a biological machine which directly registers higher-order invariants appear to register lower-order properties?

The polar planimeter can again provide an intuitive answer. Watching the planimeter in use, one might notice that the wheel rolls forward under certain conditions and backward under others. One might even contrive a mechanical "microelectrode" in an effort to determine the conditions under which the wheel rolls the fastest or furthest. Those conditions could, no doubt, be determined. But it is an unjustifiable theoretical leap to claim that these are the data from which the planimeter computes area. Skidding, rolling, and angle are not features extracted by a planimeter; their existence is only *incidental* to the act of measuring area.

Quite obviously, the suggestion is that "feature detectors" have the same incidental status. They are the artifacts of a technology and a set of assumptions about what perception involves.[1]

5. How can one deny the existence and importance of iconic memory?

As anyone familiar with tachistoscopes knows, it's all done with mirrors. If by iconic memory one means the brief persistence of neural activity that follows the end of a bright, brief exposure, iconic memory certainly exists. And, if by important one means necessary for a par-tial- over whole-report superiority in a poststimulus sampling experiment

---

[1]There is a further problem with feature detectors that concerns the entire strategy of trying to relate perceptual activity to properties of individual neurons. For a summary of the logical paradoxes that such a view entails, the reader is referred to John and Schwartz (1978).

(e.g., Sperling, 1960), it is important. Usually, however, psychologists would want to say a great deal more, explicitly or implicitly, about iconic memory. Such statements might be that iconic memory is a *purposive* store; its role is to maintain the input while the slower processes of attention and pattern recognition are brought to bear. Or, that iconic memory is the first stage in the information processing system, the first step in the act of perceiving. Statements of this latter sort are the sources of objection.

Once again, the distinction that needs to be drawn is between processes that are part of the act of perceiving and processes that are incidental to that act. That is to say, some responses that can be evoked from a perceptual system are an integral part of that system's activity, while other responses simply reveal properties of the structures that support perceiving (Turvey, 1977a).

As an example of a property of the structural support of perceiving, consider pressure phosphenes. If people press on their eyes they will have a visual experience. Presumably, the pressure stimulates receptor cells. Do we want to claim that these color phosphenes are constituents of the normal course of perceiving; that, for example, light causes pressure that, in turn, fires receptors? Surely not. Rather, neural stimulation from pressure happens to be a property of a device necessary for visual perception (receptor) but not a property of perception itself.

Iconic memory should be accorded the same status as pressure phosphenes. Under a particular set of circumstances (tachistoscopic exposure), certain cells demonstrate a property (persistence of firing). But this property has no more claim to being part of perception than pressure phosphenes. Both persistence and pressure sensitivity are incidental properties of eyeballs and not constitutive parts of seeing.

6. *It has been argued that the psychologist, as contrasted with the physicist, is concerned with the way in which different activity affects the organism's "knowledge system." A psychologist is not concerned with how the environment structures energy. That question is irrelevant to perception.*

Notice how closely the question identifies perception with a process inside the animal, an identification with which we should take issue on the basis of our objection to animal-environment dualism.

We are reminded of a story cited by Shaw (1971) in which archeologists from another planet arrive on earth when humans are extinct. They discover a clock whose hands have been broken off. These aliens want to understand the clock—how it works, what it is for. Their examination leads to an understanding of all the mechanics of the device, even to the point that they could build an identical device. But in spite of the elegance of their science, we would have to ask what these beings understand of clocks, for the essential nature of the device is unknown to them. Unless these scientists, by systematic or random search, note the activities of the celestial body whose motion the clock chronicles, that essential nature will be ignored. Put another way, to understand the device, we must not only understand how it does it, but *what it does.*

Confining investigation to the intrinsic workings of a device, be it clock or brain, omits the central rationale for its structure and function. The questions of *why* are not to be answered by looking *within.* As Mace (1977) puts it, "Ask not what's inside the head, but what the head is inside of." The reasons for structure and functioning, both psychological and biological, are to be found, at least in part, in an analysis of the environment in which they exist and upon which they operate. And in the absence of physicists who seek to describe the world in ways commensurate with animals, the job falls by default to the psychologist.

7. John Locke drew a distinction between primary and secondary qualities. Primary qualities are those that are inherent in objects (e.g., size, shape, solidity, number, motion), while secondary qualities are properties of objects that are nothing in the objects themselves, but powers to produce sensations such as color, taste, and so on.

While it may make sense to claim that primary qualities are directly perceived; isn't it nonsense to claim that secondary properties are directly perceived? After all, the qualities are not in the object so they cannot be in the stimulation.

To accept Locke's distinction is to open the door to a host of problems for both ecological and traditional psychology. It was this distinction that later permitted Berkeley to cut the knot connecting mind and reality and to deny the existence of matter as such while affirming the reality of mind. This, in turn, left the door open for Hume to deny the existence of mind. But no matter. We prefer to dispense with the distinction, not for its ontological consequences, but because it partakes of— and, indeed, is a showcase of—animal-environment dualism.

The distinction drawn by Locke requires that we begin with some catalog of properties of our ideas about objects. Next, one must decide which of those ideas "resemble" the thing itself (e.g., perceived shape resembles actual shape) and which ideas do not resemble the thing itself (e.g., a sensation of pain does not resemble a pin-prick). To the extent that we cannot believe the pain to be "in" the pin, pain is accorded the status of a secondary quality—something the pin has the power to produce.

There is so much that an ecological theorist would take issue with that we scarcely know where to start. Perhaps the most fundamental premise to which we would object is that objects have certain properties while ideas about objects have certain other properties. At issue for us is not so much whether the object in the head (idea) and the object in the world have different properties, but whether it makes sense to consider them as two objects.

To explain what it means to consider the real object and the object of perception as a single object, we shall create three categories and then eliminate one and draw the other two together. We might loosely characterize the three as the animal-neutral object, the animal-referential object, and the perceptual object. By animal-object, we mean what is usually called the "real" object. By animal-referential we mean the object defined with reference to an animal. By perceptual object we mean the object as perceived. So descriptions of the three objects might be, respectively: object 1, having a circumference of 10 cm; object 2, sized to be graspable by a human hand because of the compatibility of the object with human effectivities (intention to grasp, anatomical configuration permitting grasping, appropriately sized hand); and object 3, the object perceived as graspable.

We suppose that activity called *knowing* relates two of these objects. But which two? We think that most epistemology, Locke's included, seeks to relate object 1 to object 3. But as we have said elsewhere in a different way, object 1 is a fiction, at least as far as epistemology is concerned, in that its properties are not relevant to the survival of animals. Perforce, knowledge of object 1 cannot be taken as a reasonable consequence of evolution. (Object 1 may be an ontological fiction in that the act of describing an object in an animal-neutral way requires an animal—a describer—and so the description is not animal-neutral at all.)

The ecological approach might start with the assumption that knowing is a relationship between object 2 and object 3. But the properties of the two are the same. Object 2 is the collection of behaviors (affordances) that might be entered into by an animal with a collection of effectivities. Object 3 is the collection of effectivities that is compatible with the affordances of the environment. Thus, object 2 and object 3 become two sides of a coin; from the environment's perspective on the animal, the animal has certain effectivities. From the animal's perspective on the environment, the environment has certain affordances.

Returning to Locke, then, it is claimed that the properties of objects and the properties of ideas about objects are not different. The apparent difference rests on the neutrality of the description with reference to an animal.

8. *How can the ecological approach account for experiential dimensions of hedonic tone (humor, pleasure, amusement) that appear to have no physical stimulus referents?*

The invariants must be very higher-order indeed.

9. *Regarding higher- and lower-order invariants, what rule specifies "the ordering of abstract properties all of which, one would think, are equally abstract in their description"?* (Kolers, 1978)

Frankly, we do not know. It is quite fair to claim that we are far too casual in the use of the terms higher-order and lower-order. While we do not believe that these concepts are wholly unintuitive, the development of an explicit rule (perhaps based on dimensionality from topology or order of derivatives in calculus) is an important project for ecological psychologists in the next few years.

10. *After all, the retinal image is the input for vision. It is not satisfactory to demonstrate that the optic array has information.*

When the pattern of light on the receptor surface is conceived of as an *image,* a variety of intractable pseudoproblems emerge. Perhaps the following contrasts will make this point clear. An image is something that is seen (but *who* is doing the looking?); structured light does not imply someone (a homunculus, perhaps) looking at it. An image is a two-dimensional surface, and, therefore, one is inclined to describe it in Euclidean geometry. One feels less constrained in description by considering structured light that *happens to be* detected by two-dimensional surfaces over time. An image implies something static; structured light is more easily conceived of as dynamic. Retinal images seem to imply the stimulation of particular receptors; structured light suggests something that might be felt, as a hand might feel texture, and so on.

The central issue concerns what is seen. Image languages suggest that *images,* with all their ambiguities as described in Chapter 1, are seen, while the more ecological terms invite a notion that the *world* is seen.

11. *It is difficult to conceive of how the structure of the optic array specifies the layout of environmental surfaces. Doesn't one need a concept like image?*

One way to think about the structure of the light without reference to something like an image is to think about how structured *sound* might specify the layout of surfaces. Just as radiated light is structured by the process of reflection, radiated sound can be structured. For example, bats have taken advantage of this fact in their use of echolocation. They emit sounds which are reflected or absorbed by surfaces in the surrounds (see Figure 8-1). The patterns of structured energy arriving at the bat's ear constitute an acoustic array, just as structured light to an eye constitutes an optic array. Both contain information about the layout of environmental surfaces.

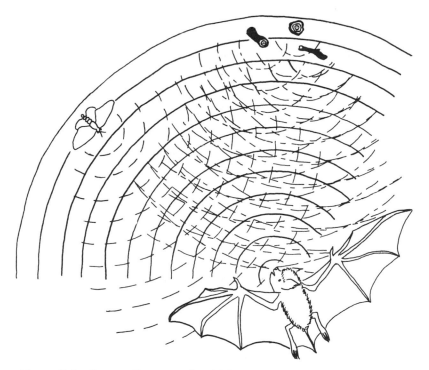

Figure 8-1. Bats radiate sounds which are structured by the process of reflection off environmental surfaces. The resulting acoustic structure specifies the environment sufficiently to guide the bat's flying, the capturing of prey, and so on. Structured sound, then, serves the same role for bats that structured light serves for humans.

The methods of detecting the layout of surfaces from the bat's acoustic array and the human's optic array are, of course, quite different. In the auditory case there is no image; the bat's auditory system registers the three-dimensional character of the world from energy structure, not from an image or picture of the world.

The nature of the information for echolocation illustrates the distinction we desire—that between structured energy and images. A bat's auditory system clearly detects the former, and the theory of direct perception argues that visual systems do, too.

12. Consider the Necker cube (Figure 8-2). We perceive a cube even though the figure is patently two-dimensional. What is the information specifying the third dimension?

First, one must be careful in phrasing. If one *really* perceives a cube, he or she must wonder how this book could possibly close properly. It is more accurate to claim that a picture (projection or image) of a wire cube is perceived. It is unambiguously specified as flat because the responses in the optic array to certain transformations (e.g., motion or the binocular rotation) are unique to flat surfaces. So the question is what is the information that specifies that the object pictured is three-dimensional.

The attention of many, but not all, human perceivers has been educated to the invariant relation between *edges* and *lines*. An edge, of course, is the boundary of two surfaces, and insofar as two surfaces are not coplanar, the edge is three-dimensional and the *information* a line provides, in specifying the boundary of regions, specifies three dimensions.

An ecological account would claim that there exists, in this figure, information about a large number of shapes. The perceiver merely selects

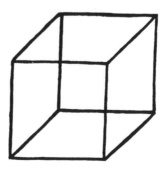

Figure 8-2. A Necker cube.

one; his or her attention is directed to that information. The perceiver is in no sense creating the third dimension, only attending to information about one of many specified three-dimensional shapes.

13. *Most investigations in scientific disciplines put forward arguments that are subject to test. Is it not true that ecological arguments do not fall into that category?*

Ecological psychology, like traditional psychology, puts forward both testable and nontestable assertions. A testable assertion for information processing might be that iconic memory lasts from .25 to 4 sec. A testable assertion for ecological psychology might be that cardioidal strain provides information about age. The assertions that are not subject to test might be that the animal is the proper unit of analysis for perception or, conversely, that the animal-environment system is the proper unit. It is the metatheory that is untestable in the usual sense. It is unfair to criticize ecological psychology for making its metatheory explicit while lauding the testability of information processing assertions whose metatheory is left tacit.

14. *Does the emphasis on rich stimulation mean that experimentation in the spirit of Gibson's theory does not allow that information be reduced to its bare essentials?*

Not at all. It is wrong to suppose that natural viewing conditions are prerequisites for any experiment. Imagine, for example, that one wants to understand how the light to the eyes might specify the flight of the ball and, thus, where a perceiver should be to intercept it. Presumably, one could generate a roster of invariants (e.g., rate of optical expansion of the texture of the ball, rate of occlusion of the optical texture of the background, change in rate of expansion, etc.). Clearly, a process of elimination to bare essentials would be an apt method for determining which optical properties constitute information.

The ecological approach simply encourages one not to make gratuitous assumptions about the information specifying the event. It encourages the seeking of dependent variables that have ecological relevance as well. Thus, an ecological psychologist would not ask perceivers to estimate the rate of optical expansion in degrees per second, they would be asked to catch balls.

The point is, simply, that great care must be exercised in whittling down a complex perceptual event to its essentials, lest the phenomenon of interest itself disappears.

15. *How can ecological psychology account for phenomena in clinical neurology? "For instance, I once had a patient who, after a blow on the head, experienced episodes of vertigo during which the visual world went spinning. His major complaint was that every so often, when his perceptions again stabilized, they left him with the world upside down until the next vertigo which might right things once again."* (Pribram, 1977)

We would like to analyze this type of question rather than answer it because we can discern two underlying assumptions neither of which should go unchallenged. First, it is assumed that the brain is wholly responsible for perception and, second, it is assumed that ecological psychologists believe that the environment is wholly responsible for perception.

Given our commitment to animal-environment synergy, the second assumption must be false. Nowhere in the ecological approach is the claim that optical structure is *sufficient* for visual perception. Clearly, perceptual systems modulate information. If part of the system is malfunctioning, that modulation may be strange indeed.

But this type of question ignores the fact that optical structure modulates perceptual systems. Unless we are mistaken, the question tacitly assumes that the brain creates information (e.g., specifying that the world is upside-down) and, by extension, must create information about a right-side-up world. At issue is the nature of the responsibilities that the theorist should impart to the brain and, more generally, to perceptual systems. The ecological psychologist requires that they detect it; the passage above seems to require that they manufacture it.

16. *Why would one object to Pribram's (1977) formulation that portrays perception as both direct and constructional? The consequence of constructional processes is an image that is as much a product of information residing in the organism as it is of information in the environment. It is this constructed image that is directly perceived.*

This theory, which might appear as the best of both worlds in having an outer, indirect perceiver and an inner, direct perceiver, is really the worst of both worlds; it forfeits whatever logical leverage either position has. The outer perceiver falls prey to *all* the problems of a theory of indirect perception, and the inner perceiver is either unnecessary (if the affordances of the environment are instantiated in neural tissue, then why not take that instantiation to be knowledge itself rather than merely that *from which* knowledge is had) or subject to most of the criticisms levied against a *single,* direct perceiver.

But there is an even more fundamental problem: the entire concept of an internal image or representation. Why is it supposed that the world, or our actions upon it, *must* involve a representation, or image-of-achievement? What experimental evidence or philosophical argument requires the postulation of internal representations? It matters little whether the creation of an internal image involves mediation; the central question is whether there is an internal image at all. For if one argues for internal images, one must also argue that these images are (somehow) perceived. Why not suppose instead that whatever mechanisms perceive the image perceive the environment? The postulation of an internal image explains nothing; it merely pushes the problem of perceiving deeper into the nervous system. Asking how cortical images are perceived puts the theorist on no sturdier footing than asking how environmental events are perceived. It only shifts the problem.

17. *Do "traditional theorists" hold that any kind of perception is direct?*

Most theories seem to imply that tactile perception is direct. That vision is learned through touch, verified through touch, or calibrated by touch suggests that the haptic system has some sort of privileged access to information about what the world is *really* like. When we feel an object we feel the object. We know of no theorist who claims that when we feel an object we construct or compute the object from data on skin deformation, joint articulation, muscle length, muscle strain, and all of the other variables that could describe how the rigid/elastic form of the body interacts with objects over time.

It is ironic but true that if the same set of assumptions that are applied to vision were also applied to haptic perception, the theory of how we get from features to visual shape perception would be simple compared to how we might get *haptic* shape perception from a succession of images from the tip of an index finger that over time explores an object. Or, how enveloping the object in one or two hands might lead to the perception of the same shape. *There* is a constancy problem. Next to it, the "problem" of visual shape constancy pales to insignificance.

We know of no reason that one perceptual system should have evolved to perceive directly, while others evolved to perceive indirectly.

Nevertheless, traditional perceptual theory is either relying on that premise or has been remiss in not articulating the mechanisms of the mediation of haptic perception.

18. *"Direct" doesn't mean nonmediated, it means not roundabout. In direct-dialing, for example, no one would suggest that the problem of mechanism is avoided. Nor can it be argued that the message gets from one phone to another without mediation. What is really meant by the term direct?*

We certainly do not mean "direct" as in the "unmediated" phone-to-phone example cited; that is, we do not go along with Plato's notion that objects can be directly apprehended without reference to the senses. Rather we mean that the structure of environmental objects and events as they relate to a behaving animal is preserved in the energy patterns stimulating perceptual systems. The converse of this view, which we have attributed to more traditional theories, is that the structure of environmental objects and events is *lost* (in the light or at the receptor surface or in the stimulation) and must be restored by the brain.

19. *Ecological psychology rejects the idea that perception involves calculations on primitive variables. But if algorithms are found that produce straightforward solutions to perceptual problems based on these variables, how can you justify the assertion that they are not used? For example, isn't the size-distance invariance hypothesis a simple account of the phenomenon of size constancy?*

Assume, for the sake of argument, that the senses do detect primitive variables. Under this assumption, the tasks for evolution and learning would be to achieve (in the brain) the algorithms for imposing meaning upon the meager deliverances of the senses. It has been argued by Turvey and Shaw (1979), that the acquisition of the algorithms is, in essence, an impossibility. They claim that, in principle, it would be impossible to *acquire* certain concepts that are, of necessity, entailed in operations that convert ambiguous data into meaningful perceptions. To reiterate, the real issue is how such algorithms could arise initially.

The determination of the size-distance invariance algorithm, for example, *presupposes* the existence of a variety of other constancy algorithms (orientation constancy, shape constancy, etc.). That is to say, in order to determine the relationship of object size and distance to retinal image size, all else (e.g., orientation) must either be held constant (unlikely under natural circumstances) or be "corrected for" (e.g., by applying an orientation algorithm). But unfortunately, the acquisition of the orientation-to-image-size relationship itself presupposes the size-distance algorithm. It seems that to learn any constancy rule, one must already know the other constancy rules. These remarks apply both to evolutionary acquisition and learning. In sum, it seems that sensitivity to nonspecific input not only represents an improbable course for evolution, but also presents serious problems as to how the algorithms that convert nonspecific input into meaningful experience might have originated. Solutions to the problem of algorithmic origins end up begging the question—they presuppose the very processes they seek to explain.

20. *The ecological approach asks psychology to dispense with memory as stored representations. Instead of this reasonable concept, we are offered a radio metaphor and a notion of the education of attention. Aren't these concepts hard pressed to account for recognizing and remembering?*

First, it should be pointed out that *memory*—as conceived as traces of past experiences—is hard pressed to account for these phenomena. Theories of pattern recognition attempt to discern how an input contacts its representation in long-term memory. The kernel problem is to figure out how an input specifies the particular memory to be evoked and not some other memory. If we take a memory to be a stored representation of an environmental event, object, or place, the problem for the pattern recognition theorist is figuring out how the input specifies which object's, place's or event's representation is to be called up. But if the object, place, or event is specified with the precision required to call up the right memory, the entire concept of a stored representation becomes superfluous. That is to say, if the input specifies the representation, it specifies the event. And if the event is specified in the stimulation, it need not be contained in the head. On the other hand, if the input does not specify the representation, pattern recognition becomes an impossibility, for the input could find no match. Thus, if pattern recognition is possible, it is unnecessary.

On the other hand, if one were to assume that the memory does not faithfully represent the experience whose trace it is—i.e., that the trace is somehow unlike the event—then pattern recognition would be revived as a legitimate problem, but this assumption renders the trace useless, for how would one know to what the trace refers? Therefore, one would need another memory to associate the trace with the event. But such a solution is untenable in that it requires a second memory, and so on, to explain how the first memory works.

Thus, it is a mistake to suppose that dispensing with the notion of traces unties us from a firm anchor and casts us adrift with two flimsy concepts. We were quite adrift already.

Inasmuch as 3,000 years of thought on the matter have yielded a concept the essence of which is "that which accounts for remembering and recognizing," the demands put on ecological theory should not, at this point, be unnecessarily harsh. The ecological solution will capitalize on the event orientation of the approach, which has already had significant impact on research (e.g., Bransford et al., 1977). The reanalyses of the foundations of memory research by Jenkins (1977) and Turvey and Shaw (1979) are important beginnings of this capitalization.

21. *Hasn't much of the "revolutionary" ecological view been proffered by others before Gibson?*[2]

The lineage of the position presented here started with Gibson and is probably traceable to the influence of Walls's (1942) book, *The Eye and Its Adaptive Radiation,* on Gibson. Walls's book makes so clear that eyes are "ingenious" reflections of ecological niches that after reading it, one simply has to abandon the "here is the eye, how does it work" approach. Rather, the obvious diversity of visual systems demands attention to the environment and patterns of energy that shaped the structure and functioning of that system. Gibson's approach to the psychology of perception responded to that demand.

Nevertheless, the ecological approach that emerged in and in response to Gibson's thinking has been presaged in part by other psychologists. A number of theories include aspects that could be considered similar to ecological psychology in certain respects. Gestalt psychology is often mentioned in this regard, and Gibson himself admitted an intellectual debt to Koffka. This is most apparent, perhaps, in the latter's emphasis on the order in nature. The environment was presumed to be describable in terms of "things" (not points and lines) just as experience was describable in terms of *Gestalten,* rather than sensations (Koffka, 1935). But for Koffka, as we noted in Chapter 1, the order of nature was lost at the retina and had to be reconstituted by organizational processes in the brain. Because experience was thought to be isomorphic with the brain field, not the environment, Gestalt psychology is a theory of indirect, rather than direct, realism (Shaw & Turvey, in press).

[2]For a thorough answer to Question 21, the reader is referred to Lombardo (1973).

The ecological emphasis on ordinary perception has often been likened to Brunswik's (1956) argument that psychology should use *representative* designs involving only naturally occurring stimuli, rather than systematic designs which include stimuli that do not actually occur in life. Although not influential in the development of the ecological perspective, this assertion is not inconsistent with it. Parallels might also be drawn to Brunswik's notion of "distal focusing" insofar as it demonstrates a concern with environmental properties. The similarity is not strong, however, as Brunswik was interested in how a perceiver estimates distal values by using an internalized hierarchy of proximal cues (Postman & Tolman, 1959). Indeed, Brunswik's measure of *ecological validity* is motivated by the presumed slippage between distal and proximal.

The pragmatic bent of ecological psychology has antecedents in functionalism. In delimiting the tasks of functional psychology, Angell (1907) expressed an interest in "what mental processes *are for* rather than what they *are* .... [That is] how mental processes further the activities of the whole organism (Harrison, 1963, p. 400)." Early functionalism has been criticized, however, for its implicit psychophysical interactionism—i.e., that the psyche controls or causes behavior. The late phase of functionalism, epitomized by Carr (1930), deemphasized consciousness to focus on behaving as an adaptive device. Psychological reactions were taken to be ways of attaining successful adaptations to the environment.

One perspective closely in concert with ecological realism is naturalistic theory.

> If the naturalistic view that all science at bottom constitutes the observation of, and experimentation upon events, whether the interbehavior of two bodies (sun and earth, for example) or [of] an organism and a sound, must be called realism, then realism or metaphysics is simply another name for science. (Kantor, 1941)

Scholars who may be labeled naturalists oppose animal-environment dualism:

> A knower with nothing it knows, or a known without a knower to know it is absurd. (Bentley, 1941, p. 13)
>
> Our position is simply that since man as an organism has evolved in an evolution called "natural," we are willing under hypothesis to include all of his behavings, including his most advanced knowings, as activities not of himself alone, nor even as primarily his, but as processes of the full situation of organism-environment .... (Dewey & Bentley, 1949, p. 104)

They deny a dichotomy of perception and action:

> ... the meaning of the object, which may be very elaborate, though not attached directly to an immediate response, is most certainly acting. (Kantor, 1920, p. 200)

And, they emphasize pragmatic knowing:

> In seeking firm names [knowings], we do not assume that any name may be wholly right, nor any wholly wrong.... We take names always as namings: as living behaviors in an evolving world of men and things. (Dewey & Bentley, 1949, p. xii)

In spite of these stunning parallels, the common positions that have been arrived at by ecological psychologists and philosophical naturalists come from two very different intellectual routes.

References

Angell, J.R. The Province of Functional Psychology. *Psychological Review*, 1907, *14*, 61–91.

Arutyunyan, G.A., Gurfinkel, V.S., & Mirskii, M.L. Investigation of Aiming at a Target. *Biophysics*, 1968, *13*, 642–645.

Bentley, A.F. The Human Skin: Philosophy's Last Line of Defense. *Philosophy of Science*, 1941, *8*, 1–19.

Bernstein, N. *The Coordination and Regulation of Movements*. Elmsford, N.Y.: Pergammon Press, 1967.

Bolles, R.C. *Learning Theory*. New York: Holt, Rinehart, & Winston, 1975; 2nd ed., 1978.

Bransford, J.D., McCarrell, N.S., Franks, J.J., & Nitsch, K.E. Toward Unexplaining Memory. In R.E. Shaw & J. Bransford (Eds.), *Perceiving, Acting, and Knowing*. Hillsdale, N.J.: Lawrence Erlbaum Associates, 1977.

Brunswik, E. *Perception and the Representative Design of Psychological Experiments*. Berkeley, Calif.: University of California Press, 1956.

Bunge, M. *Philosophy of Physics*. Boston: Reidel, 1973.

Bunge, M. Levels and Reduction. *American Journal of Physiology*, 1977, *233*, R75–R82.

Carr, H.A. Functionalism. In C. Murchison (Ed.), *Psychologies of 1930*. Worcester, Mass.: Clark University Press, 1930.

Cherry, E.C. Some Experiments on the Recognition of Speech, With One and With Two Ears. *Journal of the Acoustical Society of America,* 1953, *25,* 975–979.

Cutting, J.E., & Koslowski, L.T. Recognizing Friends by Their Walk: Gait Perception without Familiarity Cues. *Bulletin of the Psychonomic Society,* 1977, *9,* 353–356.

Dennett, D.C. *Content and Consciousness.* New York: Humanities, 1969.

Dewey, J., & Bentley, A.F. *Knowing and the Known.* Boston: Beacon, 1949; Westport, Conn.: Greenwood, 1975.

Dodwell, P.C. *Visual Pattern Recognition.* New York: Holt, Rinehart, & Winston, 1970.

Duncker, K. [On Problem-Solving.] (trans. by L.S. Lees.) *Psychological Monographs,* 1945, *58,* 5.

Easton, T.A. On the Normal Use of Reflexes. *American Scientist,* 1972, *60,* 591–599.

Eimas, P.D., Siqueland, E.R., Jusczyk, P., & Vigorito, J. Speech Perception in Infants. *Science,* 1971, *171,* 303–306.

Elton, C. *Animal Ecology.* London: Sidgwick & Jackson, 1927.

Fitch, H., & Turvey, M.T. On the Control of Activity: Some Remarks from an Ecological Point of View. In B. Landers & R. Christina (Eds.), *Psychology of Motor Behavior.* Urbana, Ill.: Human Kinetics, 1978.

Fodor, J.A. *The Language of Thought.* Cambridge, Mass.: Harvard University Press, 1979.

Forgus, R.H., & Melamed, L.E. *Perception: A Cognitive-Stage Approach.* New York: McGraw-Hill, 1976.

Fowler, C.A., & Turvey, M.T. Skill Acquisition: An Event Approach with Special Reference to Searching for the Optimum of a Function of Several Variables. In G. Stelmach (Ed.), *Information Processing in Motor Control.* New York: Academic Press, 1978.

Fukuda, T. Studies in Human Dynamic Postures from the Viewpoint of Postural Reflexes. *Oto-Laryngologica,* 1961, Supplement 161.

Galper, R.E. Recognition of Faces in Photographic Negative. *Psychonomic Science,* 1970, *19,* 207–208.

Galper, R.E., & Hochberg, J.E. Recognition Memory for Photographs of Faces. *American Journal of Psychology,* 1971, *84,* 351–354.

Gel'fand, I.M., & Tsetlin, M.L. Some Methods of Control for Complex Systems. *Russian Mathematical Surveys,* 1962, *17,* 95–116.

Gibson, J.J. *The Perception of the Visual World.* Boston: Houghton Mifflin, 1950.

Gibson, J.J. The Concept of the Stimulus in Psychology. *American Psychologist,* 1960, *15,* 694–703.

Gibson, J.J. Ecological Optics. *Vision Research,* 1961, *1,* 253–262.

Gibson, J.J. *The Senses Considered As Perceptual Systems.* Boston: Houghton Mifflin, 1966.

Gibson, J.J. The Theory of Affordances. In R.E. Shaw & J. Bransford (Eds.), *Perceiving, Acting, and Knowing.* Hillsdale, N.J.: Lawrence Erlbaum Associates, 1977.

Gibson, J.J. *The Ecological Approach to Visual Perception.* Boston: Houghton Mifflin, 1979.

Greene, P.H. Problems of Organization of Motor Systems. In R. Rosen & E. Snell (Eds.), *Progress in Theoretical Biology* (Vol. 2). New York: Academic Press, 1972.

Gregory, R.L. *The Intelligent Eye.* New York: McGraw-Hill, 1970.

Gregory, R.L. *Eye and Brain: The Psychology of Seeing* (3rd ed.). New York: McGraw-Hill, 1978.

Grillner, S. Locomotion in Vertebrates: Central Mechanisms and Reflex Interaction. *Physiological Review,* 1975, *55,* 247–304.

Gross, C.G., Rocha-Miranda, C.E., & Bender, D.B. Visual Properties of Neurons in Infero-temporal Cortex of the Macaque. *Journal of Neurophysiology,* 1972, *35,* 96–111.

Haber, R.N., & Hershenson, M. *The Psychology of Visual Perception.* New York: Holt, Rinehart, & Winston, 1973.

Harrison, R. Functionalism and Its Historical Significance. *Genetic Psychology Monographs,* 1963, *68,* 387–423.

Hochberg, J.E. *Perception* (2nd ed.). Englewood Cliffs, N.J.: Prentice-Hall, 1978.

Hochberg, J., & Galper, R.E. Recognition of Faces: I. An Exploratory Study. *Psychonomic Science,* 1967, *9,* 619–620.

Holling, C.S. The Analysis of Complex Population Processes. *Canadian Entymologist,* 1964, *96,* 335–347.

Hubbard, A.W., & Seng, C.N. Visual Movements of Batters. *Research Quarterly,* 1954, *25,* 42–57.

Iberall, A.S. A Personal Overview, and New Thoughts on Biocontrol. In C.H. Waddington (Ed.), *Toward a Theoretical Biology* (Vol. 2). Chicago: Aldine, 1969.

Iberall, A.S. A Field and Circuit Thermodynamics for Integrative Physiology: I. Introduction to the General Notions. *American Journal of Physiology,* 1977, *233,* R171–R180.

Jenkins, J.J. Remember That Old Theory of Memory? Well, Forget It!. In R.E. Shaw & J. Bransford (Eds.), *Perceiving, Acting, and Knowing.* Hillsdale, N.J.: Lawrence Erlbaum Associates, 1977.

Johansson, G. Visual Perception of Biological Motion and a Model for its Analysis. *Perception and Psychophysics,* 1973, *14,* 201–211.

John, E.R., & Schwartz, E.L. The Neurophysiology of Information Processing and Cognition. In M.R. Rosensweig & L.W. Porter (Eds.),

Annual Review of Psychology (Vol. 29). Palo Alto: Annual Reviews, Inc., 1978.

Johnston, T., & Turvey, M.T.   A Sketch of an Ecological Metatheory for Theories of Learning. In G.H. Bower (Ed.), *The Psychology of Learning and Motivation* (Vol. 14). New York: Academic Press, 1980.

Kantor, J.R.   Suggestions Toward a Scientific Interpretation of Perception. *Psychological Review*, 1920, *27*, 191–216.

Kantor, J.R.   Current Trends in Psychological Theory. *Psychological Bulletin*, 1941, *38*, 29–65.

Kaufman, H.   *Perception: The Information Paradigm*. Book manuscript in preparation, 1978.

Koffka, K.   *Principles of Gestalt Psychology*. New York: Harcourt Brace Jovanovich, Inc., 1935.

Kolers, P.A.   Light Waves. *Contemporary Psychology*, 1978, *23*, 227–228.

Koslowski, L.T., & Cutting, J.E.   Recognizing the Sex of a Walker from a Dynamic Point-light Display. *Perception and Psychophysics*, 1977, *21*, 575–580.

Krueger, L.   Is There a Future for the Past? *Contemporary Psychology*, 1980, *25*, 110–111.

Kugler, P.N., Kelso, J.A.S., & Turvey, M.T.   On the Concept of Coordinative Structures as Dissipative Structures: I. Theoretical Lines of Convergence. In G.E. Stelmach & J. Requin (Eds.), *Tutorials in Motor Behavior*. Amsterdam: North Holland Publishing Co., 1980.

Kugler, P.N., & Turvey, M.T.   Two Metaphors for Neural Afference and Efference. *Behavioral and Brain Sciences*, 1978, *1*, 1.

Kugler, P.N., Turvey, M.T., & Shaw, R.E.   Is the "Cognitive Penetrability" Criterion Invalidated by Contemporary Physics? *Behavioral and Brain Sciences*, in press.

Kuhn, T.S.   *The Structure of Scientific Revolutions*. Chicago: University of Chicago Press, 1962.

Land, E.H.   The Retinex Theory of Color Vision. *Scientific American*, 1977, *237* (6), 108–128.

Lawicka, W.   The Role of Stimuli Modality in Successive Discrimination and Differentiation Learning. *Bulletin of the Polish Academy of Sciences*, 1962, *12*, 35–38.

Lee, D.N.   On the Functions of Vision. In H. Pick & E. Saltzman (Eds.), *Modes of Perceiving and Processing of Information*. Hillsdale, N.J.: Lawrence Erlbaum Associates, 1978.

Lee, D.N., Lishman, J.R., & Thompson, L.   Visual Guidance in the Long Jump. *Rep. 7th Ann. Coaches Conv.*, Edinburgh, 1976.

Lettvin, J., Maturana, H., McCulloch, W., & Pitts, W.S.   What the Frog's Eye Tells the Frog's Brain. *Proc. I.R.E.*, 1958, *47*, 1940–1951.

Liberman, A.M., Cooper, F.S., Shankweiler, D.P., & Studdert-Kennedy, M. Perception of the Speech Code. *Psychological Review,* 1967, *74,* 431–461.

Liberman, A.M., Delattre, P.C., & Cooper, F.S. The role of selected stimulus variables in the perception of unvoiced stop consonants. *American Journal of Psychology,* 1952, *65,* 497–516.

Lindsay, P.H., & Norman, D.A. *Human Information Processing* (2nd ed.). New York: Academic Press, 1977.

Lombardo, T. J.J. Gibson's Ecological Approach to Visual Perception: Its Historical Context and Development. (Doctoral Dissertation, University of Minnesota, 1973). University Microfilms No. 74–721.

Mace, W.M. James J. Gibson's Strategy for Perceiving: Ask Not What's Inside Your Head, But What Your Head's Inside Of. In R.E. Shaw & J. Bransford (Eds.), *Perceiving, Acting, and Knowing.* Hillsdale, N.J.: Lawrence Erlbaum Associates, 1977.

McNeill, D. *The Acquisition of Language.* New York: Harper & Row, Pub., 1970.

Maier, N.R.F. An Aspect of Human Reasoning. *British Journal of Psychology,* 1933, *24,* 144–155.

Mark, L.S. A Transformational Approach Toward Understanding the Perception of Growing Faces. Unpublished doctoral dissertation, University of Connecticut, 1979.

Michaels, C.F. The Information for Direct Binocular Stereopsis. Unpublished manuscript, 1978.

Mitchell, C. Perceiving the Gradients of Black and White Faces. Unpublished doctoral dissertation, University of Minnesota, 1976.

Morowitz, H.J. *Foundations of Bioenergetics.* New York: Academic Press, 1978.

Neisser, U. *Cognitive Psychology.* New York: Prentice-Hall, 1967.

Neisser, U. *Cognition and Reality.* San Francisco: W.H. Freeman Co., 1976.

Nicolis, G., & Prigogine, I. *Self-organization in Nonequilibrium Systems: From Dissipative Structures to Order Through Fluctuations.* New York: Wiley Interscience, 1978.

Pastore, N. *Selective History of Theories of Visual Perception: 1650–1950.* New York: Oxford University Press, 1971.

Pianka, E.R. *Evolutionary Ecology.* New York: Harper & Row, Pub., 1974.

Pittenger, J.B., & Shaw, R.E. Aging Faces as Viscal-elastic Events: Implications for a Theory of Nonrigid Shape Perception. *Journal of Experimental Psychology: Human Perception and Performance,* 1975, *1,* 374–382. a

Pittenger, J.B., & Shaw, R.E. Perception of Relative and Absolute Age in

Facial Photographs. *Perception and Psychophysics,* 1975, *18,* 137–143. b

Pittenger, J.B., Shaw, R.E., & Mark, L.S. Perceptual Information for the Age Level of Faces as a Higher-order Invariant of Growth. *Journal of Experimental Psychology: Human Perception and Performance,* 1979, *5,* 478–493.

Postman, L., & Tolman, E.C. Brunswik's Probabilistic Functionalism. In S. Koch (Ed.), *Psychology: The Study of a Science* (Vol. 1). *Sensory, Perceptual, and Physiological Formulations.* New York: McGraw-Hill, 1959.

Pribram, K.H. Some Comments on the Nature of the Perceived Universe. In R.E. Shaw & J. Bransford (Eds.), *Perceiving, Acting, and Knowing.* Hillsdale, N.J.: Lawrence Erlbaum Associates, 1977.

Prigogine, I. Order through Fluctuation: Self-organization and Social Systems. In E. Jantsch & C.H. Waddington (Eds.), *Evolution and Consciousness: Human Systems in Transition.* Reading, Mass.: Addison-Wesley, 1976.

Prigogine, I., & Nicolis, G. Biological Order, Structure and Instabilities. *Quarterly Review of Biophysics,* 1971, *4,* 107–148.

Runeson, S. On the Possibility of "Smart" Perceptual Mechanisms. *Scandinavian Journal of Psychology,* 1977, *18,* 172–179.

Ryle, G. *The Concept of Mind.* London: Harper & Row, Pub., 1949.

Saldanha, E.L., & Corso, J.F. Timbre Cues and the Identification of Musical Instruments. *Journal of the Acoustical Society of America,* 1964, 2021–2026.

Schmidt, R.A. The Schema as a Solution to Some Persistent Problems in Motor Learning Theory. In G. Stelmach (Ed.), *Motor Control: Issues and Trends.* New York: Academic Press, 1976.

Seligman, M.E.P. On the Generality of the Laws of Learning. *Psychological Review,* 1970, *77,* 406–418.

Shaw, R.E. Cognition, Simulation, and the Problem of Complexity. *Journal of Structural Learning,* 1971, *2,* 31–44.

Shaw, R.E., & Bransford, J. Introduction: Psychological Approaches to the Problem of Knowledge. In R.E. Shaw & J. Bransford (Eds.), *Perceiving, Acting, and Knowing.* Hillsdale, N.J.: Lawrence Erlbaum Associates, 1977.

Shaw, R.E., & Cutting, J.E. Ecological Constraints on Linguistic Forms: Clues from the Ecological Theory of Event Perception. In U. Bellugi & M. Studdert-Kennedy (Eds.), *Biological Constraints on Linguistic Form.* Berlin: Dahlem Konferenzen, 1981.

Shaw, R.E., & McIntyre, M. Algoristic Foundations to Cognitive Psychology. In W. Weimer & D. Palermo (Eds.), *Cognition and the Symbolic Processes.* Hillsdale, N.J.: Lawrence Erlbaum Associates, 1974.

Shaw, R.E., McIntyre, M., & Mace, W. The Role of Symmetry in Event Perception. In R.B. MacLeod & H.L. Pick (Eds.), *Perception: Essays in Honor of James J. Gibson*. Ithaca, N.Y.: Cornell University Press, 1974.

Shaw, R.E., & Pittenger, J.B. Perceiving the Face of Change in Changing Faces: Implications for a Theory of Object Perception. In R.E. Shaw & J. Bransford (Eds.), *Perceiving, Acting, and Knowing*. Hillsdale, N.J.: Lawrence Erlbaum Associates, 1977.

Shaw, R.E., & Turvey, M.T. Coalitions as Models for Ecosystems: A Realist Perspective on Perceptual Organization. In M. Kubovy & J. Pomerantz (Eds.), *Perceptual Organization*. Hillsdale, N.J.: Lawrence Erlbaum Associates, 1981.

Shaw, R.E., Turvey, M.T., & Mace, W. Ecological Psychology: The Consequence of a Commitment to Realism. In W. Weimer & Palermo (Eds.), *Cognition and the Symbolic Processes II*. Hillsdale, N.J.: Lawrence Erlbaum Associates, 1981.

Shik, M.L., & Orlovskii, G.N. Neurophysiology of Locomotor Automatisms. *Physiological Review*, 1976, *56*, 465–501.

Solso, R.L. *Cognitive Psychology*. New York: Harcourt Brace Jovanovich, Inc., 1979.

Sperling, G. The Information Available in a Brief, Visual Presentation. *Psychological Monographs*, 1960, *74*, (11, Whole No. 498).

Thompson, D.A.W. *On Growth and Form* (2nd ed.). Cambridge: Cambridge University Press, 1942 (originally published 1917).

Todd, J.T., Mark, L.S., Shaw, R.E., & Pittenger, J.B. The Perception of Human Growth. *Scientific American*, 1980, *242* (2), 132–144.

Turvey, M.T. Contrasting Orientations to the Theory of Visual Information Processing. *Psychological Review*, 1977, *84*, 67–88. a

Turvey, M.T. Preliminaries to a Theory of Action with Reference to Vision. In R.E. Shaw & J. Bransford (Eds.), *Perceiving, Acting, and Knowing*. Hillsdale, N.J.: Lawrence Erlbaum Associates, 1977. b

Turvey, M.T., & Shaw, R.E. The Primacy of Perceiving: An Ecological Reformulation of Perception for Understanding Memory. In L.-G. Nilsson (Ed.), *Perspectives on Memory Research: Essays in Honor of Uppsala University's 500th Anniversary*. Hillsdale, N.J.: Lawrence Erlbaum Associates, 1979.

Turvey, M.T., Shaw, R.E., & Mace, W. Issues in the Theory of Action: Degrees of Freedom, Co-ordinative Structures and Coalitions. In J. Requin (Ed.), *Attention and Performance VII*. Hillsdale, N.J.: Lawrence Erlbaum Associates, 1978.

Verbrugge, R.R., Rakerd, B., Fitch, H., Tuller, B., & Fowler, C.A. The Perception of Speech Events: An Ecological Approach. In R.E. Shaw & W. Mace (Eds.), *Event Perception: An Ecological Perspective*. Hillsdale, N.J.: Lawrence Erlbaum Associates, to be published.

von Frisch, K. *Bees: Their Vision, Chemical Senses and Language.* Ithaca, N.Y.: Cornell University Press, 1971.

von Holst, E. *The Behavioral Physiology of Animals and Man.* Coral Gables, Fl.: University of Miami Press, 1973.

von Neumann, J. *Theory of Self-Reproducing Automata.* A.W. Burks (Ed.), Urbana, Ill.: University of Illinois Press, 1966.

Walls, G.L. *The Vertebrate Eye and its Adaptive Radiation.* Birmingham, Mich.: Cranbrook Institute of Science, 1942.

Warlick, D. Ecological Acoustics. Unpublished honors thesis, Lake Forest College, 1978.

Warren, W.H., Jr. Them's the Breaks: Acoustic Information for Breaking and Bouncing Events. Paper presented at the Eastern Psychological Association, Hartford, Conn., 1980.

Whittaker, R.H., Levin, S.A., Root, R.B. Niche, Habitat and Ecotope. *American Naturalist,* 1973, *107,* 321–338.

Whorf, B.L. *Language, Thought, and Reality.* New York: John Wiley, 1956.

Wigner, E.P. In W. Moore & M. Scriven (Eds.), *Symmetries and Reflections: Scientific Essays in Honor of Eugene P. Wigner.* Cambridge, Mass.: MIT Press, 1970.

Yates, E.E. Physical Biology: A Basis for Modeling Living Systems. *Journal of Cybernetics and Information Science,* in press.

Yin, R.K. Looking at Upside-down Faces. *Journal of Experimental Psychology,* 1969, *81,* 141–145.

Name Index

Subject Index

238 0758
Ottawa U
telephoo booth